Prison Profiteers

Prison Profiteers

Who Makes Money from Mass Incarceration

Edited by

TARA HERIVEL

and

PAUL WRIGHT

THE NEW PRESS

NEW YORK
LONDON

Requests for permission to reproduce selections from this book should be mailed to:
Permissions Department, The New Press, 38 Greene Street, New York, NY 10013.

Originally published in the United States by The New Press, New York, 2007
This paperback edition published by The New Press, New York, 2009
Distributed by Perseus Distribution

LIBRARY OF CONGRESS CATALOGING-IN-PUBLICATION DATA

Prison profiteers : who makes money from mass incarceration / edited by Tara
Herivel and Paul Wright.
        p.   cm.
Includes bibliographical references.
ISBN 978-1-59558-167-9 (hc)
ISBN 978-1-59558-454-0 (pb)
1. Prison industries—Corrupt practices—United States.   2. Corrections—
Contracting out—United States.   3. Imprisonment—United States—Finance
I. Herivel, Tara.   II. Wright, Paul, 1965-
HV8925.P58 2007
365'.973—dc22   2007035010

The New Press was established in 1990 as a not-for-profit alternative to the large,
commercial publishing houses currently dominating the book publishing industry.
The New Press operates in the public interest rather than for private gain, and is
committed to publishing, in innovative ways, works of educational, cultural, and
community value that are often deemed insufficiently profitable.

www.thenewpress.com

Composition by The INFLUX House
Printed in the United States of America

2   4   6   8   10   9   7   5   3   1

Contents

Part II: The Private Prison Industry

Part III: Making Out Like Bandits

Introduction

Although there is an expanding body of writing and analysis regarding the harms caused by mass incarceration in America, there is little discussion about the increasing number of entities that profit from and subsequently engender the growth of prisons. Beginning with the owners of private prison companies, and extending through a whole range of esoteric industries—from the makers of taser stun guns, to riot security training companies, to prison health-care providers, to the politicians, lawyers, and bankers who structure deals to build new prisons—a motley group of perversely motivated interests coalesce to sustain and profit from mass imprisonment. This anthology addresses the question of who profits from the incarceration experiment, and to whose detriment.

The United States now holds the grave distinction of imprisoning the largest number of people of any country: with just 5 percent of the world's population, it incarcerates 25 percent of the world's prisoners. Beginning in the 1970s, America embarked upon an unparalleled experiment in industrialized mass imprisonment. At that time, U.S. prisons and jails held roughly 300,000 prisoners; by 1990, that figure grew to over 1 million. Now, around 2.3 million are imprisoned in state and federal prisons and jails, with many more in military prisons, juvenile prisons, immigration prisons, and civil commitment facilities. If adults under community supervision are included, the figure shoots upward to 7 million.

While there are many industries that make money from prisons, the private prison industry is unique in that it is the only such industry founded solely in order to profit from prisons. The private interests that attach to prisons generally take the following forms: private companies like Geo (formerly Wackenhut), and Corrections Corporation of America (CCA), which compete to purchase the contracts to staff and run private prisons for profit; corporate interests that vie to sell their wares or services to prisons; and industries eager to make use of the enormous, untapped labor pool of prisoners, for whom the usual restrictions of labor protections do not apply. More difficult to categorize is the related transference of public wealth to the prison context, such as the siphoning of public monies as politicians and bankers fund private prison ventures with state-financed bonds. This volume takes a first step into the murky, unexplored territory of the prison profiteers.

Private Prison Profiteers: Who, What, Why?

The prison profiteers are a varied and aggressive group with enormous reach. What they share is a common lack of experience in the prison arena, and an undivided focus on the bottom line: less expense, more profit.

Judy Greene, a researcher, author, and fellow at the Open Society Institute, opens the discussion with an overview of the current state of the private prison industry and its leading entities, including Geo and CCA. Greene traces the industry's growth from its nascent form in the 1970s to the thriving industry of today, highlighting the industry's iniquitous aim: to foster expansion of the prison population and keep beds filled.

Author, attorney, and this volume's co-editor, Tara Herivel, examines privatized youth facilities and evaluates the relationship between state power and private industry, as it applies to youth incarcerated in private facilities. Some of the worst examples of juvenile injustice arise in this context, including the nepotistic dealings of Louisiana politicians willing to sell off the state's financial credibility and its imprisoned youth's safety for sweetheart deals and state-backed bonds. In exchange for selling off the rights to its juvenile facilities to the highest bidder, Louisiana's privately run juvenile facilities produced horror stories of Dickensian proportion, with a financial legacy that severely restricts that state's budget to this day.

The story repeats itself around the country, with different locales and players, but the same basic scenario. Among the most disturbing questions that arise is: Why have the numbers of children in private juvenile facilities increased by 95 percent in the past decade, *despite* a downward turn in juvenile crime in the same time period? It appears that, where there is profit to be made, beds will be filled by an industry willing to turn a deaf ear to abuses (or even necessity) in this setting.

Journalist Silja Talvi goes undercover to provide a fly-on-the-wall perspective on the industry-insider conference held annually by the American Correctional Association (ACA), at which many of the deals that benefit private companies at the expense of prisoners and taxpayers are struck. The ACA conference draws the foremost industry players, including Geo and CCA, and serves to connect providers as diverse as Verizon, Western Union, Smith & Wesson, and Glock with those making purchasing decisions on behalf of the prison industry. Talvi also visits workshops with titles like "Faith-Based

Juvenile Programming" and "Anti-Terrorism in Correctional Facilities"—revealing the undeniable influence of the industry's right-leaning political perspective.

Transferring Public Wealth to Prisons

Other authors track the creative transference of public monies to fund prisons and thereby enrich pro-profit prison builders in an era replete with evidence that the current rate of prison growth is financially unsustainable.

Writer and Soros fellow Kevin Pranis presents the symbiotic relationship between the promotion of private prison industries and the financial well-being of the states that fund them. In his chapter on backdoor prison financing through state bonds, Pranis shows that states are tethering themselves to privatized prison companies by providing taxpayer-funded bonds to the industry to build and maintain prisons. To ensure payment on the bonds, prison beds must be filled to capacity, creating a troubling relationship between state power, criminal justice, and private industry.

Journalist Jennifer Gonnerman investigates the phenomenon of "million-dollar blocks," as illustrated by maps representing prison spending by neighborhood. The maps make clear that people in the poorest urban neighborhoods often have the highest "price tags" per block, with an average of $30,000 per resident per year being spent to incarcerate a large percentage of these blocks' populations. With cruel irony, the prison-spending budgets for these impoverished neighborhoods are then diverted to the rural prison towns where the urban-based prisoners are housed at the expense of the poor neighborhoods from which prisoners originate.

In a similar vein, prisoner Gary Hunter and Soros fellow Peter Wagner evaluate the political and financial impact of census figures that count prisoners as "residents" of the communities in which they serve their time, rather than their communities of origin. Wagner and Hunter demonstrate that counting prisoners as residents of the prison towns in which they are incarcerated benefits politicians in the rural communities where prisons are sited by enlarging their districts with nonvoting members.

Proponents of rural prison-siting often make promises of improved economic health to their prospective prison town residents. But scholars Clayton Mosher, Gregory Hooks, and Peter Wood find that prison construction in rural locales actually stagnates or impedes economic health. By comparing income levels, total earnings, and employment growth between urban and rural communities with newly built prisons and those without prisons, the authors discovered that both rural and urban communities with newly built prisons grew at the slowest pace. Those who do benefit from rural prison siting are instead the political backers and bankers who funnel funds to prisons, the companies that hawk their wares to prisoncrats, and a handful of lucky locals in prison host communities who scavenge for the leftovers.

Kirsten Levingston of NYU School of Law's Brennan Center reveals another example of the transference of wealth between unlikely populations. Levingston illustrates the current trend of forcing defendants to pay for the very criminal justice system that seeks to incarcerate them. Levingston shows that in an era of impossibly high criminal justice expenses, criminal justice officials are shifting the costs of incarceration onto defendants, or even the untried accused.

Across the country, pretrial detainees—who may not even have been convicted yet—are increasingly forced to pay for their "room and board" while they sit in jail awaiting trial. The state now compensates itself for both immediate and prospective costs of administering criminal justice—costs that it previously assumed as its own. This is a remarkable shift in costs to the accused that benefits states and municipalities unable to sustain the crushing weight of the costs of incarceration to the detriment of our poorest, most disenfranchised citizens.

Hooking up to the Prison Gravy Train

The companies that supply services in prisons run the gamut from riot gear to transportation, from food and telephone services to medical services. In the prison context, however, engaging for-profit services means that cost-cutting measures in areas like medical treatment can mean the difference between life or death for prisoners.

Journalists Wil Hylton and Paul von Zielbaur separately present hellish pictures of the state of medical treatment for U.S. prisoners as they respectively track the results of farming out health care to substandard private medical companies like Correctional Medical Services (CMS) and Prison Health Services (PHS). With health care professionals of dubious quality and treatment to match, companies like CMS and PHS nevertheless easily avoid the industry check typically provided by malpractice suits and are enjoying healthy profits at the expense of unhealthy prisoners. The difficulty for prisoners of gathering evidence or bringing costly lawsuits keeps these prison providers flush, despite a growing body count and undeniably poor practices.

Researcher, writer, and former prisoner Alex Friedmann surveys the state of private prisoner transportation companies that are enriched by the practice of transferring prisoners. Following the track record of injuries, charges of sexual harassment, and a litany of abuses (some fatal) that trails multimillion-dollar private transportation companies like Tennessee's TransCor, a subsidiary of private prison giant CCA, Friedmann scrutinizes the link between TransCor's profit-oriented goals and the resulting increase in escapes, injuries, deaths, and lawsuits.

University of Michigan professor Steven Jackson discusses the ramifications of privatizing the prison telephone industry, with many families paying hundreds of dollars a month to cover exorbitant rates for collect calls from prisoners. With prison phone companies' contracts currently awarded by departments of corrections on the basis of the largest kickback, and with rates unequalled in any other setting, price-gouging of prisoners' loved ones enriches telecommunications firms and corrections departments alike.

Journalist Anne-Marie Cusac reviews the question of arming poorly educated and inadequately trained guards with weapons like tasers, profiling the companies that profit from supplying these weapons to prisons and jails. And, in a related chapter, Jennifer Gonnerman traces the bizarre goings-on at "riot academies": annual training sessions sponsored by private companies where prison guards learn current tactics to subdue their charges. Gonnerman tracks the explosive $1 billion growth of the law enforcement industry—which includes stab-proof vests, helmets, shields, batons, and chemical agents—that prospers in tandem with the speeding train of prison growth.

Paul Wright, former prisoner, co-founder and editor of *Prison Legal News*, and co-editor of this volume, explores pop culture's increasing "commodification" of prison culture, as the experience of prison becomes normalized in both the media and the marketplace.

Journalist Samantha Shapiro reviews the trend of linking social services with conservative Christian faith-based programming, in an article that underscores the present-day shift to the right and its direct connection to prison privatization. In her article about this growing trend, Shapiro exposes the

Bush administration's substitution of private, largely conservative, faith-based groups for traditional social service providers. State legislators who are loath to spend public dollars on prison programming eagerly enter into government contracts and grants under the rubric of the Bush administration's faith-based initiatives. As a result, GED, substance-abuse, and sex-offender programs are replaced by prison courses in "biblically based therapy sessions" and Christian sex-offender "cure" programs, with public dollars flowing into church coffers across the country.

Prison Labor

On the surface, prison jobs appear to serve a number of positive aims: they provide pocket change for people who have no other moneymaking prospects, keep prisoners busy in an idle environment, and build skills prisoners might use after release. But prison labor is generally exempt from basic labor protections—like worker's compensation, labor and industries safeguards, benefits of any kind, or the ability to unionize—a situation that has captured the interest of private businesses eager to circumvent such irritants as expensive regulations. The real beneficiaries of prison labor are the private companies who reap all the more profit to the general detriment of both captive and free-world labor, which suffers the consequences of what is essentially unfair competition.

Journalist Ian Urbina examines the federally created corporation "UNICOR" (also called Federal Prison Industries) that, using prison labor, produces everything from military gear for soldiers in Iraq to furniture for government employees. Over 21,000 prisoners are employed by UNICOR at a rate of between 23 cents and $1.15 per hour in an industry exempted by statute from federal minimum-wage laws. Founded in the early 1930s to offset the costs of running prisons, UNICOR and its captive labor pool sold $687.7 million worth of products to the U.S. government in 2002, with $400 million in sales to the Department of Defense alone.

Writer and ex-prisoner David M. Reutter investigates the use of prison labor at the state level in his article about Florida's statutorily created for-profit corporation, the Prison Rehabilitation Industries and Diversified Enterprises, or PRIDE. PRIDE was the brainchild of a former drugstore mogul who recognized profit potential in the untapped labor pool of Florida's well-stocked prisons. The Florida legislature bought into his dream of a prison-based industry that would produce cheap goods while avoiding competition with free-world private enterprise, and in 1981 PRIDE was born, enjoying the same statutorily mandated protections against liability from lawsuits, unemployment compensation, or workers' compensation for most prisoners as its federal complement, UNICOR.

Prisons present one of the most difficult subjects for scrutiny: by their nature, they lack transparency; in the case of private prisons, there is little access to or available research on the topic. Private companies that are in no manner beholden to the public interest therefore operate out of the public eye. Given the general lack of transparency in prisons, the extra hurdle presented by placing prisons in an impermeable private context effectively prevents public oversight. The handful of such protections that provide vital information about the abuses of state-run prison simply have no power in the private prison setting, where there is no duty to provide such information to the public. On occasion, a story that is outrageous enough will wind its way into the public discourse; but one horror story represents a thousand more lurking behind the prison walls.

And yet, even extreme examples of the failures of privatization still may not be enough to effect real change. Sympathetic lawmakers must also be locally available and courageous enough to take on the politically volatile topic of profits and prisons—a rare situation for most jurisdictions.

This lack of transparency also means there is little research performed in private prisons, research that is critical to lay the groundwork for change. If there is no comprehensive analysis of, for instance, trends in privatized juvenile facilities, how will we know when children are systematically and disproportionately abused and neglected in such facilities? How will we know what it costs the private prison industry to defend itself against prisoners in court? How will we know how much the private prison industry made last year, or any year? Without a comprehensive understanding of the scope and power of the interests vested in fostering the growth of the prison industry, policy makers and advocates are hindered in articulating effective arguments to diminish the use of incarceration. *Prison Profiteers* takes an initial step to uncover an industry that prefers to obscure its operations, at a significant human price.

Tara Herivel
August 2007

Prison Profiteers

Part I

The Political Economy of Prisons

Banking on the Prison Boom
Judith Greene

August 2006

Our growth is generally dependent upon our ability to obtain new contracts to develop and manage new correctional and detention facilities. This possible growth depends on a number of factors we cannot control, including crime rates and sentencing patterns in various jurisdictions and acceptance of privatization. The demand for our facilities and services could be adversely affected by the relaxation of enforcement efforts, leniency in conviction and sentencing practices or through the decriminalization of certain activities that are currently proscribed by our criminal laws. For instance, any changes with respect to drugs and controlled substances or illegal immigration could affect the number of persons arrested, convicted, and sentenced, thereby potentially reducing demand for correctional facilities to house them. Legislation has been proposed in numerous jurisdictions that could lower minimum sentences for some non-violent crimes and make more inmates eligible for early release based on good behavior. Also, sentencing alternatives under consideration could put some offenders on probation with electronic monitoring who would otherwise be incarcerated. Similarly, reductions in crime rates could lead to reductions in arrests, convictions and sentences requiring incarceration at correctional facilities.

—Corrections Corporation of America 2005 Annual Report[1]

Over the final quarter of the twentieth century criminal justice policies in the United States underwent a period of intense

politicization and harsh transformation. Draconian sentencing laws and get-tough correctional policies led to an unprecedented increase in jail and prison populations, driving the
United States' rate of incarceration head and shoulders above
that of other developed nations.

The United States has—by far—the highest prison population rate in the world.[2] The imprisonment boom that began
in the late 1970s has swelled the state and federal prison system to more than 1.4 million prisoners. Adding those held in
local jails and other lockups (juvenile facilities, immigration
detention, etc.), the total number of people behind bars rises
to almost 2.3 million.[3] Expenditures for corrections increased
by 573 percent between 1982 and 2003, with the bulk of the
increase going for expansion and operation of prisons.

Prison expansion is the lifeblood of the private prison industry. In recent years the debate over privatization of prisons has
been focused primarily on the relative costs and performance
of private prisons compared to those operated in the public
sector. But increasing attention has been paid to the role the
industry appears to play in fostering growth in the number
of people behind bars—political contributions made to politicians who set criminal justice policies—and the leadership position various industry executives filled over many years with
the American Legislative Exchange Council, a powerful lobby
for prison privatization and "get tough" penal policies. Corporations with a stake in the expansion of private prisons invested
$3.3 million in candidates for state office and state political
parties in forty-four states over the 2002–04 election cycle.[4]

The Private Prison Debate

The proponents of private prisons insist that privatization will
bring lower costs, higher-quality correctional services, and a
higher level of accountability. They argue that lower costs and

better quality will result from certain advantages they believe are inherent to privatization. Market efficiency is taken to be axiomatic by advocates for private prisons. They contend that competition between vendors for contracts creates strong incentives for managers to find innovative methods to provide improved prison administration and service delivery while at the same time "cutting the fat" from their expense budgets. Because contracts can be terminated or rebid if major performance problems arise, these proponents maintain, market discipline will keep contractors on their toes to prevent loss of business.

Proponents' arguments are often built on abstract assumptions about why privatization should work to improve correctional services. They argue that since gross operational failures—prison escapes and riots—threaten public safety and are therefore likely to attract negative media publicity, private companies that must build a marketing strategy on success will have more incentive than government to guard against security lapses and harsh treatment of prisoners. They assert that if public correctional managers hand the reins to private prison operators, they will be in a better position to demand successful performance than if they retain bureaucratic responsibility for the performance failures of their underlings. Since private firms are not encumbered with civil service and union contract requirements, proponents argue, they will assign staff more efficiently, make promotions solely on the basis of merit, and fire those who fail to perform well or abuse the human rights of the prisoners in their charge.

At the heart of the arguments for prison privatization is the notion that competition from the private sector will inevitably lead to better-quality prison services, at lower costs, across the board. The linchpin for this claim is the concept of "cross-fertilization"—the notion that innovative competition from the private sector challenges public prison managers to cut costs and improve practices, galvanizing them to introduce the modern management techniques and technology improvements claimed to be the hallmarks of the private sector.

Proponents of "managed competition" claim that public bureaucrats find the threat of privatization as potent as its implementation. The prospect that their functions may be transferred to private corporations may compel governmental agencies to improve efficiencies through innovation and may also weaken labor's bargaining power over compensation and work rules. Should public prison managers discover ways to beat the private sector at its own game, *their* innovations will be snapped up in turn by private sector competitors eager to win the race for government contracts.

In addition to this happy picture of ever-spiraling correctional improvement, proponents contend that private prison companies operate at a sheltered remove from the corrupting demands of the political process. And since they are also unfettered by the intricacies of public procurement, private prison managers are free to attain certain efficiencies and economies that lie beyond the reach of government agencies. They can build facilities faster and more cheaply, and save taxpayer dollars by cutting operational costs. In the private sector, cost savings can be wrung from expense categories over which public prison managers have little or no control. Salaries, fringe benefits, and overtime can be contained by private companies free from civil service rules and union contracts. Moreover, proponents point out that that contracts for correctional services sometimes require performance standards that may not apply to a state's own public prisons. Unlike governmental agencies, private contractors may be subject to sanctions for poor performance. Contracts may even be terminated when significant performance problems arise.

These assumptions do not go unchallenged. Elliott Sclar points out that market efficiencies are greatly diminished when—as has been the case in the private prison arena—the industry is dominated by a couple of giant competitors who wield powerful economic and political resources to gain contracts. "By sidestepping the issue of how concentrated economic power arises and sustains itself in the actual operation of contract markets, privatization advocacy often amounts to little more than an endorsement of changing rather than correcting the problems we face with public agency performance."[5]

In a survey of private prisons in the United States conducted for Congress, researchers at the Federal Bureau of Prisons concluded that innovation in private sector corrections is limited due to two primary factors. First, to manage the risks associated with prison management, most contracting agencies require that private prisons be run according to policies and standards that closely resemble those developed for the state's public prisons. Second, since private prisons have been sold on the promise of lower costs, and many states require that a set percentage of cost savings be demonstrated, private prison managers face intense pressure to pare down expenditures in order to save money and produce profits at the same time. In combination, these factors leave little or no margin for the free experimentation that might breed innovative correctional practices.[6]

From their inception, private prison management schemes have drawn criticism from penal reformers, human rights advocates, legal experts, and organized labor. Much early debate focused on assertions that prison privatization might fail to pass constitutional muster. Proponents argue that while government cannot delegate its legislative or adjudicative powers to other entities, it *can* generally pass along its prerogative to perform more mundane functions (including rule making) and to provide public services. This simply requires that governments create adequate statutory standards and retain oversight as well as the right to approve or disapprove rules and disciplinary actions. Opponents of privatization have argued that legal prerogatives that are well established under the "delegation doctrine" might fail if challenged in the context of prison privatization, since liberty interests (not property interests) are at stake. This theory has never advanced far in the courts.

Philosophical opposition to privatization is grounded in the argument that incarceration is a core function of government that should not be handed off to private interests. For those who hold this view, the authority to deprive citizens of liberty and to coerce them—or even kill them—simply should not rest in nongovernmental hands.[7]

Many who oppose prison privatization on moral grounds assert that turning the operation of prisons over to organizations that are organized for the sole purpose of generating profits will inevitably produce pressure for increased incarceration— the prison contract tail will wag the correctional policy dog. Others argue that the profit motive is immoral in the context of prisons because it places financial gain foremost, over the welfare of prisoners.

The American Friends Service Committee takes the position that prison privatization is inherently unethical:

> First and foremost, we oppose companies operating correctional facilities for the purpose of making a profit for their owners and investors. It is inherently unethical for a private corporation to profit from depriving human beings of their liberty. The very nature of the arrangement invites these companies to prioritize their profits over the needs of those in their custody.[8]

Forty-three Catholic bishops from the southern region of the United States have issued a pastoral message that raises privatization of prisons as a serious moral issue:

> We believe that private prisons confront us with serious moral issues, demanding a gospel response. To deprive

other persons of their freedom, to restrict them from contact with other human beings, to use force against them up to and including deadly force, are the most serious of acts. To delegate such acts to institutions whose success depends on the amount of profit they generate is to invite abuse and to abdicate our responsibility to care for our sisters and brothers.[9]

Opponents hold the view that private firms are *less* accountable than government agencies, pointing out that private prison firms that import prisoners from other jurisdictions have sometimes refused to inform the host-state authorities about what types of prisoners are being held in their facilities and for what offenses.

While advocates of privatization claim that public tax dollars are saved when prisons are privatized, opponents of privatization insist there is little evidence of any real cost savings. They say that many of the savings cited in cost-comparison studies are the product of faulty methodology, such as where comparisons are made to hypothetical public prisons. And while labor costs *are* lower, the savings primarily serve to boost executive compensation and corporate profits.[10]

Critics of the "cross-fertilization" argument point out that there is little room for innovation in correctional practice, and that years of experience with private corrections have produced scant evidence that application of new technology or modern business methods has resulted in significant improvements in how prisons are run.[11]

Many argue that the impact of competition on public correctional costs looks less like increased efficiency and more like a race to the bottom line. In this view, competition to cut costs serves only to lower the quality of prison services and diminish the level of security and safety.[12]

The influence of private prison firms changes the dynamics of correctional policy development in many ways. Political scientist Barbara Stolz has examined the impact of the private sector on the "corrections subgovernment"—the small circle of individuals who steer the major decisions about correctional policy and practice in a given state. These key actors are traditionally drawn from the legislative and executive branches, typically from the subcommittees responsible for corrections authorizations and appropriations, from the executive level of correctional agencies, and from those interest groups that wield enough power to influence policy—those with business and professional interests to promote (law enforcement and district attorneys organizations, correctional unions, bar associations) as well as private groups that promote the interests of crime victims or serve as public watchdogs of the interests and rights of prisoners.

Stolz contends that with the advent of private prison companies, the balance has shifted in many states' correctional subgovernments. She argues that actors with a direct professional, bureaucratic, or financial stake in the outcomes of the policy process usually manage to wield more power in the process than those with social or public interest concerns.[13] Private prison firms work hard to raise the ante in the political power game in ways that disadvantage or disempower other players. They bring the profit motive directly to the foreground of policy decisions, raising the stakes, shifting the goals, and changing the dynamics of the policy process.

Through contributions to political campaigns and employment of well-heeled lobbyists, private prison firms manage to pull into the subgovernment process new actors that are not typically involved: legislators, governors, and other elected officials. By dangling the prospect of lucrative employment prospects, they distort the normal reward structure for the public players.

Most disturbing of all, the ability to finance prison construction privately with municipal bonds and corporate loans loosens the normal fiscal constraints on prison expansion that serve to spur important debates about sentencing and correctional policies and rational allocation of public expenditures. Private prison executives are very adept at using political connections and lobbying power to short-circuit correctional policy deliberations with offers of new prison capacity "built at no cost to the state."

We Got By with a Little Help from our Friends

No private stakeholder has had a larger interest in the growth of the American prison system than the world's largest prison company, the Corrections Corporation of America. With a market capitalization of $2 billion, CCA runs the nation's fifth-largest penal system: sixty-three correctional, detention, and juvenile facilities with a total design capacity of approximately seventy thousand beds in nineteen states and the District of Columbia.

From the day of its founding in Nashville, Tennessee, CCA has traded on close political ties to public officials. When Lamar Alexander was elected governor of Tennessee in 1978 he appointed a Republican activist and supporter, Tom Beasley, to his transition team. Ultimately Beasley rose to be chairman of the state Republican Party. In 1983, eight days after Alexander was inaugurated for a second term, Beasley and Doc Crants (his former roommate from the U.S. Military Academy at West Point) set up a new company with the intention of running the state's prison system. CCA's initial investors included the governor's wife, Honey Alexander, and Ned McWherter, then Speaker of the Tennessee House of Representatives.

Since its founding, CCA has made two audacious bids to take over the entire Tennessee prison system—once in 1985 and again in 1997. Both bids failed, but the company has nonetheless prospered greatly in its home state, operating three prisons that hold adult prisoners from the Tennessee Department of Corrections, a fourth prison that holds detainees for various federal authorities and imports prisoners from other states, two large local jails, and one juvenile facility.

By 1997, when CCA made its second bid to assume state-wide prison operations, most state officials had long since divested ownership of CCA stock. But at least five had gone into business partnership with CCA chairman emeritus Beasley, owning barbecue restaurants in a chain that had been founded by Lee Atwater, campaign manager for President George H.W. Bush. These included then–governor Don Sundquist; the lead sponsor of the bill to privatize the prison system, state representative Matt Kisber; and the House Speaker, Jimmy Naifeh, whose wife, Betty Anderson, was then CCA's lead lobbyist.[14]

CCA's political contributions have sometimes appeared to be phased around the company's need for political support in times of operational difficulties. In 1999, after Wisconsin prisoners who had been shipped out of state due to overcrowding complained of brutality in the CCA prison in Whiteville, Tennessee, the company's CEO suddenly sent $4,000 in campaign contributions to Wisconsin governor Tommy Thompson and several prominent legislators.[15]

The development history of private prisons in Oklahoma gives a graphic example of the way private prison interests can dominate the criminal justice policy process, swinging the balance toward reliance on incarceration and away from more effective and humane policy choices. Facing a prison overcrowding crisis back in the mid-1980s, legislators in Oklahoma had enacted a law that required the corrections director to request that the state's governor approve an emergency release of carefully selected nonviolent prisoners whenever the prison population exceeded 95 percent of prison capacity for thirty consecutive days. This cap law triggered a release credit of sixty days to nonviolent prisoners, allowing those whose release dates were near to be considered for release back to their home communities a few weeks earlier than usual. Until the election of Governor Frank Keating in 1994, the state had struggled to manage its prison population with a combination of prison expansions and pre-parole community supervision programs—invoking the cap law when necessary to keep the prison population within affordable levels.

Prior to Keating's election, the state was host to one private "spec" prison that had been built by the town of Hinton in 1990 on the assumption that once private prisons are built, the corresponding government contracts to house prisoners would necessarily follow. Oklahoma officials had never expressed interest in contracting for private prison beds, however, so the Hinton facility operated for years with prisoners imported from other states. Keating, a conservative Republican who had served as a federal law enforcement official in the Reagan and George H.W. Bush administrations, campaigned on a program of "get tough" crime policies as well as privatization of government services. Immediately after his election CCA began lining up sites for construction of prisons on speculation that contracts would soon be available from the Keating administration.

The explicit promotion of prisons as economic development was propelled during the 1980s by the "greed is good" flamboyance that epitomized much of the investment banking industry. The spirit of freewheeling speculation and junk-bond financing entered its zenith when hundreds of tiny rural towns, desperate to stave off economic ruin triggered by mass capital flight overseas, reversed a long-standing tradition of "not in my backyard" and jumped into cutthroat competition to win the prison sweepstakes.

Prison boosterism has come to pervade the thinking of many small-town mayors and county legislators, for whom prisons represent a "clean industry" more than a penal institution. In states such as Texas and Georgia—and even Minnesota—small towns that come up losers in competitions for public prisons have responded with enthusiasm to inducements from private entrepreneurs promoting spec prison construction. Exploitation of this fervor for speculative construction greatly fueled the high-growth private prison industry through the 1990s.

Speculative expansion was a mainstay in CCA's strategy to grow its business. "One part of our company growth is from anticipating the needs of government and investing in a particular project because you know that a state or federal system has a severe overcrowding problem," said Susan Hart, interviewed about the controversial practice in 2000 before she left her post as a vice president at CCA. "We are anticipating their needs without costing government or taxpayers any capital."[16]

The company quickly entered into development deals with public officials in Holdenville and Cushing, Oklahoma. Local economic development authorities in those towns agreed to sell lease-revenue bonds to finance construction of facilities to be leased for operation by CCA. Less than a month after Keating was sworn into office, CCA broke ground and began prison construction in Holdenville.[17]

Other sectors of government in Oklahoma were at work on policy reforms they hoped might rein in the state's prison population growth rate. A sentencing commission had been created to design a new sentencing structure to provide guidance to judges in the sanctioning of offenders. Key legislators were determined to see that the resulting sentencing guidelines would be designed to better apportion the state's correctional resources, reserving prison sentences for offenders convicted of serious, violent crimes, and providing an array of community corrections supervision and treatment programs for nonviolent offenders and those convicted of petty drug crimes.[18]

CCA received its first contract with the Keating administration in 1996. The company opened the Davis Correctional

Facility in Holdenville in April. While construction was still under way on CCA's second spec prison in Cushing, LaMonte Fields, a twenty-year-old prisoner who had recently gained release under the cap law, shot and killed his girlfriend and her parents before being killed himself by police.[19]

On the heels of this tragedy Governor Keating pressured his corrections director to resign. He ordered termination of all of the state's early-release and pre-parole supervision programs. To manage the overcrowding crisis that resulted, Oklahoma officials signed a contract for beds at the private prison in Hinton, and they shipped overflow prisoners out of the state to private prisons located in Texas.

Governor Keating invited J. Michael Quinlan to "evaluate" the Oklahoma prison system. Quinlan had served as director of the Federal Bureau of Prisons during the George H. W. Bush administration, and had worked closely with Keating when the governor was an assistant attorney general in the Justice Department. After leaving government Quinlan had joined CCA as the firm's head of strategic planning. He offered his expertise at no charge to the state. Legislators complained that Quinlan's appointment presented an obvious conflict of interest, given his employment by the world's largest private prison company, which also happened to be building spec prisons in the state.[20]

Quinlan's report was highly critical of the state's classification system, saying it allotted too many prisoners to nonsecure community programs. He recommended a more stringent system that would reclassify thousands of prisoners and require a huge expansion of the state's medium-security prison capacity.[21] Soon after Quinlan's recommendations began to be implemented, two Florida-based private prison companies—Wackenhut Corrections and Correctional Services Corporation—joined CCA in the Oklahoma spec-building binge.

CCA's second prison was activated in Cushing in May 1997.

That same year the Oklahoma legislature enacted a sweeping structured sentencing reform designed to curb further prison population growth. The new truth-in-sentencing law was scheduled to take effect in July 1998, providing guidance to judges in using community sanctions programs as an alternative to imprisonment for many offenders convicted for nonviolent crimes.

The legislative sponsors of the bill hoped it might reduce the need for more private prison beds. State senator Cal Hobson was worried that once contracts were signed, legislators would find themselves pressured to keep those beds filled. "Once you're in them, they're like little junior colleges. They become just as important to those little communities, and you can't get out of them."[22]

By 1998 CCA had built two more prisons in Oklahoma and Wackenhut had built one. The state had already contracted for 2,755 private prison beds in Oklahoma and was still housing 1,017 prisoners in Texas private facilities. In April the Corrections Board approved three *new* contracts for 2,240 new private prison beds, allowing the state to retrieve all its prisoners from Texas and further expanding its in-state private prison capacity.[23] During the 1998 legislative session Governor Keating and the state's district attorneys lobbied for revision or repeal of the sentencing reform law. In June the legislature, bowing to this pressure, voted to postpone implementation of the sentencing reform law for another year.

When Keating took office the state had no private prison contracts, but by the end of his first term the state had contracted private beds costing more than $66 million a year. Governor Keating campaigned for a second term in 1998. He received $12,500 from the private prison industry for his campaign, $10,000 of which came from CCA executives.[24]

Defending his reliance on private prisons in a campaign debate, Keating noted, "As a result of repealing early release, as a result of repealing pre-parole conditional supervision, as a result of arresting and putting back into prison 3,000 chronic offenders and violent offenders, the crime rate across the board is down and down dramatically and in virtually every category for the first time ever. Why has that occurred? Because we are using private prisons."[25] That same year the governor vetoed a bill that would have required statutory contracting requirements for private prisons, including providing workers' compensation, creating emergency plans, and carrying liability insurance.[26]

In a fractious special session during the summer of 1999 the legislature finally repealed the structured sentencing reform legislation it enacted in 1997 to control the state's prison population. The law had never taken effect.[27] Shortly after repeal, the state's prison population again hit the system's capacity, despite the state having funded an expansion of more than 5,170 private prison beds. Faced with another prison population emergency that would trigger issuance of cap credits to nonviolent prisoners within sixty days of their release date, Governor Keating refused to allow releases, saying, "We have the option of leasing more private prison beds.[28]

The decision to contract for up to 720 additional beds at CCA's Diamondback Correctional Facility threw the state's prison budget $20 million in the red, locking the legislature into funding a supplemental appropriation when it convened for the 2000 session. The governor's allies in the legislature responded with a pledge to repeal the cap law during the next legislative session.[29]

By the end of 1999 the state of Oklahoma had placed 5,568 prisoners—one-quarter of the prison population—in private prisons, at an annual cost of more than $90 million. Six private prisons had been built on speculation, without state oversight or competitive bidding. Developers, bond attorneys, architects, and construction firms had made millions.

Governor Keating had received more than $29,000 in campaign contributions from the private prison industry.[30] The idea of sentencing reform in Oklahoma was dead and has remained so to this day.

If We Can't Sell a Legislator on Privatization, We'll Just Hire Him

CCA's primary competitor is the Geo Group—the world's second-largest private prison company. With market capitalization of $327 million and 51,000 beds in operation, Geo manages prisons and mental health facilities in the United States, Australia, South Africa, Canada, the United Kingdom, and Guantánamo Bay, Cuba. Geo was founded in 1983 as a division of the Wackenhut Corporation. The prison company changed its name in 2003 after the parent company was bought by a European security corporation.

When Gary Johnson was sworn in as New Mexico's governor in 1995 with an agenda that included privatization of as many state functions as possible, CCA had already established two private prisons in the state, but Johnson's embrace of privatization seemed to offer a prime opportunity for Wackenhut to compete in the state's prison bed market. In line with his goal, Johnson asked managers at the New Mexico Corrections Department to draw up a plan for privatizing the entire state prison system, and he launched a campaign to privatize any new prisons that would be built in the state.[31]

Governor Johnson's criminal justice philosophy mixed a conservative "tough on criminals" line with a libertarian position on drug use. An admitted ex-user of marijuana and cocaine, New Mexico's governor became a national spokesman for legalization of drugs. Less well known outside of New Mexico are his extreme positions on penal policy. He ran campaign ads calling for prisoners to serve "every stinking minute" of their sentences.[32]

In 1996 Johnson unveiled a privatization deal he had lined up with Wackenhut Corrections Corporation (now renamed GEO Group, Inc.)—two large prisons that he claimed would save the state $40 million. State Senate president Manny Aragon, a vocal critic of prison privatization, was firmly opposed to the Wackenhut deal. He fired off a letter to that effect to Lehman Brothers, the investment bank that had been lined up to underwrite the bonds that would be required to finance construction of the prisons.[33] Upon learning that key legislative leaders had not been convinced to back Johnson's privatization plan, Wall Street bond raters informed the governor that the bonds required to finance construction of the prisons would not receive favorable ratings.

Facility construction plans were stalled while Governor Johnson tried to gather political support. He said that his privatization plan would address the need to free the state of federal court oversight under the *Duran* consent decree. And, Johnson said, his plan would provide sufficient increased capacity to accommodate his efforts to ensure that prisoners would serve a larger portion of their sentences before being released.

Despite these arguments, Johnson's new plan still failed to win approval from Senate president Manny Aragon and House Speaker Raymond Sanchez. Both legislative leaders remained skeptical about the governor's cost savings estimates. Discussions of the governor's privatization plan continued into the fall of 1996, when a deal appeared to have been struck between the legislative leadership and the governor that would allow prison *construction* to begin in Hobbs and Santa Rosa but leave the issue of whether prison *operations* would be privatized to be determined during the 1997 legislative session. Once the deal was announced, construction commenced at Santa Rosa.

Some legislators remained strongly opposed to the deal, however, and two of them—Democratic representative Max Coll and Republican representative Jerry Alwin—filed a lawsuit to block it. Johnson's privatization plan involved creating a private nonprofit corporation, the New Mexico Private Finance Corporation, to float industrial revenue bonds for the two localities that would then lease the prison beds to the state. Coll and Alwin charged that this arrangement had been made in order to evade state limitations on bond indebtedness and avoid a vote of approval for the bonds.[34]

The administration's prison financing scheme was stalled again by the legislators' legal challenge, and the debate about prison construction spilled into the 1997 legislative session. Manny Aragon introduced his own prison construction proposal that would have funded construction of three new 600-bed prisons for public operation, with additional, smaller private facilities for special segments of the prison population—a treatment facility for mentally ill prisoners and a transition center for women prisoners. But Johnson continued to push for his plan, and the session ended in a deadlock filibuster.

Lea County then stepped forward with a plan to set up its *own* nonprofit corporation—the Lea Corrections Corporation—to issue bonds to finance construction of a 1,600-bed facility (a "county jail") to be built at Hobbs. The new plan was for Wackenhut to sign a contract with Lea County to operate the facility. Guadalupe County soon followed suit, approving a similar nonprofit scheme for the Santa Rosa site.

In June 1997, the counties' plans appeared to hit a snag when the legislative finance committee, in a straight party-line vote, passed a recommendation that no money be appropriated for *any* proposed private prison contracts. Even so, Governor Johnson signed contracts with the counties, contingent on legislative appropriations for funding, but the bond transactions were held in limbo while the legal challenge by Coll and Alwin remained pending. Finally, Wackenhut executives decided to step into the breach. Having received a pledge from the governor that state contracts would be won to fill the facilities, they decided to provide interim financing until the counties could float the bonds.

Representative Max Coll enraged Manny Aragon when he sought a subpoena to obtain information about whether Aragon's construction company was involved in contracting work at the Wackenhut prison sites. Aragon's business partner Francisco Melendez had won a contract to pour concrete at Santa Rosa, and Aragon had already revealed that his company might have a bid in to lay water and sewer lines. Wackenhut executives promptly denied receiving a bid from Aragon, and they claimed they had no idea that Melendez was associated with Aragon when they selected his firm for a contract.[35]

The legislators' challenge to the bonding schemes was dismissed in late December 1997. As the 1998 legislative session opened, the pressures to find solutions to the prison population bulge increased. New Mexico had 3,200 prison beds and 4,700 prisoners; 1,500 prisoners were being housed out of state. The idea of buying the prisons then under construction at Hobbs and Santa Rosa was raised by the governor and his Republican allies in the legislature. They proposed that the prisons would be owned by the state but be operated by Wackenhut for at least five years. The governor did not actually request money to purchase the prisons in his budget, but he did include a request for $147 million to lease 1,700 Wackenhut beds to house New Mexico's prisoners.

Democratic legislators opposed to contracting for private prison beds produced a majority vote in the Senate Judiciary Committee to table the lease proposal. But then Senate president Manny Aragon surprised his colleagues by introducing a measure to buy both prisons for $69 million. Aragon proposed to allow Wackenhut a five-year contract to operate the prisons.

But the House of Representatives leadership refused to approve this bargain. Lea and Guadelupe Counties then backed off altogether from their plans to issue revenue bonds.[36] The prisons would remain privately owned as well as privately operated.[37]

Wackenhut opened its first 300-bed housing unit at Hobbs in May 1998. One month later New Mexicans who opposed privatization were shocked to learn that Manny Aragon had secured a consulting contract with Wackenhut. Wackenhut president Wayne Calabrese expressed the company's delight about "having Manny aboard."[38]

Don't Need Our Beds? You Still Need Our Jobs

The political clout wielded by prison entrepreneurs was demonstrated again in 2001 in Mississippi, when—as in most states—a fiscal crisis loomed, driving deep cuts in the state budget for essential services such as mental health and education. Every public service sector was hit hard by the budget crisis save one: corrections. As Mississippi legislators slashed the public schools' budget for textbooks and classroom supplies, they were able to find an extra $6 million to increase funding for prison contracts. Private prison companies as well as local sheriffs who built county correctional facilities to harvest the dollars provided for housing state prisoners prospered, while schoolchildren went without.[39]

Legislators had eagerly embraced the mid-1990s "truth-in-sentencing" trend. They enacted a package of new laws to crack down on crime and youth violence, eliminating parole for all offenders sentenced to prison—violent and nonviolent alike—and requiring that they serve 85 percent of their sentence before gaining release. They voted funds to expand the prison system by more than 4,000 additional beds, half in new state prison beds and half by contracting for two private prisons.

Slowly pushing back release dates
to make money.

The "get tough" campaign sent the state's prison population growth rate into overdrive, and legislators continued to pump money into the budget for yet more prison capacity. In 1997 they decided to share the private prison bounty with powerful local sheriffs. They created a new system of county-level lockups, authorizing the state Department of Corrections to bid contracts for beds in small "regional correctional facilities."

Between June 1994 and June 2001 the prison budget more than doubled, but population growth slowed somewhat. Prison managers had been keeping the contractors happy and the private and regional contract facilities nearly full. But that left the state's own prisons with more than 2,600 empty beds and a shortage of funds.[40]

In light of the budget crisis, then-governor Ronnie Musgrove and his corrections chief, Robert Johnson, decided it was time to tighten the correctional belt, ratcheting down the state prisoner count at all contract facilities, private as well as regional, to minimum-occupancy payment guarantees, specified at about 80 percent of full occupancy in most of the contracts. Both private prison executives and regional contract-facility lobbyists mobilized themselves at the legislature.

A former state legislator retained by six regional prison contractors to provide legal advice lobbied, he said, on behalf of "the littlest and the poorest" regional prisons. CCA's lobbyist begged for a guarantee of at least 930 prisoners, which he claimed his client would need just to break even. Wackenhut president Wayne Calabrese flew in from Palm Beach Gardens on the Florida coast to wine and dine key state senators.[41]

Lawmakers responded. They voted to increase the minimum-occupancy guarantees for contract facilities. Wackenhut and CCA would be guaranteed a minimum occupancy payment for 900 state prisoners, an increase of about 100 each. Ten regional contractors got their guaranteed occupancy payments hiked by 30 prisoners each. The budget bill directed that correctional managers would pay for 600 more contract beds, at an annual cost of $6 million, whether or not there was a need to fill them with prisoners.

Commissioner Johnson charged that legislative conferees had voted to squander scarce tax dollars to pay contractors for housing "ghost" prisoners. Governor Musgrove denounced them for investing in private prison corporations instead of in teachers and students as he vetoed the bill. Two days later the legislature voted to override his veto.

Two years later, longtime national Republican political boss Haley Barbour waged a successful campaign as a fiscal conservative to unseat Governor Musgrove. After he took office Barbour moved to slash the DOC budget, but he hiked payments for private prison beds. By 2006 the Mississippi correctional system consisted of twenty prisons. All but three are operated under contracts—six with private companies and eleven with county officials.

Crime Rates Down? Immigrant Detentions R Us

Private prison companies represent just one sector of the business interests that have profited greatly from the U.S. prison boom. But it is the only sector that was founded for the explicit and paramount purpose of profiting from this phenomenon, creating a financial momentum that strives to grow its market share even while a declining crime rate and a slowing economy have combined to moderate the prison population growth curve.

State prison population growth slowed to a near halt as state fiscal crises hit in 2001, and growth rates have remained relatively modest in most of the states. Yet business is booming for private prison companies thanks to anticipation of a rapid increase in the federal market for immigrant detention. Immigration authorities have focused an increasing share of Immigration and Customs Enforcement resources on the mandatory detention and removal of so-called criminal aliens—immigrants convicted of "aggravated felonies," which, as defined in federal immigration law, are crimes that need not be either aggravated or felonies. In the name of border security and the "war on terrorism," many drug war strategies and tactics are being retargeted to immigrant enforcement. In 2005, border patrol agents were told to wind down their long-established policy of releasing many immigrants from countries other than Mexico on their own recognizance.

The current crackdown on immigrants shares many characteristics with the war on drugs, a failed campaign which is responsible for a great deal of the growth in incarceration of people of color over the last two decades. Just as the media were used to alarm the public about a national "crack crisis" in the mid-1980s and garner its support for the war on drugs, hyped-up media coverage of an "illegal immigration crisis" is serving to construct and conflate the identity of immigrants as criminals, gangbangers, and terrorists.

Conservative pundits and politicians are using false statistics and anecdotal stereotypes to argue for new laws and increased funding for enforcement of criminal and immigration laws by state and local police. New "joint task force" operations have been created to focus and coordinate campaigns against alleged immigrant gang members, expanding the number of people and groups who are subject to racial and ethnic profiling.

Enforcement strategies that were ineffective in the war on drugs are no more effective when redeployed against undocumented immigrants because the demand for immigrant workers in the United States will not be abated by supply-side tactics. But—as with the drug war—the punitive crackdown on immigrants is producing explosive growth in jail and prison capacity.

Fractious immigration policy debates and anti-immigrant

militia operations have increasingly dominated the media spot-
light over the past year, sending the price of stock in the Corrections Corporation of America and the GEO Group soaring.
An immigration reform bill approved by the U.S. Senate in
May 2005 proposed an increase of 20,000 detention beds. An
entrepreneurial "immigrant gold rush" along the Texas border with Mexico has already spawned some 7,500 proposed or
recently constructed private prison beds intended for housing
immigrant detainees.[42]

The rise of the private prison industry came on the heels of
a sharp departure by the United States from the penal policies
of the world's other industrialized democracies. The astonish-
ing upward shift in our incarceration rate has swept this country into the uncharted territory of mass incarceration. Profits
by no means created the machinery of mass incarceration—no
more than defense contractors invented war—but the huge
profits to be made by incarcerating an ever-growing segment
of our population serve the system very well. Profits oil the
machinery, keep it humming, and speed its growth.

Million-Dollar Blocks:
The Neighborhood Costs
of America's Prison Boom
Jennifer Gonnerman

November 16, 2004

The Remeeder Houses make up one of the poorest blocks in Brooklyn. Six-story buildings rise from the rectangular patch of land between Sutter and Blake avenues, and between Georgia and Alabama avenues in East New York. More than 50 percent of the project's residents live below the poverty line. Unemployment is rampant. Run-down, overcrowded apartments are the norm.

By another measure, though, this block is one of the priciest in the city. Last year, five residents were sent to state prison, at an annual cost of about $30,000 a person. The total price tag for their incarceration will exceed $1 million. Criminal-justice experts have a name for this phenomenon: "million-dollar blocks."

In Brooklyn last year, there were 35 blocks that fit this category—ones where so many residents were sent to state prison that the total cost of their incarceration will be more than $1 million. In at least one case, the price tag will actually surpass $5 million. These blocks are largely concentrated in the poorest pockets of the borough's poorest neighborhoods, including East New York, Bedford-Stuyvesant, and Brownsville.

In recent years, as the U.S. prison population has soared, million-dollar blocks have popped up in cities across the country. Maps of prison spending (like the one on the following pages) suggest a new way of looking at this phenomenon, illustrating the oft-ignored reality that most prisoners come from just a handful of urban neighborhoods. These maps invite

Prison Expenditure by Block
Brooklyn, New York

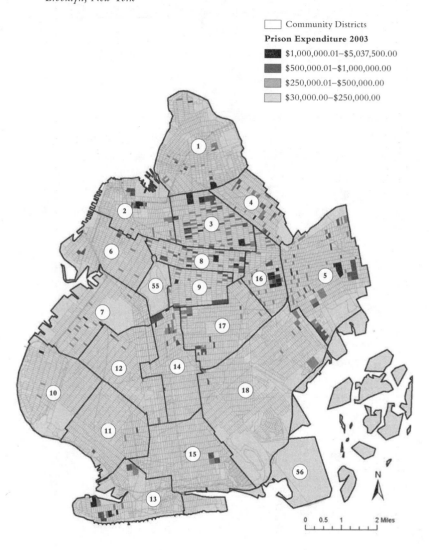

☐ Community Districts

Prison Expenditure 2003

■ $1,000,000.01–$5,037,500.00
■ $500,000.01–$1,000,000.00
■ $250,000.01–$500,000.00
☐ $30,000.00–$250,000.00

0   0.5   1   2 Miles

CD	Population 2000	Prison Admissions 2003	Admissions Per 1,000 Residents	Expenditure Per Community District
1	160,338	183	1.1	$19,045,000
2	98,620	153	1.5	$14,175,000
3	143,897	565	3.9	$58,935,000
4	104,358	318	3.0	$32,402,500
5	173,198	492	2.8	$50,522,500
6	104,054	105	1.0	$8,855,000
7	120,063	131	1.1	$13,185,000
8	96,076	328	3.4	$35,267,500
9	104,014	152	1.5	$15,697,500
10	122,542	31	0.3	$4,030,000
11	172,129	47	0.3	$4,686,250
12	185,046	45	0.2	$5,830,000
13	106,120	116	1.1	$11,545,000
14	168,806	128	0.8	$16,340,000
15	160,319	41	0.3	$5,680,000
16	85,343	287	3.4	$32,182,500
17	165,753	176	1.1	$18,925,000
18	194,653	107	0.6	$8,995,000
TOTAL	2,465,326	3,406	1.4	$355,298,750

One Tenant Leader's Take

Ronald Ward has never heard of a "million-dollar block," but he's lived on one for years—in the Howard Houses in Brownsville, Brooklyn. When he talks about crime, he doesn't talk about statistics or dollars or maps. He talks about what he's seen: young men selling drugs out of his lobby; parole officers who have become a regular presence in his project; men who have come home from long prison stays, only to end up selling drugs once again.

"Most of the crime is committed against the people who live here—the muggings, the burglaries," says Ward, 61, a tenant leader who has been living in the Howard Houses for 43 years. "Crime here is really so rampant." There is one particular crime that he is less eager to discuss. Fourteen years ago, his 20-year-old son was out driving a cab when two men got in, pointed a gun at him, then shot him in the head. His son died three weeks later. "Losing a child—I had never experienced that kind of trauma," he says.

When Ward learned that he lived on a million-dollar block, he wasn't surprised. Many of his project's residents go to work every day, he says, but "we've got people with problems." Empty refrigerators, crack addiction, illiteracy. If legislators asked him how to stop the cycle of imprisonment, he says he'd tell them: "Stop the racism." And he'd advise them to improve the schools. "If you don't educate people, you keep them powerless," he says. "They need to understand the system they're living in. When people become aware of that, then they can get out of it."

numerous questions: How is the community benefiting from all the money being spent? And might there be another, better way to spend those same criminal-justice dollars?

These maps have attracted attention nationwide from state legislators struggling to balance their budgets. In a few state capitols, prison-spending maps have begun to influence the dynamics of the political debate, suggesting new ways to think about crime and punishment, recidivism and reform. One state, Connecticut, has even gone so far as to change its spending priorities, taking dollars out of the prison budget and steering them toward the neighborhoods with the highest rates of incarceration.

Prison-spending maps highlight the fact that money spent on million-dollar blocks winds up in another part of the state—far from the scene of the crime. In New York State, about 60 percent of prisoners come from New York City, but virtually every prison is located upstate, in rural towns and villages, places like Attica, Dannemora, and Malone. As Todd Clear, a professor at John Jay College of Criminal Justice, puts it: "People who live on Park Avenue give a lot of money to people who live in Auburn, New York, in order to watch people who live in Brooklyn for a couple of years—and send them back damaged."

Most likely, nobody would now be mulling over the concept of million-dollar blocks if not for a 42-year-old Brooklynite named Eric Cadora. Back in 1998, Cadora was working at a nonprofit agency in Manhattan called the Center for Alternative Sentencing and Employment Services, or CASES. He taught himself mapping software and studied the various ways mapping was used, including by the New York City Police Department to identify crime hot spots.

About crime mapping, Cadora says, "People weren't coming at it from a policy reform perspective—and the whole idea of [prisoner] re-entry and community wasn't part of the issue. Most of the issue was about getting tough." Cadora wanted to try a different approach. He decided to create a new set of maps, which he hoped "would help people envision solutions rather than just critiques."

With criminal-justice data he obtained from a state agency, he embarked on his first mapping project: Brooklyn. Colleague Charles Swartz helped, and together they made a series of maps illustrating where prisoners come from and how much money is spent to imprison them.

"The reasons we did the money maps weren't to say, 'Gee, we spent too much money on criminal justice,'" Cadora explains. "Because what's too much? The question was to say, 'Look, you can now think of the money you're spending on incarceration and criminal justice as a pool of funds'"—that is, funds that could be spent in a different way. He adds, "What struck me, looking back at a year's worth of prison admissions, was that these were the results of a bunch of individual decisions, but it turns out to amount to enough financial investment to be thought of as an actual spending policy."

In 1999, Cadora began sharing his maps with criminal-justice agencies and nonprofit organizations. Word spread. Soon other states were calling. Five years later, Cadora's maps are well-known in criminal-justice circles and demand for his maps continues to grow. By now, he and Swartz have made maps for agencies in Rhode Island, Florida, Arizona, Connecticut, Louisiana, Kentucky, and New Jersey.

The money that taxpayers spend on prisons pays for the incarceration of some very violent people—the sorts of criminals who neighbors are eager to see go away. These dollars are also used to lock up individuals who commit nonviolent crimes—possession of a few vials of crack, for example. Soon these individuals will be released from prison, and they'll go back to the same neighborhoods. Statistics show there is a strong likelihood they will be locked up again.

Professor Clear, who has worked closely with Cadora, says the maps suggest a different sort of solution: "Use some of that money to improve the places those people came from in the first place, so that they are not crime-production neighborhoods." This might sound like a fantasy scenario—and a few years ago, that's all it really was. Just a radical idea, to which Cadora and a colleague gave a wonkish name: "justice reinvestment."

But budget shortfalls have a way of encouraging politicians to re-evaluate even the most popular policies, and many states have concluded that they simply cannot afford to keep so many people in prison. For the most part, states that have shrunk their prison populations have then steered the savings into a general fund. One state, however, has reinvested in the neighborhoods that are home to the bulk of its prisoners.

Until recently, Connecticut had a $500 million budget deficit and more prisoners than it could house. State Representative Michael P. Lawlor, a Democrat from East Haven, joined with fellow legislators in 2003 to introduce a bill that would scale down the inmate population and funnel the savings into social programs. To win over their colleagues, the legislators invited Cadora to present his maps.

"A picture is worth a thousand words," says Lawlor, a former prosecutor who chairs the Judiciary Committee. "I think Eric is able to graphically depict the insanity of our current system for preventing crimes in certain neighborhoods. We're spending all of this money and not getting very good results. I think when you look at it the way Eric is able to depict it in those neighborhood graphs, you can see how crazy this all is."

Connecticut legislators passed the bill this spring. To shrink the prison population, they adopted several strategies, including reducing the number of people sent to prison for violating probation rules. And they steered the savings into services designed to curb recidivism, including mental-health care and drug treatment. Programs in New Haven—which has many high-incarceration neighborhoods—will receive $2.5 million.

"It's a huge precedent, even though it's a small state," says Michael Jacobson, former commissioner of the New York City Department of Correction, who worked as a consultant for the Connecticut legislature and wrote about the experience in his book, *Downsizing Prisons: How to Reduce Crime and End Mass Incarceration.* "It's the first state that through legislation has simultaneously done a bunch of things that will intelligently lower its prison population, and then reinvest a significant portion of that savings in the kind of things that will keep lowering its prison population. No other state has done anything like that."

The idea may be starting to catch on. In Louisiana, three state senators introduced a bill in 2004 that proposed to trim the prison population, save more than $3 million a year, and then spend that savings on helping ex-prisoners find jobs. The bill did not pass, but the idea caught the attention of Governor Kathleen Babineaux Blanco, a Democrat, whose state has the highest rate of incarceration in the country. She invited representatives of three foundations, including Cadora, to a luncheon at the governor's mansion. At the request of her office, Cadora will be creating many more detailed maps of Louisiana.

A map of million-dollar blocks, with stark concentrations of color, can quickly convey a sense of how self-defeating many criminal-justice policies have become—how, for example, spending exorbitant amounts of money locking people up means there's far less money available for programs that decrease crime, like education, drug treatment, mental-health care, and job training. But these maps don't tell the whole story, since they don't show what happens after prisoners are set free.

New York's state prisons release around 28,000 people a year.

Nearly two-thirds of them return to New York City. They arrive wearing state-issued clothes—a plain sweatshirt and stiff denim pants—and they come back to the same streets they left. They bring home all the memories and lessons of prison life, plus the system's parting gift, $40. Usually, they discover that the neighborhoods they left behind have not changed, and that life on the outside can be incredibly difficult. If the past is any predictor, half of them will be back upstate within three years.

Doing Borrowed Time:
The High Cost of Backdoor Prison Finance

Kevin Pranis

January 2007

Much public attention has been devoted in recent years to the "industrial" side of the prison boom, from the fortunes of private prison operators to the profits generated by telecommunications companies from lucrative phone contracts. Less attention has been paid to the sector of the prison industry that gets paid each time a prison is financed or built. Unlike those who make their money from operations, firms that get paid on the front end may have little stake in the ultimate use or financial viability of a new prison or detention project. They profit whether the beds are empty or full.

Declining public enthusiasm for costly prison expansion plans has closed off traditional options for financing new prison construction. But this trend has created new opportunities for a cottage industry of investment bankers, architects, building contractors, and consultants to reap large rewards with "backdoor" financing schemes. A review of recent prison, jail, and detention expansion initiatives shows that federal, state, and local governments are using backdoor financing mechanisms to borrow hundreds of millions of dollars to build facilities that the public does not want and cannot afford.

Paying for Prisons: Corrections Takes the "Public" out of Public Finance

Until the mid-1980s, prisons were generally built in one of two ways. State officials either took the "pay-as-you-go" approach by funding new construction out of general revenues; or they borrowed money through the sale of general obligation bonds.[1] A general obligation bond is an unlimited repayment pledge that is backed by the "full faith and credit"—including the taxing power—of the issuer. Failure to pay debt service on a general obligation is rare among large government entities and is tantamount to bankruptcy. The issuance of new general obligation bonds often requires approval by taxpayers in the form of a bond referendum.

As correctional populations and costs mounted in the 1980s and 1990s, states had greater difficulty funding expansion out of their operating budgets or winning public approval for new debt. State officials responded to these developments by issuing another type of debt—revenue bonds—to finance new prison construction.

Revenue bonds are limited obligations that are backed only by assets and income streams specified in the issuing documents. Revenue bonds were originally designed to provide a source of financing for projects that could generate sufficient revenues to pay for themselves over time. The classic example is a bridge that generates enough income from tolls to cover the cost of operations, upkeep, and debt service on the bonds issued to finance its construction. Revenue bonds can be issued without public approval because they are not backed by the full faith and credit of the government.

Prisons, jails, and detention centers would seem to be poor candidates for revenue bond financing since they are largely or entirely funded with tax dollars. Yet in 1980, New York governor Mario Cuomo responded to voters' rejection of a $500 million prison bond referendum by turning to the state's Urban Development Corporation (UDC).

The UDC is a nonprofit corporation established after the assassination of Martin Luther King Jr. to expand access to af-fordable housing. The governor used the UDC to issue rev-

enue bonds to build upstate prisons—a very different kind of
low-income housing. The "revenues" backing the bonds came
from leases between the UDC and the state's Department of
Correctional Services.

Under such lease-revenue arrangements, the state has no legal obligation to repay the debt incurred by its bonding authority, and the legislature can terminate the lease at any time
by choosing not to appropriate the necessary funds. Revenue
bond financing allows officials to dispense with restrictions on
general obligation debt such as constitutional debt limits and
public referenda requirements.

Behind the legal fiction, however, is a moral obligation to
investors who purchased the bonds. The consequences of failing to meet such a moral obligation can be as serious as the
consequences of failing to meet a legal obligation. They range
from a costly downgrade of a state's bond rating to investors'
reluctance to make further investments in the region.

Revenue bonds and other backdoor financing schemes
became more popular during the 1990s when state officials
found themselves squeezed by mounting corrections costs and
a growing anti-tax chorus. The Web site PublicBonds.org reports that by 1996, more than half of new prison debt was being issued in the form of certificates of participation, a type of
lease-revenue bond.

Some local governments continue to issue general obligation debt to finance jail expansion. But no state has built a
new prison with general obligation bonds since the turn of
the century, and few have put the question to voters. It's not
hard to figure out why. A 2002 proposal to build a $25 million
new prison in Maine was defeated by a two-to-one margin,
while California governor Arnold Schwarzenegger was recently forced to pull a $2.6 billion prison proposal from a bond
package after failing to find support for the measure within his
own party.

Instead, states pursuing a prison expansion agenda have done so through increasingly complex, and costly, backdoor finance schemes. State officials are not alone: backdoor financing is playing an increasingly important role in prison and jail expansion at the federal and local levels as well as in the private sector.

Officials in Shelby County, which includes the city of Memphis, Tennessee, were recently courted by the nation's leading private prison companies with offers to build a massive new jail. A plan advanced by the Geo Group (formerly Wackenhut Corrections) would have established a nonprofit bonding authority to issue revenue bonds, while Corrections Corporation of America offered to build the facility using its own credit line in exchange for a fifty-year lease agreement. In 2005, CCA made a similar proposal to the leaders of Richmond, Virginia.

Even private prison companies, which can serve as vehicles for backdoor prison financing, are themselves seeking ways to keep prison debt off their books and to push risk back onto the public sector. Several have sought to finance new prisons through, or sell existing prisons to, local economic development authorities and then lease the facilities back. Such arrangements not only give private prison companies access to low-interest, tax-free financing but also allow them to avoid becoming saddled with costly, vacant real estate if a contract is terminated. Correctional Services Corporation, for example, sold several facilities to local bonding authorities before being acquired by the Geo Group in July of 2005.

Finally, the process employed by the U.S. Marshals Service (USMS) and the Department of Homeland Security's Bureau of Immigration and Customs Enforcement to secure detention beds has encouraged speculative detention growth. Less than a quarter of USMS detainees are housed in federal facilities according to statistics published by the Office of Detention Trustee, which manages federal detention contracts. The rest are housed in state, local, or privately owned facilities under contracts and intergovernmental agreements. The promise of profitable federal immigration detention business has spurred counties in Texas and elsewhere to "supersize" their jails and build new facilities solely intended to serve the federal detention market.

Cost 1: Policy Makers Binge on Easy Prison Credit

Easy access to investment capital permits policy makers to commit to thousands of new prison beds that will cost billions of dollars to operate over the coming decades while putting, as they say in the car commercials, "nothing down." The lucrative nature of backdoor prison finance deals also brings together powerful financial interests that have a large stake in pushing the deals through.

North Carolina has financed construction of five prisons since 2001 by engaging a private consortium to float bonds, build facilities, and sell them to a state bonding authority. The North Carolina Infrastructure Finance Corporation then issued its own bonds to finance the purchase of the prisons for the state. The deals generated millions of dollars in fees for developer Carolina Corrections and the investment bankers at Lehman Brothers who sold both sets of bonds.

A few years ago, Arizona found itself caught between a rapidly growing prison population and record budget deficits. Lawmakers responded by turning the bulk of new prison finance over to the private sector. Private prison companies have arranged financing for 2,400 new beds that operate under long-term contracts with the state over the past half decade, while the state has built 1,000 new public beds using proceeds from the sale of lease-revenue bonds.

Backdoor financing arrangements drive up the long-term

costs of prison expansion. Complex deals require more work from investment bankers and attorneys than straightforward state bond sales. Outsourcing also increases the risk to investors, who in turn demand higher rates of return and/or costly bond insurance. *Not good for tax payers*

But such schemes provide short-term benefits to elected officials. Backdoor financing keeps prison debt off the books, avoiding constitutional caps, and concealing major long-term obligations from normal budget scrutiny. Decisions about prison expansion remain beyond the reach of the voters who will bear the costs of operating the prisons. Finally, backdoor financing generates large transaction fees for investment bankers and others with deep pockets and close ties to state officials.

Backdoor prison financing encourages overbuilding and has a corrosive effect on criminal justice policy making. In both Arizona and North Carolina, bipartisan groups of legislators were considering sentencing reform proposals that could have reduced or eliminated the need for prison expansion. Given the intense budget pressures each state faced and the lack of public support for further prison spending, reform seemed to be the obvious choice. But once big-ticket expansion plans gathered momentum, advocates of sentencing reform had difficulty getting a serious hearing for their ideas.

A perverse loophole in the law has pushed officials in one Texas county to *over*build a jail in order to secure financing. In 2004, Willacy County was being pressured by the Texas Commission on Jail Standards to fix persistent problems with its plumbing and with overcrowding of female detainees in its 45-bed jail. The county was in a quandary. A budget crisis had forced local officials to borrow $1.5 million for operations, pushing the county's debt load and tax rates to the maximum allowed by law—80 cents per $100 of assessed property valuation. Unable to issue county obligation bonds to finance a new jail, officials faced the unappetizing prospect of being shut down by the commission and spending millions of dollars to transport detainees and house them elsewhere.

They chose another option that might at first seem counterintuitive—borrow two or three times as much money, at a higher interest rate, to build a jail twice the size needed. The larger jail could then be marketed to the federal government and, as the county's investment banker put it, be "paid for by the inmate population at no cost to the taxpayer."

County judge Simon Salinas considered the scheme's chances of success to be slim. With no other means to bring the jail up to state standards, however, local officials decided to take the gamble. The new jail was built, but the detainees did not come. In May 2006, the county was forced to pay bondholders $137,000 out of its general funds, and commissioners reported that the county risked losing control of the facility.

Cost 2: Backdoor Finance Locks in Excess Prison Capacity

State policy makers know only too well that pressure from local communities and other interested parties makes prisons easier to open than to close. Reginald Wilkinson, who until recently ran Ohio's Department of Rehabilitation and Corrections, had to go all the way to the Ohio Supreme Court to vindicate the department's right to close prisons over the opposition of the prison guards' union.

But closing a prison, jail, or detention center can be doubly difficult if the facility was financed off the books. Louisiana lawmakers discovered this unfortunate fact when they tried to shut down the nation's most notorious juvenile detention center.

In 1995, the Louisiana Department of Corrections entered into a "cooperative endeavor agreement"[2] with the City of Tallulah and Trans-American Development Associates (TADA), a group of businessmen with close ties to then-governor Edwin Edwards, for the construction, financing, and operation of a secure juvenile facility.[3] The Swanson Correctional Center for Youth—Madison Parish Unit, better known as the Tallulah facility, was financed and then refinanced with bonds backed by the state's operating contract with TADA.

Tallulah became notorious for abusive conditions, and the problems did not end when the state took over operating the facility. But state legislators who wished to withdraw funding for the facility—including $3.2 million in annual payments to the owners for debt service—were hamstrung in their efforts. State officials received letters from rating agency Standard and Poor's and bond insurer Ambac warning that a decision to break the juvenile prison lease could damage the state's bond rating.

The state could simply have shut down the Tallulah facility while continuing to make lease payments. But such a move would have put lawmakers in the politically unpalatable position of appropriating millions of tax dollars each year for an empty prison (a step that lawmakers were eventually forced to take anyway). Youth confined at Tallulah were left to suffer for another year while the bond controversy delayed closure of the facility. When lawmakers did act, the bill to close Tallulah came attached with a rider requiring the state to reopen it as an adult prison.

If the construction of Tallulah's youth prison had been financed out of the state's capital budget, it would have been a simple matter to convert the site into a learning center (a demand made by local residents) or abandon it entirely. The state would still have been obligated to repay the debt incurred to build the facility, but the payments would be smaller—courtesy of cheaper public financing—and buried in the tens of millions of dollars spent each year to service state debt. Lawmakers instead found themselves trapped in a costly lease, one that

Predatory lending on a large scale of bad decision making!

could not be terminated without damaging consequences to the state's credit rating, for a prison that must be kept filled in order to justify the lease payments to voters.

Arizona officials have entered into similar arrangements: since 2000, they have signed off on the sale of $132 million in private prison bonds backed entirely by state lease payments. Even if bond rating agencies and insurers were willing to let Arizona out of the leases, fear of a damaging default could prevent the state from canceling contracts with private prison operators. Most of Arizona's state-contracted private prisons have been financed or refinanced with bonds issued by county industrial development authorities. The bonds are not legally county obligations, but a default could still scare away investors and raise the cost of borrowing for both public and private groups in the region.

Cost 3: Immigrant "Gold Rush" Creates Speculative Detention Bubble

The emergence of prison and detention markets and easy access to investment capital have combined to create the conditions for speculative expansion, especially at the local level. No state has seen more speculative prison growth—or more fallout from speculation—than Texas. The state made headlines in the early 1990s when a detention scheme promoted by a group of investment bankers and developers collapsed, resulting in one of the largest-ever bond fraud and conspiracy cases.

A decade later, Texas' speculative detention market is hotter than ever thanks to a federal detention "gold rush." One group of investment bankers has played a particularly active role— helping to inflate the detention bubble by setting up a string of questionable deals that span the state. Over a five-year period, a Connecticut bond house known for putting together "tough" deals and a Dallas firm with substantial experience financing private prisons sold nearly $200 million of revenue bonds for eight rural Texas counties and one small city.

The proceeds of the bond deals underwritten by Herbert J. Sims and Co. and Municipal Capital Markets Group (MCMG) were used by the sparsely populated localities to build, acquire, or refinance for-profit jails and detention centers that derive the bulk of their income from housing federal detainees or other states' prisoners. The team's first Texas deal financed construction of a speculative detention center in the Texas Panhandle that has faced financial problems and allegations of abuse. The second transferred ownership of an existing private prison to the host county and loaded the facility with $13 million worth of debt.

The team's fourth Texas detention deal landed the underwriters and their partners in the pages of the *Bond Buyer*. On November 7, 2002, the La Salle County Public Facilities Detention Corporation issued $21.9 million of taxable revenue bonds to fund construction of a 500-bed detention center for U. S. Marshals Service detainees whose cases were being heard in nearby Laredo.

The project gave many causes for concern. The county had an intergovernmental agreement with USMS for the use of the facility, but no firm commitment for how many beds the agency planned to use or for how long. The county's partner in the project, Emerald Correctional Management, had very little experience in private corrections. La Salle's top elected official had been barred from doing business with the Department of Housing and Urban Development for misuse of low-income housing funds. Finally, the deal featured generous financial terms—including 12 percent interest rates and large payouts for those who put the deal together—that benefited everyone but taxpayers.

Opponents of the project won a major victory when county treasurer Joel Rodriguez, who had voiced serious concerns about the enterprise, defeated incumbent county judge Jimmy Patterson in the Democratic primary. Patterson and his allies responded by pushing the bond deal through over the objections of county attorney Elizabeth Martinez. When Martinez refused to sign an opinion drafted for her by outside counsel, the opinion was simply included without her signature among the bond documents.

The sale of the bonds generated $1.3 million in underwriting fees for Sims and MCMG, along with a $700,000 consulting fee for former Webb County commissioner Richard Reyes. Local officials were forced to defend and eventually settle a lawsuit filed by local residents Donna Lednicky and Sean Chadwell under the state's Open Meetings Law. Meanwhile, payment of a USMS Cooperative Agreement Program grant that was critical to financing the facility was delayed by an environmental lawsuit that rancher Greg Springer filed against the law enforcement agency. The county was ultimately forced to issue an additional $5.45 million in bonds due to cover the delays and cost overruns.

The La Salle bond sale was followed quickly by two more controversial transactions. In January 2003, officials in nearby Crystal City borrowed $14 million to finance a $9 million purchase of an existing private detention center whose assessed value was just $6 million. The sale generated protests by local residents, but also large payouts to bond underwriters, the city, its public finance corporation, and a consultant.

A July 29, 2003, article in the *Bond Buyer* warned that experts believed a wave of detention deals in the Southwest posed "a growing risk to bondholders and the counties that stand behind the projects." Two weeks later, Hudspeth County officials borrowed $23.5 million through a public finance corporation to build a 500-bed speculative detention center ninety miles from El Paso. Local residents questioned the project's feasibility and sued unsuccessfully to block the bond sale. Business slowed somewhat after 2003, but Sims and MCMG continued to execute detention deals, including a $24.22 million revenue bond issue to fund construction of a jail in Polk County and a $31.41 million revenue bond refinancing for Garza County.

The rapid growth of local detention finance schemes is a recipe for disaster. The most telling failure may be the near-default of a 3,000-bed, $90 million detention project in Reeves County. Reeves was one of a few detention center projects whose bonds could secure an investment-grade rating because of what was considered an effective management team, a strong client relationship with the Federal Bureau of Prisons (BOP), and growing demand for contract beds in the area.

Then in late 2003, the detention center suddenly found itself on the brink of default after the BOP declined to sign a contract for 1,000 new beds that had been added to the facility. The county was ultimately forced into the arms of the Geo Group, which took over bond payments and management of the project. Reeves' sudden reversal of fortune caught analysts by surprise, and revealed how little those charged with the "self-regulation" of public debt know about the detention market.

Why the Economics of Prison Expansion Escape the Bond Markets

The current wave of prison expansion is financially unsound. Public enthusiasm for incarceration has waned, and it is plausible that long-term demand for beds could fall below the current supply. The federal appetite for new prison and detention beds continues unabated, but lawmakers have not yet shown a willingness to fund them at a level that would take up the slack in the much larger state prison market.

These developments may not be of great concern to investment bankers and bond counsel, who make money on both good and bad deals. They should be of great concern to bond *investors*, who risk losing their shirts if supply greatly exceeds demand. Yet investors seem blissfully ignorant of the dangers. Their failure to appreciate the risks of long-term investments in prison expansion may be rooted in the differences between prisons and other bond-financed projects.

The bulk of municipal bonds are issued to fund projects that meet public needs in a direct and obvious way, such as sewer and water systems, highways, and schools—most people flush toilets, drive to work, and send their kids to school on a daily basis. Consumers of these services may argue over what the quality should be and how much they should pay for them. But it's safe to assume that they will keep paying as long as there is money in the bank.

It is more difficult to determine how many prison beds the public needs and is willing to pay for. Researchers have found little correlation between incarceration and measures of public safety such as crime rates, and to the degree that a relationship exists, it doesn't necessarily go in the right direction. Opinion research has shown that the public is deeply ambivalent about the wisdom of current high incarceration rates and reluctant to throw more money into a system that delivers such poor results.

But bond investors are getting all of their information from bond issuers who have a financial stake in making prison bonds look as safe as possible. Prison bond documents are full of information about the remarkable pace of prison population growth over the past quarter century. They contain little or no information about sentencing and correctional policy reforms, shifts in public opinion, or other trends that would weaken the case for new prisons.

If investors knew that modest sentencing and correctional policy reforms could pull the floor out from under prison population growth in Arizona, they might think twice about buying private prison bonds issued by the Pinal County Industrial Development Authority. If financial analysts understood the extent of speculative detention growth in Texas, they might have been less sanguine about the prospects for a major bed expansion at Reeves.

The risks backdoor prison finance poses to both investors and governments are very real. A review by staff at Good Jobs First, a nonprofit economic development think tank, found that prisons financed with certificates of participation accounted for a third of all lease-backed bond defaults in the 1990s. A decade ago, a $74 million speculative scheme to build 500-bed prisons in six Texas counties collapsed when five of the six were unable to house the necessary numbers of prisoners. The fiasco gave rise to one of the largest-ever bond fraud and conspiracy cases and resulted in a partial bailout by the state, which acquired substandard jails at 50 cents on the dollar.

More recently, the bond ratings of three Texas counties— Hayes, Hood, and Kerr—were downgraded after local officials decided to walk away from lease-purchase agreements. Hayes County built a juvenile detention center twice the size it needed with the intention of renting the remaining beds to other counties. But Texson Management Group, which set up the deal, went bankrupt and left the county holding the bag. In 2003, Standard and Poor's downgraded Hayes County's bond rating from A-plus to BBB-minus based on the county's failure to meet its moral obligation to repay the debt. Crystal City has already been denied a loan to buy trucks and police cars because of concerns the city's detention deal raised for a local bank.

Build It and They Will Come
(but Not in Time to Pay the Mortgage)

The belief that prison expansion is inevitable could become a self-fulfilling prophecy, at least in part. Once prisons, jails, and detention centers are built, the political pressure to fill them is enormous. Backdoor financing only heightens these pressures by aligning bond investors, insurers, and rating agencies with the communities that see prisons as a source of jobs and economic development.

This is not to say that new prisons will be a sure bet for investors or local governments that engage in backdoor finance schemes. The lack of rational planning processes virtually guarantees that there will be slippage between supply and demand for prison and detention beds.

The best-financed, best-informed and best-connected market players will be able to survive the slippage and even thrive on it, picking up valuable prison real estate at rock-bottom prices. Meanwhile, less well-positioned counties and investors will fall through the cracks when they make bad market bets or simply get squeezed out by more powerful competitors. Worst of all, long after their bonds have gone into default, with damaging consequences to local economies, the prisons will still be there demanding to be filled—with immigrants, kids, the mentally ill, or another population du jour.

The bigger question for the financial markets is not why they turn a blind eye to risky prison financing deals but why they don't pay more attention to the broader implications of growth in the use of incarceration. Prisons are a drop in the public finance bucket, but the cost of *operating* prisons and jails makes up a significant and growing share of state and local spending.

According to the most recent available figures, for every dollar spent on state prison construction, $16 was spent on operations.[4] The hundreds of millions of dollars that are being borrowed for backdoor state prison expansion will draw down *billions* of dollars in operating costs, draining states of the resources needed for services that strengthen their long-term economic outlook. Seen in this light, high and rising incarceration rates should be understood by bond markets as a threat to the long-term fiscal health of state and local governments.

Fortunately, activists and advocates across the country understand what the financial markets are missing. They have begun to develop strategies to challenge backdoor financing of prisons, jails, and detention centers by putting the public back in public finance.

When Oregon proposed building new prisons with revenue bonds, the Western Prison Project held a public series of meetings to discuss a possible taxpayer lawsuit and flooded the state treasurer's office with phone calls, ultimately drawing attention to and postponing the bond sale. Colorado's Criminal Justice Reform Coalition filed suit against a sale of certificates of participation for a supermax prison under that state's tough constitutional protections for taxpayers. And North Carolina anti-prison activists tried to persuade legislators that a scheme to privately finance construction of three new prisons was overpriced, fiscally unsound, and undemocratic.

None of these efforts ultimately succeeded in blocking the financing of new prisons, but all helped raise a public debate over what was previously an invisible issue. Local campaigns to oppose the construction of new jails and detention centers from Memphis, Tennessee, to Laredo, Texas, have also highlighted financing concerns. In 2004, advocates and activists concerned with prison finance gained a new tool to break down prison finance deals—a Web site that contains a wealth of information on revenue bonds and their use in prison expansion.

Ultimately, increased attention to the issue may persuade both policy makers and Wall Street that backdoor prison finance is not in anyone's long-term interest. If not, we will all pay the price for many years to come.

Making the "Bad Guy" Pay: Growing Use of Cost Shifting as an Economic Sanction

Kirsten D. Levingston

March 2, 2007

State recoupment laws, notwithstanding the state interests they may serve, need not blight in such discriminatory fashion the hopes of indigents for self-sufficiency and self respect.[1]

At some point, we have to be able to say to people who have been incarcerated, and served time on probation or parole upon release, you have paid your debt to society. We have got to help people move on to leading productive lives."[2]

For people with loads of debt from court fines, supervision fees, restitution, and other charges related to their crime, getting out of prison is no fresh start. . . . They come out of the gate already at a disadvantage."[3]

Ex-prisoner Wilbert Rideau became known as "the most rehabilitated prisoner in America during his long and complex journey through Louisiana's criminal justice system, which began when he was 19 and ended when he was 64."[4]

Rideau was tried, convicted, and sentenced to death three times for kidnapping and murder, but three different appellate courts reversed those convictions because of blatantly unconstitutional conduct by judges and prosecutors.[5] Following the trio of reversals, Rideau was ultimately convicted of manslaughter at his fourth trial in 2005, an offense that carried a maximum sentence of twenty-one years. By then Rideau had already served forty-four years, one of the longest sentences in Louisiana history, and consequently left Angola prison on January 15, 2005, a free man.[6] But despite this distinction and despite his undisputed rehabilitation, the judge in his case nevertheless felt Rideau still owed a debt to society—$127,905.45, to be precise.[7] As a kind of twisted parting gift, Judge David Ritchie saddled Rideau with nearly $61,000 of costs "associated with impaneling, housing, feeding, transporting and providing security for the jury,"[8] and a $67,000 bill to "reimburse the Indigent Defender's Board for all costs associated with [Rideau's] defense, including witness fees and expenses."[9] The Louisiana appeals court vacated the trial court's six-figure assessment against Rideau, finding the trial court overstepped its legal authority. While the relevant Louisiana statute authorized recoupment of some "costs of prosecution or proceeding," the appellate court concluded this did not mean "'every' cost incurred by the State in maintaining the judicial system," as apparently interpreted by Judge Ritchie.[10] The state's appeal of this decision to the Louisiana Supreme Court, seeking reinstatement of Judge Ritchie's order, was pending at the time of this writing.[11]

Rideau's case was extraordinary in most respects, including the six-figure assessment levied against him, but common in at least one: the system's attempt to recoup costs from the prosecuted.

Across the country, in the face of expanding expenses and shrinking budgets, federal and state criminal justice officials are becoming more aggressive in shifting a range of criminal justice system costs onto defendants.[12] Criminal financial obligations are not aimed solely at benefiting victims and punishing offenders; increasingly, policy makers are using them simply to keep the system in the black.

A Georgia sheriff, for example, collected $18 a day in room

and board fees from those awaiting trial until former pretrial
detainees challenged the practice, which was not authorized by
any state statute or policy.[13] Mickel Jackson, one of the plaintiffs, was jailed for three months and paid half of the $1,471
cost of his jail stay before the state dropped the charges against
him.[14] The sheriff had compelled Willie Williams, jailed for
nine months before posting bond, to sign a promissory note
agreeing to pay over $4,600 or risk going back to jail.[15] "Tax-
payers," according to the sheriff, "should not have to bear the
burden of feeding and housing lawbreakers."[16] Clinch County
settled the case, agreeing to return about $27,000 to those
forced to pay the unauthorized jail fees.

Though the practice was unauthorized in Clinch County,
some argue that shifting costs in this way makes sense. After
all, they say, those arrested, charged, and prosecuted are responsible for the ballooning costs of jails, courts, prison, and
community supervision. "In essence, an inmate is being asked
to reimburse the State because the inmate 'has made it necessary for the State to keep and maintain him at a large cost,'"
the Supreme Court of Washington explained in a 2001 case
challenging automatic deductions from inmate accounts to
cover costs.[17] While the notion of charging "users" for the systems' cost may have some appeal, it ignores critically important
policy and practical realities.

Powerful interests profit directly from keeping our jails and
prisons full—private prison investors, powerful correctional
officers' unions, telephone companies, and various service industries (such as medical, transportation, and food service
industries)—all gain directly from keeping prisons in business. As correctional systems grow, however, so does the burden on taxpayers who fund them. Why, disgruntled taxpayers
might ask, are policy makers not finding less expensive and
more effective ways to keep the public safe? Why, taxpayers
might wonder, won't policy makers devise alternatives to jails

and prisons that solve the underlying problems contributing to involvement in the system instead of making them worse? Rather than answer these important questions, increasingly jurisdictions now seek to quell taxpayer concern about system costs by shifting those costs away from taxpayers and onto the "bad guys" who use the system. By shifting costs in this way, officials are not only immunizing themselves from taxpayer complaints but also muzzling calls for change and demands to develop more cost-effective alternatives to criminalization and incarceration, since they can always pass along costs to the users. The resulting status quo most greatly benefits a limited yet influential few—those who profit from full jails and prisons.

Concern over shielding "hardworking taxpayers" from the costs of getting the "bad guy" figures prominently in cost-shifting rationales. Yet the distinction between "taxpayers" and "bad guys" may be an illusory one. Someone may be holding down a taxpaying job one day and behind bars the next. And, where compelled to pay book-in fees or a per diem for room and board in pre-trial detention, one is paying fees *before* being convicted of any offense. Probationers, for whom employment is often a condition of release, pay taxes but are still charged fees for probation services. Family members—who pay into commissary or personal accounts for a detained or incarcerated loved one, only to have those dollars intercepted by corrections officials to cover inmate room and board—are often taxpayers.

Ora Lee Hurley's situation offers an illustrative example of the hazy divide between "bad guy" and "taxpayer" and the counterproductive cycle fee assessments create. Hurley is a prisoner held at the Gateway Diversion Center in Atlanta because she owes a $705 fine. As part of the diversion program, Hurley was permitted to work during the day and return to the Center at night. Five days a week she works fulltime at a restaurant, earning $6.50 an hour and, *after taxes*, nets about $700 a month. Room and board at the diversion center is $600, her monthly transportation costs $52, and miscellaneous other expenses eat up what's left. Hurley's attorney explains, "This is a situation where if this woman was able to write a check for the amount of the fine, she would be out of there. And because she can't, she's still in custody. It's as simple as that." Though she works while in custody, most of her income goes to repay her diversion program, not the underlying fine that landed her there in the first place.[18]

While the notion of charging "users" for the systems' cost may have some appeal, it ignores critically important policy and practical realities. In addition to allowing them to limit the public's financial burden caused by alleged wrongdoers,[19] policy makers and justice administrators argue that imposing cost-covering fees allows them to avoid raising taxes,[20] to ensure that crime victims are properly compensated,[21] to appear fiscally responsible,[22] and to teach moral lessons[23] and fiscal responsibility.[24] These goals, however, remain elusive.

The Chief Justice of Rhode Island warns that the pressure to generate revenue "hardly leave[s] our courts disinterested if we are forced to collect fines and costs for our operating revenue."[25] A criminal court judge from Ohio explains, "For people with loads of debt from court fines, supervision fees, restitution, and other charges related to their crime, getting out of prison is no fresh start." He warns, "They come out of the gate already at a disadvantage."[26]

Court-imposed debt is usually layered onto other disadvantages. According to a 1997 survey of state prisoners conducted by the Department of Justice, "68 percent of people in prison had not completed high school, 53 percent earned less than $1,000 in the month prior to their incarceration, and nearly one half were either unemployed or working only part-time prior to their arrest."[27] A 2006 report by the New York State Bar Association found it "fair to conclude that about 80% of all defendants charged with a felony in the United State are indigent," based on Department of Justice data collected in 2000.[28] Saddling those least able to pay with an extra cost—beyond that assessed in general taxes—for running a justice system ostensibly designed to serve the public is both inequitable and unlikely to generate the desired revenues. Predictably, researchers have found that "[s]taggering amounts of economic sanctions are unpaid, more than $4.5 billion in fines at the federal level and more than $166 million in New Jersey alone."[29]

The current approach of levying costs has a particularly devastating effect on populations of color, communities disproportionately represented in the criminal justice system. At the end of 2005, 60 percent of state and federal prisoners were African American or Latino.[30] African American women were more than twice as likely as Latina females and over three times more likely than white females to have been in prison on December 31, 2005.[31] The Census Bureau's most recent income and poverty figures show that African American households had the lowest median income in 2005 ($30,858), 61 percent of the median for non-Latino white households ($50,784).[32] Median income for Latino households was 71 percent of the median for non-Latino white households.[33] In 2005, the poverty[34] rate was 24.9 percent for African Americans, with 9.2 million people in poverty, and 21.8 percent for Latinos, with 9.4 million in poverty.[35] For non-Latino whites, the poverty rate was 8.3 percent, or 16.2 million people in 2005.[36] These prison and economic demographics show that communities of color are both disproportionately incarcerated and disproportionately impoverished.

Legislators often create new fees and increase existing assessments without much, if any, information about the system-imposed debts criminal defendants already face, or how those debts affect people's lives. Nonetheless, in 1988, the National Institute of Corrections (NIC), which provides information and support to local, state, and federal corrections officials, observed that economic sanctions against people involved in the criminal justice system were expanding in five specific ways. First, NIC noted "growth in the sheer variety of monetary sanctions," particularly sanctions designated "fees" or "special assessments." Second, NIC saw an increase in the courts' use of economic sanctions, especially fines, restitution, and reparations to the victim.[37] Next, NIC saw a dramatic increase in the percentage of defendants against whom the courts levy multiple economic sanctions as a result of a single offense. Fourth, they noted an increase in the size of fees in many, but not all, jurisdictions. Finally, they observed economic sanctions had grown from being a practice employed in a few states to becoming standard practice in most states. The number of states charging a probation fee, for example, grew from nine in 1980 to twenty-four in 1986.

This trend continues: in 2003 alone about a third of the states enacted laws assessing costs against criminal defendants for court security, probation supervision, appointed counsel, transfer of parole or probation supervision to another state, inmate medical and dental expenses, sex offender registration, electronic monitoring fees, and costs of incarceration, such as room and board. In addition to enacting new fees, some states increased existing assessments.[38] Illinois doubled its monthly probation fee (to $50),[39] Kansas doubled its assigned counsel application fee (to $100)[40] (which all defendants seeking a court-appointed lawyer to represent them at trial must complete). Minnesota upped its assigned counsel fee from $25 to $200,[41] and Oklahoma quadrupled its monthly electronic monitoring fee to $300.[42]

Legislators often create new fees and increase existing assessments without much, if any, information about the system-imposed debts criminal defendants already face, or how those debts affect people's lives.

George Keiser, chief of the Community Corrections/Prison

Division at the National Institute of Corrections, has studied the issue for decades. "Legislation imposing financial obligations has typically been passed incrementally," Keiser observes, creating "a danger in tacking fees upon fees with no end in sight." He suggests reviewing "the mandates in place before introducing new financial penalties."[43]

With the growth of the adult correctional population—over seven million adults are in jail, in prison, or supervised in their community[44]—in the near term policy makers will continue to feel pressure to balance large, costly criminal justice system budgets. The temptation to shift the financial burden to the most politically powerless among us—those caught up in the criminal justice system—is fierce. While the move may be popular with taxpayers and legislators eager to avoid raising taxes, any short-term gains in revenue come at the cost of long-term community survival. Even the courts and criminal justice administrators who are the intended beneficiaries of cost-shifting economic sanctions are beginning to realize the futility of saddling those who are reentering society with debt so crippling that debt that will erase any chances of successful reintegration.

A first step in understanding whether assessing cost-related fees is the appropriate way to defray those budget costs is identifying the actual fees being assessed.

An Overview of Criminal Financial Assessments

I've never seen so many people interested in $15![45]
—*Probationer's disbelief at paying multiple tiny fees, as expressed on the wall of a probation office bathroom*[46]

A first step in understanding whether assessing cost-related fees is the appropriate way to defray the skyrocketing budget costs of state criminal justice systems is identifying the actual fees being assessed. An increasingly popular method for meeting the costs of expensive criminal justice systems is to recoup administrative costs from those arrested, prosecuted, incarcerated, and supervised within criminal justice systems.[47] While states usually enact legislation authorizing assessment of fees at each stage of the criminal justice process, these charges resemble land mines—they are "hidden" and "scattered throughout every state code,"[48] and they have the capacity to financially destroy those they come in contact with. The New York State Bar Association has concluded that "the financial penalties imposed [upon people in the criminal justice system], directly or indirectly, as a result of a criminal conviction, are among the least recognized of the collateral consequences."[49] As a result, it is difficult for any given defendant, defense attorney, or even policy maker to fully comprehend fully the financial sanction attached to a conviction or sentence. To cure this and other problems created by hidden and scattered collateral consequences, the American Bar Association recently recommended that state "legislature[s] should collect, set out or reference all collateral sanctions in a single chapter or section of the jurisdiction's criminal code" in order to "provide the means by which information concerning the collateral sanctions that are applicable to a particular offense is readily available."[50]

The National Institute of Corrections' first comprehensive analysis of economic sanctions, released in 1988, provided an overview of the types of financial consequences levied upon arrest, conviction, and sentence.[51] Fines, costs, and restitution, perhaps the most familiar forms of economic sanctions, are usually formal penalties explicitly set forth in the court's judgment and sentence of the defendant, as with the assessments Wilbert Rideau faced. Fines are the traditional monetary penalty, usually imposed according to severity of crime, to punish an individual. According to Bergstrom and Ruback,

"Nationally, fines are imposed in 25% of all felony convictions: 20% of violent offenses, 24% of property offenses, 27% of drug offenses, 19% of weapons offenses, and 27% of other offenses."[52] Court costs are fees adopted and imposed by jurisdictions on most convicted persons, to cover a variety of court expenses that may include maintenance of court facilities, service of warrants, and law enforcement officers' retirement funds.[53] Restitution is a court-ordered "payment by the offender to the victim for financial losses, and embodies both the just desserts notion of offense-based penalties and concern for the victim,"[54] and may be collected at probation or parole stages.[55]

Service fees, a second category of charges, may arise before or after conviction and cover the costs that arise when someone in the criminal justice system is required to use certain services. Pre-conviction service fees include the jail book-in fee levied at the time of arrest; jail per diems assessed to cover the cost of a pre-trial detention stay in jail; public defender application fees, charged when someone seeks court-appointed counsel; and the bail investigation fee, assessed when the court determines the likelihood of the accused appearing at trial. Post-conviction service levies include pre-sentence report fees to defray the cost of gathering information about the defendant that influences his sentence; public defender recoupment fee, charged to offset the cost of appointed counsel; and residential fees levied on convicted persons in a residential or work release center (such as Ora Lee Hurley's), which is usually a percentage of gross income, or a flat fee for room and board. Upon release additional service fees attach, including parole or probation supervision fees, often a monthly assessment during the period of supervision.

Special assessments, a third category, are automatically levied on every offender who comes before that court or on all persons guilty of a particular offense. These levies usually include victim advocate and victim compensation fees, revenues charged to support victim advocate offices in jurisdictions and amass funds set aside to compensate victims.[56]

Given the range of economic sanctions now commonly utilized by jurisdictions across the country—fines, costs, restitution, service fees, and special assessments—people entering the justice system are unlikely to leave it without facing a financial obligation they did not have before going in. Increasingly, those debts are unrelated to achieving the criminal system's putative goals of punishment, deterrence, incapacitation, and rehabilitation. Rather, those assessments are designed to defray system costs.

Two service fees—jail fees and probation fees—are particularly ripe for discussion. Those fees are gaining in popularity in jurisdictions across the country and accumulate quickly, since jurisdictions usually assess jail fees on a daily basis and probation fees on a monthly basis. As the Clinch County sheriff demonstrated in forcing pre-trial detainees to sign promissory notes to pay for room and board or return to jail, fee payments linked to freedom are particularly critical. These fees are discussed in the next section.

The Growing Cost of Detention and Supervision

To understand the impact of jail and probation fees, it is important first to understand the demographics of the populations forced to pay them. As previously noted, as of 2005 there were more than seven million people in the federal, state, or local adult correctional population, either incarcerated or in the community.[57] What these figures mean is that 1 in every 136 U.S. residents was in prison or jail.[58] There were 1,446,269 people in prison, and 747,529 people in jail,[59] figures representing a 1.7 percent growth in prison and a 4.7 percent growth in jail populations.[60] More than 4.1 million people were on probation, and 784,408 people were on parole.[61] By year end 2005 both the probation and parole populations had grown, 0.5 percent and 1.6 percent respectively.[62] Fifty-five percent of those on probation are white, 30 percent are African American, and 13 percent are Latino.[63] Parole data show whites accounted for 41 percent, African Americans 40 percent, and Latinos 18 percent of adults on parole.[64] Along with the burgeoning population of people in jails and prisons or on probation or parole, the cost of the criminal justice system has grown, leaving policy makers and legislators scrambling to find new sources of revenue without jeopardizing their political futures by raising taxes.

Jail Fees Are Common, and Costly

In 2005 the U. S. Department of Justice, National Institute of Corrections, surveyed state jails across the country "[t]o explore the extent to which local jails are charging fees to jail inmates," "[t]o learn the actual amounts of the fees that are being charged and the revenues that are being generated," and "[t]o learn jail managers' views on the effectiveness of charging fees."[65] This 2005 survey does not reflect a representative national sample; however, it does provide "substantial information on jails' current practices related to charging inmates for programs and services."[66]

The report classifies jail fees as either a "'program fee' . . . charged to jail inmates who are participating in a program that is not a basic element of jail operations, or who are receiving a program-related service,"[67] or, alternatively, as "'[n]on-program fees' . . . assessed in relation to everyday facility operations and services."[68] The purposes of non-program fees are to offset administrative costs, the costs of housing prisoners, costs of providing routine services (such as phone service and haircuts), the expense of medical services, and to deter the frivolous use of medical services.[69] Ninety percent of the jails that responded were charging jail inmate fees, with the most common charges being in the non-program fee category for health-related services, such as prescriptions (59 percent of respondents) and physician visits (59 percent of respondents), and participation in work release programs (58 percent of respondents).[70] These findings corroborate those of a 1997 NIC study of the largest jails nationwide that found "charging of inmate fees is both prevalent and increasing among the agencies surveyed," with the most common charges imposed for medical care and participation in work release programs, and the most revenues generated by telephone services, work release programs, and home detention.[71]

The table at right summarizes the prevalence of jail fees and was created by the 2005 NIC Jail Fees Report of 2004 jail revenues. The NIC report captured program and non-program categories, as well as the number of agencies assessing the fee and the total annual revenues received from all survey respondents.

State jail officials regularly collect fees from inmates by deducting the fees from funds—often deposited by family members—in inmate accounts and by taking cash directly from them upon arrest. In a 2006 lawsuit challenging collection practices in Kenton and Campbell counties in Kentucky, a federal court upheld the jails' right to deduct money directly from commissary accounts of jail prisoners.[72] Kenton County attorney Garry Edmondson called the decision "an important victory for all counties," concluding, "The order recognizes that inmates, not the taxpayers, should bear the costs of their own incarceration."[73]

Dean v. Lehman, a 2001 case decided by the Washington State Supreme Court, also addressed the legality of automatic deduction of funds from prison accounts. RCW 72.09.480(2), a 1995 state statute, "authoriz[ed] specified deductions from any outside funds sent to DOC inmates."[74]

Non-Program Fees Ranked by Prevalence in the Response Sample

FEE CATEGORY	NUMBER OF AGENCIES ASSESSING THIS FEE	REVENUES
Medical care (Including several subcategories of services)	121	$1,506,000
Telephone use	87	4,465,000
Per diem (Including comprehensive per diem fees plus separate food- and housing-specific fees)	77	7,213,000
Booking	73	4,346,000
Photocopying	69	137,000
Barber/hair care	52	31,000
Bonding	33	631,000
Escort	31	28,000
Notary service	20	303
Laundry	12	136,000
Check processing	5	6,000
Detoxification on intake	2	25,000

Source: Barbara Krauth and Karin Stayton, U.S. Department of Justice, National Institute of Corrections, *Fees Paid by Jail Inmates: Fee Categories, Revenues, and Management Perspectives in a Sample of U.S. Jails*, 17 (Connie Clem, ed., 2005) available at http://nicic.org/Downloads/PDF/Library/021153.pdf.

Husbands and wives depositing funds into their spouses' prison accounts challenged the statute, convincing a lower court to invalidate it as a violation of tax law requirements, an unconstitutional taking of property, and an unlawful withholding of earned interest on the prisoner savings account.[75] On appeal, however, the state's high court reversed the lower court in part, holding that the automatic deductions were not a tax and therefore violated neither tax law nor the state and federal takings clauses. The Washington Supreme Court explained that "the deductions authorized by [the statute] are essentially akin to a direct 'user fee,' in that they allow the DOC to recoup its expenditures, but no more. In essence, an inmate is being asked to reimburse the State because the inmate 'has made it necessary for the State to keep and maintain him at a large cost.'"[76]

Elsewhere, at Hampton Roads Regional Jail, Virginia, a federal court upheld a fee of $1 per day directly deducted from pre-trial detainees' jail accounts to pay for housing costs.[77]

Federal courts have invalidated jail book-in fee procedures allowing officials to take funds directly from prisoners upon their arrest. In 2006, the court struck down a Washington jail booking fee statute,[78] finding it and Spokane jail policies implementing the provision "facially unconstitutional in that they deprive persons of their property without due process in violation of the Fourteenth Amendment."[79] In striking down the statute on due process grounds, the court weighed three factors.[80] The court found a "significant" private interest at stake—"a person's interest in the continued possession and use of his money."[81] The court evaluated the "risk of erroneous deprivation" and the "probable value . . . of additional or substantive safeguards,"[82] concluding because the deprivation is immediate and automatic there is great risk of error that could be cured if safeguards, such as a pre-deprivation hearing or determination of guilt, were in place.[83] Finally, the court found the state lacked a specific need for immediate, pre-hearing seizures in the absence of a pre-deprivation hearing or determination of guilt.[84]

The Hamilton County, Ohio, program of confiscating from an arrested individual any cash on hand to pay up to $30 for a book-in fee was struck down by a federal court as a violation of due process, with the court concluding "the detainee's 'obligation' to pay for costs of being booked-in cannot be finally determined until after that detainee's conviction."[85]

This brief review of select cases is by no means comprehensive; however, it reveals two themes that arise when courts consider the legitimacy of jail fees. The legality of jail fees hinges on how courts classify the fee—as punishment, tax, or user fee. It also depends upon whether procedural safeguards are in place to ensure state officials do not abuse their fee collection powers or take money from someone other than a "bad guy."

Still, the dissenting opinion in the Washington Supreme Court case upholding automatic deductions offers a straightforward critique of the problem with automatic deductions from prisoner accounts that could easily apply to all forms of cost-related assessments:

> I have scratched my head more than once trying to determine what public good is promoted by a statute that essentially authorized the seizure of 35 percent of every cent that a prison inmate's spouse sends to the inmate. While I do not know this fact for certain, I feel comfortable believing that many, if not most, of the spouses of inmates are low income individuals and that some may even be beneficiaries of forms of public assistance. Consequently, the money they send to the prisons may not be easy for them to acquire. When the State takes almost half of this money from the grasp of the inmate, the needs of the inmate will often have to be met by another contribution from the spouse. These spouses, who are mostly women, must then dig deep again if they are to offset the State's cut. In doing so they undoubtedly deprive themselves of funds that could be devoted to the purchase of necessities for them and their children. Such a scheme strikes me as not only unwise but unfair.[86]

The Cost of Staying out of Jail

While there are currently no contemporary studies of probation fee collection practices, evidence of national trends, most
notably that documented by the Vera Institute of Justice, suggests the number of jurisdictions charging probationer supervision fees has grown since a 1986 NIC survey concluding
that nearly half of states then had probation supervision fees
in place.[87] That survey found twenty-four states assessed fees
for adult supervision services, typically "rang[ing] from $10
to $50 per month," five states assessed fees for adult investiga-
tions/pre-sentence reports, typically "rang[ing] from $75 to
$300 per report," five states assessed fees for specific programs
(e.g., drug/alcohol monitoring or treatment programs), and
three states assessed fees for juvenile supervision and investigation.[88] According to the American Probation and Parole
Association, "Most long-range economic forecasts point to a
continued increased competition for declining public revenues.
In this economic environment, it is reasonable to conclude that
the trend towards charging supervision fees will continue."[89]

Probation administrators have expressed differing opinions
about the use of probation service fees, with some being "ada-
mantly oppose[d]" to them, while others believe supervision
fees help secure programs "central to fulfilling [their] mission."[90] The role of probation departments in recouping fees
from probationers varies from jurisdiction to jurisdiction. In
some, probation agencies may not be responsible for collection
of fees; in others, they may collect payments on all economic
sanctions, from victim restitution to court costs and probation
service fees. Payment of the range of economic sanctions is often a condition of successful probation.

One study has found that "[p]robation officers generally believe that collecting fees takes too much time and infringes on
their ability to do what they consider to be important duties."[91]

To increase the likelihood of fee recovery some counties use collection of fees as a method of evaluating their probation officers' overall performance.[92]

The monthly payments sought by probation are sometimes steep, as are the consequences for their nonpayment. In Louisiana, for example, individuals on probation may be required to pay a probation supervision fee of up to $100 per month, and a court can condition probation on payments to various system-related funds including those for indigent defense, the criminal court, victim compensation, and privately funded crime stoppers organizations, as well as reimbursement for other court and law enforcement costs.[93] If a condition of probation is violated, the individual is subject to arrest, which can lead to imposition of additional probation conditions, increased supervision, incarceration, or revocation.[94] In Ohio, a court can order probationers to pay up to a $50 monthly supervision fee as a condition of probation. Failure to pay may warrant the imposition of additional community control sanctions[95] or a modification of the offender's sentence.[96] In Arizona, for example, officials will extend a person's probationary period until restitution has been fully paid off.[97] Nonpayment or late payment may lead to the imposition of collections fees and interest, creating a financial hole for probationers.[98]

A Texas study established that "70.8% of those with unstable employment histories . . . had negative probation outcomes."[99] Paradoxically, it also found that Harris County judges were more likely to impose miscellaneous fees and fines on probationers with unstable employment histories than those with stable histories.[100] Another study shows that probationers in rural counties have a higher chance of being assessed probation supervision fees than those in urban counties.[101]

Arizona has made its county probation agencies responsible for collecting all economic sanctions, and has even determined the precise order in which sanctions are to be paid. Payment of restitution, for example, is given the highest priority, while payment of the "prison construction and operations fee" is number seven on the list.[102] Arizona discourages court modification of payment orders, instructing probation officers to "neither request that the Court adjust the payment amount or frequency of payment, nor request that the Court delete or exonerate any delinquency or order of Probation Service Fee during the term of probation."[103] The American Probation and Parole Association has noted that "[o]f all factors affecting collections, the degree of access to fee payments is the most significant. Organizations which are able to keep part or all of the supervision fees collected, collect more."[104]

terrible   In 1997 the Georgia legislature passed a law placing supervision of misdemeanor probationers in the hands of private companies. The supervision fee the company charged contributed to Sabrina Byrd's jailing in 2003. Byrd, a single mother of three, had never been involved in the criminal justice system. That changed, however, when she failed to pay misdemeanor fines associated with failure to leash her dogs. Since she was unable to pay the fees, which totaled $852, the court placed her on probation and devised a payment plan requiring her to both pay down the fines and pay a monthly service fee of $39 charged by a private probation supervision company. The $124 monthly payment imposed by the court was too much for Byrd to pay. She stopped showing up for probation meetings and was arrested and jailed for violating her probation.[105]

Byrd's snowballing experience in the criminal justice system was both predictable and common. Over a decade earlier, in 1986, the National Institute of Corrections predicted just such a scenario would result from probation supervision fees. "The added stress caused by inability to pay may cause probationers to miss appointments, thus negating any positive effect of supervision and sometimes resulting in revocation for failure to comply with the conditions of probation."[106]

Current fee trends appear to weaken our constitutional protection against jailing people for being poor.[107] One could argue that people such as Byrd are imprisoned not for being poor and unable to pay but for their failure to attend probation meetings. But Byrd's economic status and status as a probationer were inextricably intertwined. If she had the money to pay the fine in the first place, she would not have been placed on probation, and if she had not been on probation, she would not have had to make an additional $39 payment to the private probation company on top of her fines. And, of course, but for the court's supervision she would not have landed in jail.

The Cost of Nonpayment

Each state has its own unique methods for recovering criminal economic sanctions and punishing default. The Brennan Center's research in New York, Florida, and Washington illustrates some of these methods. Perhaps most notably, imposition of nonpayment consequences may fail to absolve all or part of the underlying financial obligation and, perversely, may even result in the increase of debt. In New York, for example, a person cannot escape his or her economic sanctions solely by serving the term of confinement imposed for failure to pay.[108]

Our research suggests the two most common formal consequences for people owing criminal economic sanctions are civil judgment and incarceration. In Washington, for example, since financial obligations constitute a judgment against someone who is convicted, collection may be accomplished through methods such as payroll deduction, wage assignment, and seizure of assets.[109] However, unlike traditional civil judgments, which may be enforced only up to a period of ten years, in Washington the ability to collect may be extended.[110]

In Florida a court may order someone's property to be seized to satisfy any financial obligation,[111] or impose a civil

restitution lien in addition to traditional civil liens.[112] Under
Florida's civil restitution framework, convicted people incur
liability for damages and losses to crime victims, the state, its
local subdivision, and possibly others. Those parties may seek
a court-ordered civil restitution lien against the defendant.[113]
The range of damages assessed is statutorily prescribed[114] and
remains on the real and personal property in the debtor's possession or that she comes to possess subsequent to conviction
until the debt is fully paid.

The amount a defendant owes is likely to increase over time.
For example, in Florida interest accrues on a civil restitution
from the date of entry,[115] and in Washington, unless a court
determines otherwise, interest will accrue upon unpaid financial obligations at a rate of 12 percent from the date of judgment until final payment.[116]

In a vicious financial cycle, those behind in payments may
have to pay costs associated with civil collection methods or
incarceration. If a Florida locality refers collection to a private
collection agent or private attorney to collect unpaid financial
obligations, for example, a collection fee plus an attorney's fee
may be added to the balance owed.[117] A person will likely face
civil proceedings for failure to satisfy monetary penalties such
as these, which are normally enforceable against a person's assets in the same manner as any other civil judgment, such as
seizure of or lien against property.[118]

States including New York, Washington, and Florida also
may authorize incarceration for willful nonpayment or as part
of contempt of court.[119] Since a financial obligation is a condition of sentence or probation, a person may be subject to
additional penalties such as electronic home monitoring, community service, curfew, and any other sanctions available.[120]
Officials may also revoke probation or community-based sanctions, such as community service, curfew, suspension or revo-

cation of driver's license, and electronic monitoring, for someone in default on payments.[121]

People assessed criminal economic sanctions face clear and potentially devastating repercussions to their finances and even their freedom if they are unable to pay a criminal debt. The consequences do not stop there; outstanding debt affects people's livelihoods and their families, and even undermines our democracy. *unfair cycle*

The key to repaying criminal sanctions is having the funds to pay. We know those arrested and prosecuted are often poor and undereducated, with minimal employment histories. For people with a criminal record it is even harder to land a job and earn the funds to repay criminal sanctions. Potential employers can easily access information about criminal histories using modern technology,[122] unearthing information that stops an application dead in its tracks before an applicant is fairly considered.[123] According to the New York Bar Association, increasingly employers are also conducting credit history background checks that reveal "information about civil judgments, unpaid debts and often contain information about the individual's credit rating, criminal history, and employment history."[124] If, as the president of the National Workrights Institute says, "a bad credit report can cost you a job no matter how qualified you are," the combination of outstanding debt and a criminal conviction can be an insurmountable hurdle for job hunters.[125]

In addition to employer attitudes, a growing number of legal restrictions prevent people with convictions from securing jobs across an array of occupations and professions.[126]

For example, legal restrictions affect the ability of individuals with criminal records in New York to receive any of more than one hundred state licenses,[127] and in 2005 New York enacted a law "prohibiting the employment of any person convicted of a felony in the preceding 10 years in the field of nursing homes or home care."[128]

Unable to find employment, an individual with outstanding economic sanctions may be put in a position where he must choose between using limited resources to pay off criminal debt or meet financial obligations to his family. Child support, for example, is a common financial obligation hovering over formerly incarcerated parents that may compete with criminal sanctions for payment.[129] According to the New Jersey Institute for Social Justice, "a study of 650 incarcerated parents with child support orders in Massachusetts found that the parents enter prison owing an average of $10,543 in unpaid child support. If the orders remain at pre-incarceration levels they will accumulate another $20,461 in debt over time, plus 12 percent interest and six percent in penalty charges."[130] In addition to child support, the garden-variety expenses of life—housing, food, clothing—may be sacrificed in order to pay off criminal debt.

Finally, outstanding criminal sanctions infect our nation's democracy. At least nine states explicitly condition the right to vote on the payment of court-imposed financial obligations: Alabama, Arizona, Connecticut, Delaware, Florida, Kentucky, Maryland, Virginia, and Washington. In another nineteen states, it is possible, but unclear, that people with criminal convictions need to pay off outstanding court debts before being allowed to vote. These states have some "discharge from sentence" or "completion of sentence" language that makes it unclear whether payment of outstanding criminal sanctions is an absolute condition on the right to vote. Those states include Alaska, Arkansas, Georgia, Idaho, Kansas, Minnesota, Mississippi, Missouri, Nebraska, New Jersey, New Mexico, North Carolina, Rhode Island, South Carolina, South Dakota, Tennessee, West Virginia, Wisconsin, and Wyoming.

Are Economic Sanctions Sound Public Policy?

Quite apart from the question of whether economic sanctions are legal or whether government effectively collects the fees is the question of whether economic sanctions designed to cover the cost of the criminal system are sound public policy. Whatever their political expediency or revenue-generating force, some criminal justice system advocates and administrators are clearly troubled by this transfer of costs to people in the criminal system, and the consequences of the debt may ultimately be more expensive—in terms of lost dollars and lost futures—than the system's cost itself.

As stated at the start of this chapter, policy makers and justice administrators defend the imposition of cost-covering fees as a means to limit the public's financial burden caused by wrongdoers, to avoid raising taxes, to ensure crime victims are properly compensated, to appear fiscally responsible, and to teach moral lessons and fiscal responsibility. Given the ever-expanded use of the fees, at a minimum we must evaluate whether cost-recovery sanctions are achieving these lawmakers' stated goals and whether society as a whole benefits from their use. This chapter's preliminary review of the evidence suggests cost-recovery sanctions are missing these public policy marks.

Does Imposition of Cost-Recovery Sanctions Limit the Public's Financial Burden?

Evidence suggests it may not, for two main reasons. First, recovering monies from people may be akin to drawing blood from a stone. When one cannot find a job and is faced with other mandatory financial obligations, such as child support, one simply may not have money left to pay the system's costs. The public savings suggested in the budget ledgers, therefore, may never materialize. Moreover, because cost-recovery sanctions are often levied against the poor, further research is needed to determine whether payments made actually originate from other sources of public dollars, such as public benefits. Whether the public is paying the cost of the criminal justice system directly or indirectly, through the transfer of other public benefit dollars to pay down criminal debt, the evidence suggests cost-recovery sanctions do little to relieve the public's financial burden.

Does Imposition of Cost-Recovery Sanctions Limit Taxpayer Burden?

The evidence suggests taxpayers, albeit a potentially narrower slice of them, are paying their taxes as well as the cost-recovery sanctions that allegedly reduce their tax burden. Individuals assessed the fees may also be taxpayers, holding down taxpaying jobs while on work release or under community supervision, and still assessed additional costs to cover the system. Family members of those in the system face a triple threat—they pay taxes (which cover the cost of the system), contribute to jail and prison trust accounts (which officials intercept to cover the cost of the system), and may help released brothers, mothers, daughters, and fathers to repay old fees and new ones (such as probation supervision costs).

Does Imposition of Cost-Recovery Sanctions Ensure Crime Victims Are Properly Compensated?

Imposition of cost-recovery sanctions actually seems to undermine the penological goals of the system, including crime victim compensation. These additional financial burdens create a competition among victims and justice system administrators for pieces of a small pie.

Does Imposition of Cost-Recovery Sanctions Allow Policy Makers to Appear Fiscally Responsible?

This rationale for promoting cost-shifting to people in the system is an interesting one, focused on appearances rather than sound policy. Even if appearances were a legitimate basis for making policy, the evidence suggests these impositions do not reflect favorably on policy makers. To the contrary, cost-shifting demonstrates a willingness to place political expediency over true fiscal responsibility, which requires tough decisions about cutting costs and raising revenues. The ability to impose costs on the criminal system's captive audience allows policy makers to avoid these hard questions about how to create a cost-effective criminal justice system, as well as to avoid disappointing those with a fiscal interest in keeping jails and prisons full.

Does Imposition of Cost-Recovery Sanctions Teach Moral Lessons and Fiscal Responsibility?

For many people leaving prison, criminal economic sanctions hang over their heads like the sword of Damocles, ready to drop at any moment. High criminal debt and low earning potential combine to frustrate efforts to achieve financial and social stability and to live up to one's obligations to family and community after involvement in the system. Research in the child support context illustrates a tipping point at which the size of debt relative to income creates an unwanted backlash. Studies show that compliance with child support orders is strongly linked to ability to pay, and that compliance was significantly lower when monthly orders were more than 20 percent of a parent's income compared to when orders were 15 percent or less of income.[131] If criminal financial obligations are aimed at furthering responsibility, they cannot be so burdensome as to make work futile. These sanctions are shows of force of the system's power to punish, control, and prevent an individual from shaking loose from its yoke. Do they provide lessons in morality or in fiscal responsibility? For the individuals facing cost-recovery assessments and their families, criminal debt simply provides another obstacle to overcome before achieving greater financial and social stability.

In addition to policy makers' justifications for cost-recovery sanctions, the utility of the assessments may be considered a "[f]unction of [t]emporal [f]ocus and [t]arget," a useful rubric developed by Pennsylvania State University professor R. Barry Ruback and Mark H. Bergstrom of the Pennsylvania Commission on Sentencing.[132] "Past-oriented sentencing alternatives are concerned with what the offender did . . . [and such sentences] directed at the victim generally focus on restitution to the victim, which in almost all circumstances is monetary compensation."[133] Such retrospective victim-focused sanctions include special assessments and restitution. "Past-oriented sentences directed at society generally focus on reimbursement of costs of prosecution and on community service."[134] Cost-recovery sanctions fall here on the spectrum. "Past-oriented sentences directed at the offender generally focus on punishing the offender."[135] Fines and forfeiture fall here. In an important observation, Ruback and Bergstrom note that "[f]uture-oriented sentencing alternatives are concerned with predicting and reducing the likelihood of future offending."[136] These "sentences directed at society generally focus on deterrence and reintegration [and] generally require offenders to pay fees for treatment and rehabilitation"[137] and for services like probation supervision.

By highlighting the system's putative goals—punishment, incapacitation, deterrence, and rehabilitation—this model aids in understanding the tension cost-recovery sanctions create. They are past-oriented sanctions aimed at benefiting society by reimbursing taxpayers, yet they interfere with a victim's ability to be made whole. Cost-recovery sanctions are future-oriented as well, assessed to cover supervision costs and often collected when people return to their communities. Consequently, collecting them interferes with future-oriented goals of reintegration, rehabilitation, and greater public safety.

Policy Makers Must Reconsider the Use of Cost-Recovery Sanctions

Twenty dollars here, $15 there—for a busy legislator focused on ending the fiscal year in the black, enacting these types of monetary sanctions may appear to be sensible, relatively painless financial fixes. But as lawmakers continue to shift more and more of the costs of the criminal justice system onto those arrested, charged, prosecuted, and incarcerated, it is critical that they understand the entire economic sanctions picture and resist the current piecemeal approach. Across the country, both those burdened with the debt as well as state policy makers, probation officers, judges, and court administrators increasingly understand the big picture, and are troubled by it. They are urging reconsideration of existing cost-recovery fees and cautioning against creation of new ones.

Policy makers can heed their call by (1) conducting (and regularly updating) an inventory of all criminal fees, fines and economic sanctions on their books, (2) performing an impact analysis when a new economic sanction is proposed that includes assessment of the population most likely to face the sanction, the amount of sanctions already paid by that population, and the proposal's effect on public safety, and (3) instituting a moratorium on new sanctions or sanction increases until the proper research and impact procedures are in place. Without protections such as these, responsible decision making in the area of criminal economic sanctions is simply not possible.

Prisons, Politics, and the Census

Gary Hunter and Peter Wagner

August 2007

Prisons have become a growth industry for rural America, with a new prison opening in a small town every fifteen days over the last decade.[1] Now a $60 billion industry,[2] prisons have developed the economic muscle to bend state priorities to their needs. There are now so many people in prison that legislators who have prisons in their districts are able to short-circuit the democratic process that would otherwise govern the prison industry.

Since the first census in 1790, the Census Bureau has counted prisoners as residents of the town where the prison or jail is located. This might have made sense two hundred years ago, when there were few people in prison and the data was only used to determine the relative populations of each state and the size of its congressional delegation. It would not have mattered if an incarcerated person was counted at home in New York City or in prison in rural Attica as long as he was counted in the right state.

The importance of accuracy in counting citizens to determine voting districts has long been recognized as vital to a thriving democracy. In the 1960s, the Supreme Court struck down state legislative district plans that gave some citizens more access to government than others, declaring the "One Person One Vote" rule and the principle that "legislators represent people, not trees or acres. Legislators are elected by voters, not farms or cities or economic interests."[3] From that point forward, districts were to be based on population, not counties, history, or economics.

Drawing districts based on population requires accurate data, and states looked to the Census Bureau to provide counts for each town and neighborhood. But the centuries-old flaw in how the Bureau counts prisoners soon undermined the ability of states to draw districts that contained the same number of actual residents.

Where Prisoners are Counted Matters

By the 1980s, the prison population was starting its big upswing from the War on Drugs, and by 1990, three out of every thousand people counted by the census were in prison. Concentrated in new and ever-larger prisons in rural areas, this portion of the population was now big enough to matter.

Many state constitutions define residence for a prisoner as the place he or she resided prior to incarceration.[4] This approach reflects the involuntary and short-term nature of incarceration, and a concern that including the residents of correctional facilities could distort the local democratic process. In New York, for example, the state constitution declares that for "the purpose of voting, no person shall be deemed to have gained or lost residence . . . while confined in any public prison."[5]

The impact on census data is large because prisoners tend to be demographically different from the average population of the country, and because prisoners tend to be incarcerated in communities far removed from their homes. Although few communities are "average," incarcerated people are far from the average demographic. Ninety-two percent of people incarcerated in federal and state prisons are men.[6] Blacks and Latinos are only a quarter of the U.S. population, but are almost 63 percent of the nation's incarcerated.[7]

82   *Prison Profiteers*

According to an analysis of U. S. Census 2000 data, there are twenty-one counties where at least 21 percent of the reported census population is actually incarcerated people from outside the county.[8] In 173 counties, more than half of the African American population reported in the census is incarcerated.[9]

Distorting Democracy at the State Level

Every prisoner counted as a resident of the prison district decreases the number of "real" residents required for the prison district. As the number of real residents declines in a district, the weight of a vote in that district increases as compared to the residents elsewhere in the state.

Including disenfranchised nonresident prisoners as population for purposes of redistricting creates prison districts with substantially fewer constituents than elsewhere. The real residents of the prison district have more access to their legislator than other state residents.

Each decade, state legislatures use census data to redraw congressional and state legislative districts. The current practice of crediting prisoners to the prison location results in drawing legislative districts near prisons that have large numbers of nonresidents. One legislative district in New York is 7 percent prisoners;[10] a legislative district in Texas is 12 percent prisoners;[11] and 15 percent of one Montana district is prisoners imported from other parts of the state.[12] The existence of these legislative districts with artificial populations increases the voting strength of the real prison-district residents and dilutes the voting strength of residents in every other district in the state. The urban communities that have large numbers of residents incarcerated outside their districts see their voting strength diluted beyond that of the average district in a state, though it is impossible to calculate this precisely because the necessary census data on origin has never been collected.

Distorting Democracy in Rural Counties

The impact on local legislatures, such as county boards, is even more pronounced. Because the district sizes tend to be relatively small, a single prison can have a significant impact. The Prison Policy Initiative, of which the second author of this chapter is the executive director, has noted a number of districts in which the majority of the population are prisoners from other parts of the state. Such analysis has found that rural residents who live in the same community as a prison but in a different county legislative district frequently see their votes on local issues diluted quite severely.

New York's St. Lawrence County includes 3,120 state prisoners within only two of their fifteen legislative districts. The population of District 2 is more than one-quarter prisoners. Although the legislative districts average 7,462 county residents, District 2, in Ogdensburg, has only 5,639.

St. Lawrence County's inclusion of the prisoners was the subject of local controversy in part because the county had previously excluded the prisoners. The legislature changed course in order to shift the balance of power in the county. In response, about 2,000 citizens signed a petition opposing their legislature's plan to include prisoners in population counts. The petition was thrown out on a technicality, and the legislature went ahead with its districting plan, but many of the incumbents who were responsible for this were defeated in the following county election.

Significant vote dilution from the prisoner miscount is not confined to New York. Dodge County, Wisconsin, has a district that is 59 percent prisoners, and Waupun City within the county has an aldermanic district that is 79 percent prisoners. As a result, the small neighborhoods near the prisons get to dominate county and city affairs far out of proportion to the numbers of actual residents.

With the exception of St. Lawrence County as discussed above, every time the rural public has learned that prison populations were being used to dilute their votes in the county legislature, the actual residents of the county demanded that the districts be drawn without the prison populations.

As three residents of New York's upstate Franklin County— Dan Jenkins, Mark Flack Wells, and Norman Gervais— explained in a 2004 letter to the Census Bureau:

> Franklin County has always excluded state prisoners from the base figures used to draw our legislative districts. To do otherwise would contradict how we view our community and would lead to an absurd result: creating a district near Malone that was ⅔rds disenfranchised prisoners who come from other parts of the state. Such a district would dilute the votes of every Franklin County resident outside of that area and skew the county legislature. We know of no complaints from prisoners as a result, as they no doubt look to the New York City Council for the local issues of interest to them.[13]

Distorting Policy Decisions in Favor of Prison Expansion

The most troubling aspect of miscounting prisoners in this fashion is the potential to change the balance of political power between communities who stand on opposite ends of state crime control policy. Removing electoral clout from urban communities that are the most negatively affected by aggressive incarceration policy, and giving that clout to rural communities, has the potential of launching a cycle of prison growth with no democratic restraints.

Sixty-five percent of the nation's prison population is either African American or Latino. Locating these unwilling residents in small, predominantly white towns fundamentally shifts the balance of political power through the redistricting process. The policy impact of miscounting African American and Latino prisoners is clearest in New York State, where African Americans are sent to prison in New York for drug law violations at a rate 34.5 times higher than whites. The Latino rate is 25.7 times higher than the rate for whites.[14] As a result, in a state that is 62 percent white,[15] African Americans and Latinos account for 93 percent of prison sentences for drug offenses in New York State.[16]

Despite their proven failure, significant reform of the draconian Rockefeller drug laws has been stalled for years by a small number of powerful state senators with large prisons in their districts. When urban and minority legislators from New York City proposed reforming the laws, the prison district senators accused their critics of plotting a "jail break."[17] Of the seven rural New York State senators whose districts contain large prisons, four of them sit on the powerful criminal law committee where they have successfully stalled reform of the state's Rockefeller drug laws for years.

Crediting prisoners to the prison districts bears a striking resemblance to the original "Three-Fifths" clause of the United States Constitution, which allowed the South to obtain enhanced representation in Congress by counting disenfranchised slaves as three-fifths of a person for purposes of congressional apportionment. When credited to the South, the extra population gave the South parity in Congress and the Electoral College. It assured Thomas Jefferson's victory over John Adams in 1800, facilitated Missouri's admission to the Union as a slave state, and otherwise gave the South "important political leverage in Congress"[18] to create a national stalemate that prevented the creation of a democratic solution to the slavery problem. What might have been resolved peacefully in the 1790s became the Civil War in the 1860s precisely because the South received extra political clout from counting people it did not consider to be residents.

Opposition to Census Reform

Not surprisingly, most of the opposition to reform comes from legislators whose districts contain prisons. What is surprising is the lack of pretense these legislators give to providing actual representation to the prisoners in their districts. Indeed, the evidence indicates that representatives of such districts do not merely ignore their incarcerated constituents, but advocate policies inimical to their interests. The leading defenders of the Rockefeller drug laws (that require long mandatory prison sentences) are upstate New York senators Dale Volker and Michael Nozzolio, heads of the State Senate Committees on Codes and Crimes, respectively.[19] The prisons in their districts together account for more than 17 percent of the state's prisoners.[20]

Senator Volker has been particularly blunt in rejecting the notion that he represents the interests of the 8,951 prisoners assigned to his district, 77 percent of whom are Black or Latino (4,447 Black, 2,427 Latino).[21] As reported in a 2002 interview: "The inmates at Attica prison in western New York State are represented in Albany by state Sen. Dale Volker, a conservative Republican who says it's a good thing his captive constituents can't vote, because if they could, 'They would never vote for me.'"[22]

Some rural politicians oppose changing the census, arguing that doing so would transfer much-needed funds back to urban communities and thus bankrupt their towns. Small-town mayors who have staked their town's future on building new prisons are quick to claim any perceived benefit as the direct result of the decision to build the prison. Such politicians often base their assertion on general espousals by the Census Bureau that encourage people to participate in the Census because the data are used in the distribution of federal and state funds. While technically true that census data influences funding, how prisoners are counted does not play a significant part in funding formulas.

California's *Vacaville Reporter* followed this issue in its story about census reform by interviewing the city manager in Vacaville, where 10 percent of the town's population are prisoners. Not surprisingly, the city manager argued that counting prisoners at their home addresses would cost the prison city significant funds. But the *Vacaville Reporter* dug further and interviewed Ken Campo, the city's finance manager, who explained that the fiscal impact of counting prisoners at home would be small because only a small portion of the budget relies on per capita funding. "We'd lose some gas-tax funds from the state, but not much else."[23]

Detailed reviews of state, federal, and local funding streams reveal that where prisoners are counted has only an occasional impact on governmental financial distributions and that the impacted funds do not affect urban communities.[24] Although census data does play a role in the distribution of more than $1.5 trillion each decade in federal funds, the vast majority of these funds are unaffected by where prisoners are counted because most prisoners are incarcerated in the state in which they lived prior to incarceration. Medicaid and the federal highway system account for the majority of the partially population-based funds, but these funds are distributed as block grants to states based on the total population of the state and other factors unrelated to incarceration. The majority of other federal funds are in tailored programs that match the program to the need. The low incomes of prisoners do depress per capita income statistics, but most government programs that are concerned with poverty rely on statistics such as "household income" and "poverty" which are automatically calculated without prisoners.

In contrast, state sales taxes are often affected by the decisions of the Census Bureau. Most states distribute sales taxes with portions going directly to the state's general revenues, portions returning to the point-of-sale localities, and portions going to municipalities or other local governments on the basis of population. Thus, communities that host a prison receive an additional, unearned portion of the state sales tax.[25]

In sum, the prisoner miscount has a small impact on funding, but it does not drain urban funds to enrich rural communities. Rather, the impact is predominantly a modest distortion in how funds are distributed within rural communities. Such discussion of how the census impacts funding ultimately serves to distract urban and rural people from the real problem: how relying on the prisoner miscount radically distorts policy and democracy at the state and local levels.

Calls for Change

In spite of the objections of those who benefit, and a stubborn bureaucratic Census Bureau, calls for reform are growing. Key Census Bureau advisors have called for change, including the Census Bureau's African American advisory committee and the prestigious National Research Council of the National Academies.

In 1999, then Census Bureau director Kenneth Prewitt opposed an eleventh-hour attempt to change how prisoners were counted in the census.[26] But better conceived proposals presented during the 2010 Census–planning process have since gained his support.[27]

The *New York Times* has written nine editorials highlighting how the prisoner miscount harms democracy, and has been joined by the editorial boards of papers as diverse as the *Milwaukee Journal-Sentinel*, the *Flint Journal* (Michigan) and the rural *Jackson City Patriot* (Jackson County, Michigan).

Fearing that the Census Bureau may not act in time to fix the 2010 Census, some states are preparing interim solutions. Bills are currently pending in New York, Illinois, and Michigan that would create a special state census to gather the home addresses of incarcerated people and correct the federal census prior to redistricting.

Urban and rural legislators around the country are starting to lobby the Census Bureau directly. For example, in a recent letter to the Census Bureau sent by New York State Senator Eric Schneiderman and St. Lawrence County New York Legislator Tedra Cobb, the senators asked the Census Bureau to address its method of counting prisoners. The senators suggested alternative methods, like counting prisoners as residents of addresses outside of the facility. The senators also requested publication of the subsequently gathered redistricting data for prisoner populations, which would provide more detailed counts to assist the state and its counties in properly accounting for prison populations prior to redistricting.

The importance of where the Census Bureau counts prisoners was discovered too late to change the 2000 Census. Given the rapid approach of the 2010 Census, it is possible that a complete change in how the census counts prisoners may need to wait until 2020. But justice may not be so long off, as the *New York Times* editorial board predicted, "Voters who come to understand how this system cheats them are unlikely to keep rewarding the politicians who support it."[28]

Don't Build It Here:
The Hype Versus the Reality
of Prisons and Local Employment
Clayton Mosher, Gregory Hooks, and Peter B. Wood

January 2005

According to the Economic Research Service of the Department of Agriculture, 245 prisons opened in 212 of the nation's 2,290 rural counties between 1991 and 2001. Over the past two decades, prison hosting has been advertised as a sure-fire catalyst for economic recovery and growth, particularly for economically depressed rural areas that have seen a loss in primary industry jobs. A brochure published in 1989 by the California Department of Corrections designed to encourage communities to host prisons asserted that prisons brought economic benefits, "including 600 to 1,000 new jobs and an annual payroll of $20 to $52 million, a large share of which remains in the community." Similarly, an article discussing prison construction in the state of New York claimed that a typical 500-bed correctional facility employs 350 people with an annual payroll of $12 million and that "in rural counties of northern New York, existing correctional facilities are contributing $75 million to the local economy."

Belief in the positive economic impact of prisons is so strong that a town in Illinois developed a rap song and purchased television advertising as part of a public relations blitz for legislators deciding where to locate a prison. In Texas, students in a Sunday school class reportedly got on their knees and prayed that a new prison would open in their area. In the same state, some towns offered free golf club memberships to prospective prison officials if the facilities were located there. In California, approximately 140 residents of a southern community traveled more than 600 miles to the state capital, Sacramento, to hold a rally, chanting, "We want the prison." In the mid-1990s, nineteen communities in Washington State were competing for a juvenile rehabilitation center; in Florida, fifteen towns offered free land for a new state prison; in Missouri, twelve communities were vying for three prisons. In a 1999 "prison derby" in the state of Illinois, twenty-seven communities competed to secure a new prison. And communities that win the "prison prize" appear to be eternally grateful. For example, in Tamms, Illinois, which houses the state's supermaximum-security prison, a billboard for the local bank promised "super-max-imum savings," while a local restaurant offered the "supermax burger" on its menu. A billboard outside Tamms displays the message "Welcome to Tamms, the Home of the Supermax—Thank You Governor Edgar."

Do Prisons Deliver? A National Study of the Economic Impact of Prisons

While in recent years prisons have been almost universally viewed as economic panaceas for struggling communities, inadequate empirical analysis has been undertaken to determine whether they actually deliver the purported economic benefits. Most studies examining the economic impact of prisons have been based on a limited number of correctional facilities in a limited number of jurisdictions. In order to address this deficiency, our research involved the collection of data on all existing and new prisons built in the United States since 1960, and we examined the impact of prisons on employment growth in the approximately 3,100 counties in the contiguous United States for the 1969–94 period. (It is important to note that our research focuses on the specific economic benefits associated with employment growth. We do not address the potential economic benefits to communities that may be associated, for example, with prisoners being included in census counts, which is a topic addressed by other chapters in this volume.)

Given that the tendency to lobby for prisons has been more common in rural jurisdictions, our statistical analyses compared metropolitan with nonmetropolitan counties. In the first set of analyses, we examined income per capita, total earnings, and total employment growth (without statistically controlling for other factors that could affect economic growth). Among urban counties, there was little difference in the average annual change in income per capita between counties housing a prison and those not housing a prison. We also found that urban counties without a prison had the highest annual rate of growth, while those with a newly built prison grew at the slowest pace. In rural counties, for both income per capita and total earnings, those without a prison grew at a faster pace, and employment grew more slowly in counties in which a new prison was built.

Our next set of analyses attempted to isolate the impact of prisons on employment growth by introducing a number of statistical controls for other potential influences on economic growth in counties. Controlling for a number of social, geographical, and economic factors that could affect employment growth, including population size, economic infrastructure, and the educational level of the workforce, among others, our statistical analyses examined employment growth, again comparing metropolitan and nonmetropolitan counties. The analyses with statistical controls determined that prisons did not play a prominent role in employment growth. For nonmetropolitan counties—the counties in which the majority of prisons have been built in recent years and the counties that have typically been the ones competing to attract prisons in order to boost local economic growth—there is no evidence that prisons have had a positive impact. Neither established prisons nor newly built facilities made a significant contribution to employment growth in rural counties.

Even if prison construction does not have a positive impact on employment for all nonmetropolitan counties, it is possible that prisons could provide tangible benefits to the most economically depressed rural counties. To explore this possibility, we distinguished nonmetropolitan counties experiencing slow employment growth during the previous decade from those growing at a faster pace. Our analyses showed that among faster-growing counties, there was no evidence that prisons made a significant contribution to a change in total employment. Among the slower-growing counties, prisons appeared to do more harm than good: new prisons in these counties actually impeded private sector and total employment growth.

Although it has largely focused on smaller geographical areas, additional research has supported our primary finding that prisons do not contribute to economic growth. For example, in New York State, a Sentencing Project report by researchers Ryan King, Marc Mauer, and Tracy Huling on the impact of thirty-eight new prisons that opened between 1982 and 2000 found no substantive or statistically significant impact of prison construction on reducing unemployment, nor were there positive effects with respect to per capita income. Similarly, a report on the impact of prison construction in Missouri found that, aside from the expected increases in population in jurisdictions with prisons (primarily as a result of the arrival of prisoners in these jurisdictions), counties with prisons evidenced no increases in personal income, and actually had larger increases in unemployment, than counties without prisons.

Why Have Prisons Failed to Provide Economic Benefits?

Our analyses did not allow us to determine why prisons did not result in the economic benefits they were purported to offer. We speculated, however, that one possible explanation is that prison construction may serve to crowd out alternative economic activity. With communities in a number of states competing to attract prisons, corrections bureaucracies are shifting infrastructure costs to local governments. In order to attract prisons, communities are forced to supply the facilities with electrical service, roads, and other things necessary to operate these facilities. Under such pressures, rural counties desperate for jobs are diverting substantial portions of what in most cases are already limited infrastructure budgets to support a detention facility. As a result, the infrastructure may be ill-suited for other potential employers, and local governments may have few remaining funds for additional investments in local infrastructure.

A second possible explanation for the lack of positive impact of prisons on economic growth, confirmed in the previously mentioned Sentencing Project study of prison construction in New York and at least two other studies, is that the jobs created by prison siting—both those related to facility construction itself and jobs within the prisons—are not taken by local residents. Most prison construction firms are from out of state and typically bring their work crews with them. Construction workers, especially on large projects, are a highly mobile and skilled workforce that moves with their employer to new construction sites. With respect to the jobs within correctional institutions, the Sentencing Project study noted that jobs in rural prisons are highly desirable, so prisons can have seniority waiting lists of several years. This report noted that in Malone, New York, most of the 750 prison jobs went to people outside the town because of prison seniority rules. Malone's director of community development commented, "Did we get 750 jobs? We didn't get 100." In essence, King, Mauer, and Huling conclude that the effect of a prison in a community is largely artificial in nature and amounts to an employment transfer. Professor and prison researcher Ruthie Gilmore's study of prison towns in California similarly found that less than 20 percent of the jobs on average are taken by current residents of a town with a new prison.

Prisons also fail to create jobs in rural areas because they have limited economic multiplier effects. Prison workers who move from elsewhere rarely end up residing in the actual prison town. These workers are more likely to live in neighboring communities (up to fifty miles away) that offer more amenities but have no prison. Thus, their consumer behaviors (shopping, banking, housing, etc.) will have more of an impact on markets outside the prison community.

Another possible reason for the lack of positive economic benefit of prisons is the existence of prison industries. As researcher Tracy Huling notes, prisons may actually pit local residents in competition with prisoners for employment. All fifty states now operate their own prison industries, and there is a wide range of work activities engaged in by prisoners. Among the prominent companies that use or have used prison labor are Dell computers, the Parke-Davis and Upjohn pharmaceutical companies, Toys R Us, Chevron, IBM, Motorola, Compaq, Texas Instruments, Honeywell, Microsoft, Victoria's Secret, Boeing, Nintendo, and Starbucks. Prisoners in California have served as booking agents for TransWorld Airlines, while Microsoft has used prisoners to assist in the shipping of Windows software. Honda pays $2 an hour to prisoners in Ohio to do the same jobs that members of the United Auto Workers union were once paid $20 an hour to do. Prison officials in some states such as Washington even advertised their prisoners by asking, "Are you experiencing high employee turnover? Worried about the cost of employee benefits? Getting hit by overseas competition? Having trouble motivating your workforce? Thinking about expansion space? Then the Washington State Department of Corrections Private Sector Partnerships is for you." (A Washington State Supreme Court decision in May

2004 held that the state's free venture prison labor program was unconstitutional.)

Oregon is the state that perhaps best exemplifies the prominence of prison industries and the negative impact of prisoner labor on public and private sector jobs. In 1994, Oregon voters approved Ballot Measure 17, requiring that all prisoners in the state work forty hours per week, and that the state's prisoner work programs be conducted so that they would realize a net profit. Labor activist and professor Gordon Lafer notes that in Oregon, thousands of jobs previously in the public sector are being filled by prisoners, who are now responsible for all data entry and record keeping in the secretary of state's corporate division. Prisoners also answer the phones when members of the public inquire about corporate records, and state agencies employ prisoners for desktop publishing, digital mapping, and computer-aided design work. In the same state, companies can hire prisoner work crews. At least partially as a result of the fact that a prominent company in Linn County, Oregon, was relying on prisoner labor, the county lost approximately a thousand jobs in the four-year period spanning 1997–2001. In this particular case, given that a crew of prisoner workers costs $400 per day, Linn County Mills saved $466,000 off the cost of minimum wage plus 30 percent payroll taxes over a one-year period. If the costs of using prisoners were compared with normal wages, the company saved between $600,000 and $900,000, money that enhanced its profitability and its bottom line.

There are also several examples of companies that locate within prisons and subsequently close down their outside operations. For example, the Texas-based company American Microelectronics employed approximately 150 workers at its headquarters in Austin as well as its branch operation in Lockhart's prison. After shutting down its operations for forty-five days, the company permanently closed its Austin headquarters and moved the entire operation to Lockhart's prison. In Washington State, Omega Pacific, a carabiner manufacturing company, laid off thirty workers from its Redmond plant near Seattle and moved to the Airway Heights Corrections Center near Spokane. Interestingly, the company's catalog indicated that its products came from "our new home located on an arid plateau above the Spokane Valley," but neglected to mention that this new home was inside a prison. In Wisconsin, the Fabry company employed 205 workers at three plants in the Green Bay area in 1996. By April 1997, less than one year after the company began hiring prisoners, it had reduced its labor force at these plants to 120 employees. The company also reduced the wages of its remaining employees by up to $5.50 per hour. In Georgia, a recycling plant fired workers who were originally hired as part of a welfare-to-work program and replaced them with prison labor.

Additional evidence that the presence of prisons may lead to lower levels of employment in communities in which prisons are located was provided (inadvertently, we believe) by the mayor of Connell, Washington, where the Coyote Ridge Correctional Center is located. In an interview with an Associated Press reporter who had documented our findings that prisons did not provide economic benefits, the mayor noted that prison work crews were paid $1.10 an hour to help maintain the city's public works and commented, "If it wasn't for them, we wouldn't be able to keep our parks up."

The Cultural Commodification of Prisons
Paul Wright

November 1999

Most humans fear the unknown. For those who have not been incarcerated, prisons are dark, fearful places. For those who have been incarcerated and released, prisons are a known factor: brutal and dehumanizing, but survivable for most. The intimidation and deterrence effects of prison are enhanced by keeping it distant, remote, and unknown, but at the same time a nearby, immediate threat of imaginable evil. On the surface, these seem to be contradictory and impossible goals.

Amazingly, American pop culture has largely succeeded in not only having it both ways but simultaneously ensuring that the general population of nonprisoners does not believe that what occurs in prisons affects them. Popular culture, mainly through film and television but also with cheerleading from the corporate media and opportunistic politicians, has ingrained two conflicting images of prison into the collective American consciousness. When it is for the purpose of social control, to get the weak and poor into line, prison is the dark, barred world of brutal, sweaty, muscled, tattooed men, a world of sodomy, stabbings, and razor wire, the world conjured up when the interrogating cop whispers to the young suspect, "You know what they do to young boys like you in the penitentiary, don't you?" Prison and jail remain very much a man's world. While the number of imprisoned women has steadily increased in the past two decades, mainly due to determinate sentencing, men still make up around 94 percent of the nation's prison and jail population. As a means of social control, women tend to be medicalized, while men are criminalized. This world was alluded to when federal prosecutor Gordon Zubrod told a Canadian television interviewer that three Canadian men who were resisting extradition to the United States on fraud charges "would face a long, hard prison term as the boyfriend of a very bad man." An angry and outraged Canadian judge named Bruce Hawkins denied the extradition request, stating, "No right-thinking Canadian would endorse the use of homosexual rape as a means of persuading Canadian residents to abandon their rights to a full extradition hearing." By contrast, in American culture, the implicit threat of homosexual rape, when made by a government official in the daily course of his duties, is nothing extraordinary and deemed to be a normal part of life in prison.

However, when seeking to ensure that the lives of prisoners always remain worse than those of the poor who are not yet in prison, a different picture emerges. Tough-on-crime politicians and pundits depict prisons as lush country clubs where prisoners lounge around in comfort between leisurely sets of tennis and weight lifting, dining on steak and lobster, watching cable television, and leafing through pornographic magazines. An entire industry of politicians, victims' revenge groups, and law enforcement agencies are dedicated to unmasking the country club prisons. They have ready accomplices within most of the media.

The net result of having it both ways is that most of those who are not in prison and not likely to be there anytime soon view conditions as not nearly draconian enough, while those already incarcerated or facing the prospect of imminent imprisonment perceive it as entirely too harsh already. Nothing better illustrates this than tough-on-crime hacks such as Fife Symington, former Republican governor of Arizona, and Jim Tucker, former Democratic governor of Arkansas, groveling for mercy before sentencing judges as they beg and plead for compassion they themselves have never shown other convicted criminals. Tucker claimed poor health would doom him to death from inadequate medical care if he was imprisoned. Symington successfully argued for a reduced sentence (he never actually went to prison because President Clinton pardoned him for defrauding banks and investors of millions of dollars) by claiming that his very status as a former public official would subject him to harm in prison. Such attempts to avoid going to prison indicate that the tough-on-crime demagogues believe neither their own lies nor the cultural imagery of prisons they have devoted their political careers to propagating.

Prison as Cultural Commodity

The prison as concept is an idea ingrained into people's consciousness of what prison might be. The prison as commodity emerges when the prison culture itself is marketed and sold for mass consumption. Aside from the millions actually locked up, those on parole or probation, and ex-cons are the millions of people who feed and maintain the imprisonment machine and whose livelihoods depend on a growing carceral population: the lawyers, police, judges, courtroom personnel, prison and jail guards, administrators, police state bureaucrats, and so on. At least 750,000 people are directly employed by prisons alone in the United States. Another 800,000 or so are police. This does not include the people who build and maintain prisons and jails, those who supply the goods needed for the daily maintenance of the prison system, the doctors who contract medical services to prisons, and others.

The rise of prison culture is exemplified by the Academy in Alpharetta, Georgia, which sells "the prison experience" to those men who want to know what it is like to be in prison without actually being imprisoned. The company boasts of its wide variety of restraint and bondage equipment and the fact that its employees are real-life police officers and prison guards. Men (no women are allowed) pay almost $2,000 to spend a weekend "in prison" at the Academy, being abused, humiliated, and mistreated. This is the ultimate private prison.

Likewise, on September 24, 1998, the Style section of the *Wall Street Journal* carried a feature article on the latest fad among well-to-do home owners and interior designers: stainless-steel plumbing fixtures identical to those used in prison and jail cells. Costing over $1,000 apiece, the stainless-steel prison toilet, sans lid, is a hot fashion statement among the wealthy and stylish. An ordinary porcelain toilet, by contrast, costs as little as $60. Acorn Engineering, a manufacturer of prison plumbing fixtures, said it had received so many calls from designers it was developing a new line of jail toilets for home use.

New York architect Daniel Rowen used a stainless-steel flip-up jail seat as a towel rack in a New York City apartment he designed. The project won an award from the prestigious American Institute of Architects. Fans of prison furniture as home decor claim to like the minimalist aesthetic, saying it has "beautiful, clean lines."

Architect Peter Pawlak has cautioned, "You have to be careful. It can start snowballing. You don't want to start making it [the home] into a prison."

In a phenomenon repeated in many cities across America, Flint, Michigan, celebrated the opening of a new jail with a jail party. The city's well-to-do citizens paid hundreds of dollars each to spend the night in the new jail, with champagne and hors d'oeuvres. Documentary filmmaker Michael Moore captured the jail party on film in his classic documentary *Roger and Me*.

Unlike the items that tend to be expensive and consumed by the wealthy, prison fashion is a true mass-market commodity. Popularized by gangsta rappers, many of whom are themselves on their way into or out of prison, the baggy, ill-fitting clothes of the prison yard are sold as a cool fashion statement. The most blatant and successful example is the Prison Blues line of clothing, made by the Oregon prison system using prisoner slave labor. Oregon prison officials market the clothes with catchy slogans like "Made on the inside to be worn on the outside." One ad shows a picture of the jeans next to an electric chair with the caption "Sometimes our jeans last longer than the guys who make them." The Nevada Department of Corrections has jumped on the gangsta clothes bandwagon and markets its own line of clothes under the label Most Wanted. Their other marketing attempt is making motorcycles, Big House Choppers (which have yet to register any sales).

Chain Gang Apparel, Inc., is a Huntsville, Alabama, company that makes and sells striped prison uniforms identical to those worn by prisoners on the state's chain gangs. Perhaps with no irony, these fashions are most popular among the poor black and Latino youth most likely to wind up wearing prison clothes inside a real prison.

Chambers of commerce in Leavenworth, Kansas, and Cañon City, Colorado, compete with theme parks as tourist attractions, marketing their many prisons as must-see sites for tourists. Expensive ad campaigns use catchy slogans such as "How about doin' some time in Leavenworth?" and "You don't have to be indicted to be invited" to sell the idea. Tours of actual prisons are not offered. Instead, tourists can see prison museums and prisons that were closed due to their age. The Colorado Territorial Correctional Facility in Cañon City has a museum that displays prison memorabilia from the past and sells handicrafts made by today's prisoners. Around fifty thousand visitors pay the admission fee to visit the museum each year.

In music and music videos, prison is a frequent theme, especially among the hip-hop artists and heavy-metal rockers who cater to the young male audience most likely to wind up in prison. Is art imitating life or foretelling the future?

On HBO, the dramatic series *Oz* took place behind bars. Ryan O'Reilly is considered one of the most villainous characters on the show. In a *New York Times* interview, actor Dean Winters, who portrayed O'Reilly on the show, said "he was surprised by the fan adulation he receives for playing the character, especially when he is on the street. 'They [fans] come up to me and profess their undying love for O'Reilly. I mean, you have to wonder about these people.'"

Details magazine interviewed hip-hop singer Treach, who appeared on the show. Treach says, "I hope the show scares the shit out of people. When you go to the penitentiary, it's a whole 'nother lifestyle."

The Fox Television series *Prison Break* follows in these footsteps and has built a very successful show with millions of viewers based on a wrongly convicted death row prisoner whose brother is going to help him escape from prison. Lest prisoners, the most captive of all television audiences, get any ideas, many prisons have banned the show. Fox Television has marketed the show by having actors dressed in orange jumpsuits walk through the streets of major cities.

In 2002 7Up aired a commercial produced by Young and Rubicam called "Captive Audience" that featured a comedian playing a 7Up spokesman distributing the soft drink in a prison who drops a can of soda in front of a cell and states, "I'm not picking that up," implying that he would be risking rape if he bent over. The ad ends with a cell door slamming, trapping the soda spokesman in a cell with another man who refuses to remove his arm from around him. The commercial aired during youth-oriented programming on the networks MTV, UPN, FOX, and WB. The allusion to prison rape being used to peddle soft drinks was deemed perfectly acceptable by 7Up in its campaign to attract younger consumers. The ad was pulled after Stop Prisoner Rape and other human rights groups, including *Prison Legal News*, protested.

RBC Records has used a technique known as "viral marketing" to promote white nationalist bands such as the Woodpile to audiences by pitching the band's music to prisoners and their friends in hopes that the buzz will spread outside the prison walls and lead to increased record sales. Brian Shafton, an RBC spokesman, states that some prisoners are influential trendsetters. "Prisons are great because you have an incredibly captive audience that has a lot of entertainment time on its hands. These people are definitely influential, and not just in the prisons." The technique was first developed by black hip-hop labels to promote their musicians. As Nelson George, author of *Hip Hop America*, told the *Los Angeles Times*: "In this country, black people have been getting incarcerated justly and unjustly since we got here," he said. "The prison system has impacted black culture. And its influence on hip-hop is a subset of that."

Is anything beyond commodification? When a fashion designer recently unveiled a line of clothes modeled on Nazi concentration camp uniforms, it caused some outrage, which boosted publicity and sales. Clothing maker Benetton regularly uses images of war, famine, and disaster in its promotional campaigns. A recent Benetton ad campaign featured American death row prisoners. If the Holocaust, famine, and war can be marketed and sold, anything can—even prisons.

The Social and Political Impact of the Cultural Commodification of Prison

American prisons cannot be compared to Nazi extermination camps in that quick death is not their industrial purpose. The use of the death penalty in the United States is not yet statistically significant (the government killing a few dozen people each year in ritualized executions is statistically, but not morally, insignificant in a system that arrests, processes, convicts, punishes and imprisons millions of people each year, more so when it takes place in a geographically large nation of 300 million people). However, increased sentences, overcrowding, brutality, disease, and inadequate medical care all translate into death by incarceration. The increased popularity and use of sentences of life without parole, natural life, and mandatory prison sentences of thirty, forty, and ninety years before release all translate into one thing: death behind bars. The majority of the American anti-death-penalty movement opposes active state measures that lead to a convict's death but for the most part supports death by incarceration as a humane alternative. The end result is the same: death at the hands of the state. It just takes longer. Many judges currently impose sentences after calculating a defendant's age and how long he or she is likely to live. Accordingly, a sentence is then imposed that ensures the defendant will die behind bars. The number of people now destined to die behind bars as a result of these actuarial calculations is unknown but likely exceeds 100,000.

By commodifying prison as pop culture, mass imprisonment is made socially acceptable and connected to blue jeans, theme parks, music, entertainment, and resorts. Industrialized incarceration is the antithesis of freedom. Yet when imprisonment is equated with a lifestyle choice, few will question its fundamental nature.

Solutions?

How do we decommodify prisons as culture? The first step is to realize that pop culture is indeed political and makes policy choices seem neutral and natural when in reality they are neither. Critical awareness and analysis of pop culture among the consumers of pop culture, especially youth, is important. Then comes the attempt to counteract commodified prison culture: explaining the political and social implications of wearing Prison Blues jeans, going to Prison World on vacation, and so on. It is especially important that poor youth, the ones who populate American prisons for the most part, realize that imprisonment is not "natural." Rather, it is a policy choice that has been made instead of living-wage jobs, affordable housing, health care, and a social welfare system. In short, it is something that can be changed. Sadly, the likelihood of change at this time appears to be slight given the inability of those who do question prison culture to reach a large audience, much less reach it with the repetition and pervasiveness needed to change current attitudes.

Part II

The Private Prison Industry

Prison Labor Fuels American War Machine

Ian Urbina

January 2004

On April 16, 2003, George W. Bush visited the shop floor at the Boeing plant in St. Louis, Missouri. His ninety-minute appearance drew several hundred men and women who help make the military's $48 million F-18 Hornet fighters, thirty-six of which were deployed during the Iraq war. The purpose of Bush's visit was twofold: to offer thanks to the blue-collar workers equipping U.S. soldiers for their foreign adventures and to provide reassurance in an atmosphere of climbing unemployment.

One week prior to Bush's visit, the St. Louis plant announced layoffs for about 250 people. Already in 2003, Boeing had eliminated 5,000 positions nationwide, in addition to the 30,000 jobs the company cut in 2002. Bush's "Hardware in the Heartland" tour, which included stops across the industrial Midwest, was part of a post-war campaign strategy to capitalize on the U.S. military prowess demonstrated in Iraq. "Sure, he talked about his domestic agenda," a White House official told *Time* magazine concerning the Boeing appearance, "but there were F-18s in the background."

But the "Hardware in the Heartland" tour skipped a number of locales where thousands of hardworking men and women were contributing more than their share to the war effort. While the Boeing employees sat listening to Bush's remarks, just fifty miles to the northeast 265 workers in the apparel factory in Greenville, Illinois, were far from idle. Averaging more than 1,000 desert-tan camouflage shirts per day, 194,950 of which were bought in 2002 by the Department of Defense and worn by the U.S. infantry in the Middle East, these workers were not allowed many breaks. Equally harried were the 300 workers at the Kevlar helmet factory in Beaumont, Texas, who fill 100 percent of the U.S. military's demand for battlefield headgear. A factory in Marion, Illinois, also kept in rapid motion, soldering millions of dollars worth of cables for the Pentagon's TOW (tube-launched, optically tracked, wire-guided) missiles and Patriot missiles. Presidential plaudits were not forthcoming for these workers—all of whom are prisoners in federal prisons.

Captive Labor Force

Were it not for this captive labor force, the military could hardly meet needs ranging from weapons production and apparel manufacture to transportation servicing and communications infrastructure. U.S. soldiers are equipped with guns to fire, clothes to wear, vehicles to drive, radios to call, and maps to help them navigate, thanks in large measure to the 21,000 prisoners working for Federal Prison Industries (FPI), also known as UNICOR, a quasi-public, for-profit corporation run by the Bureau of Prisons. In 2002, the company sold $678.7 million worth of goods and services to the U.S. government, over $400 million of which went to the Department of Defense.

Created in 1934 by federal statute, UNICOR's central purpose is to turn a profit in order to offset costs in the expensive prison system, while also bolstering prison security by keeping a sizable percentage of the federal prisoner population as busy as possible. Prisoners who labor for UNICOR do so voluntarily and are paid on a relative scale set by UNICOR under its authorizing statute, but that scale is absurdly low—roughly between 23 cents and $1.15 per hour—because UNICOR is not subject to federal or state minimum wage requirements. Nor is the prison labor pool afforded the usual workers' benefits and rights, like L&I, workers' compensation, health care, the right to organize, and so on, which allowed UNICOR to recoup profits in the range of $62 million in 2004.

Government reliance upon prisoners for war production is hardly new. UNICOR/FPI started lending a hand in World War II, as prison factories ran two and three shifts per day for military manufacturing, increasing output threefold before the armistice was declared. In four years, FPI produced more than $75 million worth of everything from aircraft to dynamite cases, parachutes, cargo nets and tents, all for shipment to troops in the European and Pacific theaters. As early as May 1941, the Atlanta federal penitentiary alone was producing eight to ten train carloads of war matériel per day. During the Korean War, 80 percent of FPI output went to defense, with sales reaching over $29 million, and the number of prisoners employed by the corporation topped a then-unprecedented 3,800.

More recently, FPI has been no less vital. During the 1990–91 Persian Gulf conflict, prisoners produced belts, camouflage battle-dress uniforms, lighting systems, sandbags, blankets, night vision eyewear, chemical gas detection devices, and bomb components. Even after the September 11 attacks, prisoners took a role in relief work, their labor supplying virtually all the protective goggles worn by recovery staff at the New York and Pentagon sites.

No Ordinary Contractor

Over the years, FPI has grown exponentially, now ranking as the government's thirty-ninth largest contractor—in no small part due to the quantity and diversity of apparel items it manufactures for the Department of Defense. The company has churned out more than 150,000 Kevlar helmets between 2002 and 2004, more than $12 million worth. Aside from the battle-dress shirts sewn at Greenville, the company is also a major supplier of men's military undershirts, $1.6 million of which it sold to the Pentagon in 2002. In that year, FPI made close to $3 million fashioning underwear and nightwear for the troops. Prisoners also stitch together the vestments donned by military pastors and the gowns cloaking battlefield surgeons. If an item of clothing is torn in combat, it will likely be sent to the prison shop in Edgefield, South Carolina, where it is mended at a cost of $5 per shirt or pair of trousers. In 2002, 700 prisoners based at FPI laundry facilities located in Florida, Texas, and Alabama washed and pressed $3 million worth of military apparel.

Federal prisoners also do their part to ensure that U. S. forces are never outgunned. FPI factories produce a variety of components for weaponry ranging in size from 30 mm to 300 mm, the latter the caliber of battleship guns. FPI is there to help with more sophisticated hardware as well. To bombardiers and gunners in training, the company supplies practice targets and devices used to simulate battle conditions. In the lead-up to the 1990–91 Persian Gulf war, prisoners at the Marion facility and elsewhere ramped up production of cable assemblies for Patriot missiles. More recently, the company broadened its output to include the remote control panels, as well as the launchers, for the TOW and other guided missile systems. (It is not just the technology that has developed over the years. Though there has been no formal and updated review, most military officials report that the workmanship of FPI's weapons parts has improved markedly since the early 1990s, when a Defense Department inspector found that FPI cables sold to the army failed at nearly twice the rate of the military's next worst supplier.)

In today's military, virtually all ground troops are equipped with small microphone headsets that wire them to each other and to off-site command centers. FPI sold $7 million worth of essential components for these headsets to the Defense Department in 2002—but this is only a tiny fraction of the company's massive business with communications procurement officials at the Pentagon. FPI has fourteen prison factories employing more than 3,000 prisoners manufacturing electronics equipment. In 2002 alone, these workers crafted $30 million worth of the wire assemblies that go into all types of land, sea, and airborne communication systems. Prisoners working for FPI also provide the Defense Department with thousands of dollars' worth of services in mail sorting, and the company averages more than $4 million per year in printing services, generating everything from letterhead and envelopes to military maps, calendars, and training manuals.

Unfair Competition

From Humvee repair to the manufacture of millions of dollars' worth of electrical cords for the army, FPI offers a wide array of goods and services. But along the way, FPI has picked up a bevy of critics. One of the foremost complaints about the company stems from the unusual relationship it maintains with the U.S. government under its enabling legislation. According to the legislation that founded FPI in the era of President Franklin D. Roosevelt, the company enjoys a special "mandatory source status" that requires federal agencies to buy its products even if the same items can be purchased cheaper elsewhere. Many businesses claim that this special status gives FPI an undue competitive advantage. In 1997, this issue came to a head. After FPI doubled its stake in the military glove market over the course of several years, private glove manufacturers joined with a range of other apparel and furniture makers to fight the unfair competition. Supporting their outcry was the Defense Personnel and Support Center, in charge of most of the military's apparel purchasing, which complained that FPI's products were on average 13 percent more costly than those of commercial companies. Eventually, a General Accounting Office investigation revealed a pattern of higher prices, slower delivery, and lower-quality goods from FPI than from the private sector.

Though problems remain, most Defense Department purchasing representatives interviewed (none of whom would speak on the record) report that FPI has cleaned up its act significantly, while the mandatory source requirements have also been loosened. In the case of the glove industry, the company agreed to permit more than $7 million of the government contracts to go to outside firms.

Although FPI's relationship with the nonprison labor market still remains strained, with the skyrocketing prison population, FPI struggles to find enough new products and consumers to keep its workforce occupied. FPI's competitors in the textile industry are in no less of a bind, with more than 200,000 jobs heading overseas since 2001. Increased trade with China, a country infamous for its prison labor, has decimated the industry, leaving many domestic manufacturers on the defensive. For example, imports now account for at least 70 percent of U.S. glove sales; however, since the Defense Department is required to buy U.S.-made goods, it is one of the few remaining safe havens where glove and other apparel makers can retreat from overseas sweatshop and other prison labor competitors.

FPI's military glove production is not the only source of controversy. Skeptics also point angrily to the desert-tan battle trousers worn by the troops in Iraq and elsewhere in the Middle East. Out of the 1.3 million pairs of these trousers bought by the Defense Department last year, all but 300,000 were produced by FPI, which means that at least three out of four active-duty soldiers in the region wear pants made by the prisoners of the FPI factories in Atlanta and in Beaumont and Seagoville, Texas. These sorts of numbers have earned FPI critics from a range of perspectives. FPI competitors, such as Propper International, point out that they use free labor to make the exact same trousers for the government at $2.39 less per pair. Organized labor questions why the government should buy from a company that depends solely on prisoner workers while paying subminimum wages (from 25 cents to $1.15 per hour), skirting workplace safety standards, and enjoying exemption from the payroll and Social Security taxes levied on other employers.

In 1997, FPI lost a rare battle when, due to the "volume and tenor" of complaints, it withdrew plans to begin making American flags at its jailhouse tailor shops. FPI had completed a thorough market study, and the bulk of its flags were to be destined for the Veterans Administration, to be draped over coffins at military funerals.

Meese Versus China

FPI argues, and some studies support its contention, that its work programs not only help with prison security but also are superior to old-fashioned prison activities such as breaking rocks, since manufacturing jobs equip prisoners with job skills they can use upon their release. Prison labor is voluntary, and most prisoners jump at the chance for a job with FPI, since it is one of the few legal ways to earn money while incarcerated. However, the question remains whether these for-profit programs have an overall adverse effect on the prospects for rehabilitation of prisoners. Where prison factories can turn a profit, there is less incentive to invest in more expensive ways to fill the time, such as counseling, drug treatment, and literacy programs. In California, for example, where prison for-profit work programs are increasingly popular, prisoner educational and vocational programs have been cut statewide by almost 20 percent, with a loss of roughly $35 million for prison educational spending and three hundred fewer prison teachers.

Some advocates of for-profit prison labor, including Edwin

Meese of the Enterprise Prison Institute, contend that programs such as those of FPI have a huge potential to boost the economy. While serving as attorney general under President Ronald Reagan, Meese oversaw the implementation of stiffer sentences for drug offenders—a major cause of the historic swelling of the U.S. prison population. In Meese's view, if prison work programs were reformed in the right way, they could avoid competing with free American workers while beating countries such as China at their own game. By expanding for-profit prison factories but limiting them to the production of items that would otherwise be produced in foreign sweatshops or prison factories, the United States could actually stem the flow of jobs and profits abroad. Critics respond that such plans drive wages down at home for free workers while also undermining the potential for useful job training for prisoners, since the majority of the repetitive and low-skill jobs prisoners hold are the very same jobs that will all be either overseas or inside the prisons by the time a prisoner is released.

Politics of Exploitation

FPI's military production raises security concerns as well. Some wonder if the Defense Department's overdependence on prison labor will dry up the nation's "warm industrial base," a term referring to the small commercial manufacturers that specialize in stepping up production during times of war. They fear that as these small specialty factories disappear, the military runs the risk of being caught with its pants down if prison riots or prisoner work stoppages should happen to coincide with future drives toward military intervention.

Prisoners are often involved in highly sensitive work involving the physical safety of soldiers in the field. In 2002, FPI earned $12 million in sales of body armor to the Defense Department, and in 1999 prisoners patched holes in $30,000 worth of faulty parachutes. The screening of who works at FPI prison factories seems lax at best. As an experiment, this reporter contacted three of the men convicted for the bombing of the World Trade Center in 1993. Two of the prisoner laborers not only had worked in FPI factories but also reported being compelled to do so by prison officials who coerced their labor under threat of punishment. Some prisoners and their advocates have complained that prison staff use work programs as a punitive device and that refusal to perform results in threat of physical abuse or solitary confinement. Compelling certain high-profile prisoners serves the additional purpose of keeping them busy and making them easier to monitor.

Among those who said they were compelled to work in a FPI factory was Mohammad A. Salameh, who was convicted of the 1993 World Trade Center bombing in 1993. Salameh put up a long legal fight before he was finally excused from working for the company. In letters to this reporter, Salameh pointed out that since he, along with more than 29 percent of the total federal prison population, is not even a legal resident of the United States, he should not be legally permitted—much less forced—to work for the company. Ultimately, when the Bureau of Prisons released Salameh from the job, they admitted in court documents to having forced him to work for FPI. Officials argued that the compulsory labor was justified since higher-risk prisoners were easier to monitor if they were kept busy. Under such policies, it certainly seems that the potential and incentive for sabotage of FPI's military products would be high. Ironically enough, it is such practical and security concerns that could eventually weaken FPI's grip on production for the Pentagon.

As the U.S. occupation of Iraq stretches on with nary an exit strategy in sight, however, it is hardly surprising that the politics of prison labor are also nowhere in view. Neither the period of occupation nor prison production offers much in the way of telegenic triumphs for White House politicos to exploit. Around the same time that U.S. troops north of Baghdad were storming Saddam Hussein's notorious Abu Ghraib prison, George W. Bush was winding up his "Hardware in the Heartland" tour with a stop in Santa Clara, California, to rally the employees of United Defense, builders of the Bradley Fighting Vehicle. A raucous cheer ran through the crowd when Bush noted that the company also produces the Hercules tank recovery vehicle, one of which had played a starring role in the war's most famous (and famously staged) cinematic tableau—the toppling of a statue of Saddam Hussein in Firdous Square in central Baghdad. With American casualties mounting in Iraq and little good news about domestic employment either, even the Bush administration must understand that a reprise of such photo-op moments would be in poor taste. So the 21,000 prisoner employees of FPI, despite their vital importance to Bush's wars, remain distinctly behind the scenes.

On the Inside with
the American Correctional Association
Silja J. A. Talvi

January 2005

*There is no doubt that good work is done at the penitentiary. . . .
It only remains to go unto perfection.*
—*Unnamed speaker at the 1874 Congress of the National
Prison Association, later renamed the American
Correctional Association*

*[We] linger at the gates of correctional Valhalla—with an abiding
pride in the sense of a job superbly done! We may be proud, we
may be satisfied, we may be content.*
—*Harold V. Langlois, American Correctional Association
(ACA) president, 1966*

We'll have a hard time holding on to what we have now.
—*Gwendolnn C. Chunn, ACA president, Winter ACA
Conference, 2005 (referencing the unprecedented prison
expansion boom of the 1990s)*

It was the third day of the American Correctional Association's
winter fair in sunny Phoenix, Arizona. The spectacular south-
western sunrise and balmy outside temperatures aside, the inside of the Phoenix Civic Plaza didn't feel like a particularly
pleasant place to be—that is, unless you happened to be in the
business of profiting from the $50 billion per year prison in-

dustry, particularly as a member of the American Correctional Association.

In 1870, the National Prison Association was founded by a group of reform-minded prison wardens who saw promise in rehabilitation, religious redemption, and the importance of treating prisoners like human beings. The first national congress of the National Prison Association brought together 230 people in Cincinnati, and featured a keynote speaker who put it thusly: "It is left to the philanthropic and Christian sentiment of the age to devise ways and means to elevate the unfortunate and wayward to the true dignity of manhood."

The organization was renamed the American Correctional Association (ACA) in 1952, and by the time of the 2005 winter conference in Phoenix, the number of attendees had swelled to over four thousand. The 2005 conference again found the ACA touting its purported principles: "humanity, justice, protection, opportunity, knowledge, competence, and accountability." The organization stresses that it brings together individuals and groups "that share a common goal of improving the justice system." But with the prison industry now bringing in annual revenue of over $50 billion, the ACA seems most intent on improving profits.

Today's ACA is a sleek version, complete with online certification courses for detention facility employees (starting at $29.95) and an expensive prison accreditation process that claims to instill transparency and accountability. Members are enticed to earn accreditation in order to receive up to a 10 percent discount on prison liability insurance.

Keeping litigation costs down is only one way prison corporations profit from incarceration. In addition, for-profit prisons also increase revenues by contracting with other corporations to provide substandard or overpriced services to prisoners. In some states, companies such as Starbucks and Nintendo pay prisons to employ prisoners at wages far below market rates.

Taking advantage of the unprecedented prison boom of the late 1980s and 1990s, prison administrators, politicians, lobbying firms, and corporate boards created a prison-industrial complex in which everyone benefits except the prisoners. In 1980, federal and state prisons incarcerated 316,000 people. In 1990, that number had grown to 740,000, not including jail populations. By 2000, the number of prisoners had surpassed 1.3 million. Prison construction accompanied this growth: more than one thousand prisons are now in operation, and each new prison comes with a bevy of contracts for construction and services.

The ACA conference is where many of these transactions are cemented.

Noting that the prison population may have reached its apogee, ACA president Gwendolyn C. Chunn told members at the conference, "We'll have a hard time holding on to what we have now." But attendees seemed more than willing to try; everyone at the conference seemed to be riding high on the promise of growth, expansion, and profits.

Just Business

This conference's theme was "Corrections Contributions to a Safer World," and the conference program didn't try to hide the gathering's militaristic bent. The cover of the 201-page ACA booklet featured a soldier with an enormous phallic tank gun superimposed over the blue planet Earth. And ACA's three keynote speakers were prominent conservatives or military officers: retired general Anthony Zinni; Michael Durant, the pilot of *Black Hawk Down* fame; and disgraced Homeland Security nominee Bernard Kerik, who would later plead guilty to corruption charges associated with his tenure as chief of the New York City jail system.

The conference was financially supported by private prison

giants such as the Corrections Corporation of America (CCA), the GEO Group (formerly known as Wackenhut), Correctional Services Corporation (CSC), and Correctional Medical Services. The titles of the dozens of overlapping workshops indicated what ACA defined as the latest trends in corrections: "Faith-Based Juvenile Programming," "Anti-Terrorism in Correctional Facilities," and "Can't Simply Paint It Pink and Call It a Girl's Program."

One workshop—"Intensive Medical Management: How to Handle Prisoners Who Self-Mutilate, Slime, Starve, Spit and Scratch"—featured footage of a nonviolent paranoid schizophrenic prisoner in Utah forcibly extracted from his cell and then tied down to a restraint chair. After being strapped down naked for sixteen hours, the prisoner died. The session was facilitated by Todd Wilcox, the medical director of the Salt Lake County Metro Jail, who used the imagery as an example of how to avoid costly litigation. "Don't get personal with this," Wilcox said. "It's just business." He reminded the audience how important it is to sever the "emotional leash" that guards and nurses can form with prisoners. He also referred to some mentally ill prisoners with "Axis II disorders" as "the people we affectionately call 'the assholes.'"

Pain for a Price

The real draw of the ACA conference was the exhibitors, who had two full days to showcase their wares. The exhibition hall corridors had been given names such as "Corrections Corporation of America Court," "Verizon Expressway," "Western Union Avenue," and "The GEO Court Lounge," where one could sip Starbucks coffee and eat free glazed donuts.

Here, the discussions were all about increasing profit margins, lessening risks and liabilities, winning court cases, and new, improved techniques and technologies for managing the most troublesome prisoners. In the glaringly bright exhibit hall, attendees buzzed around booths, snapping up freebies and admiring the latest in prison technology.

Exhibitors hawked restraint chairs, tracking systems, drug detection tools, suicide prevention smocks, and prison facility insurance. Dozens of companies competed to sell private health care systems, pharmacy plans, commissary services, and surveillance systems. Of particular interest were behavior modification programs, juvenile boot camps, and Internet and phone services. Interest in the latter brought in the "big boys" of telecommunications: Sprint, AT&T, NEC, MCI Communications, Verizon, Global Tel*Link, and Qwest. With prison phone contracts generating an estimated $1 billion a year, such a lucrative field could hardly be ignored.

The range of products went on from one corridor to the next: storage systems, money wiring, surveillance, security transport, fencing, prison medical packages. (Industry giant Prison Health Services brought in rescued owls and hawks to draw crowds. What was the connection to prison health? "Oh, nothing!") Vendors who couldn't afford dog-and-pony shows handed out free bags, pens, toothpicks, mugs, tape measures, and sugar-coated churros. The exhibitors who didn't need giveaways to draw crowds included weapons manufacturers Smith and Wesson, Glock, and Taser International.

Two smiling exhibitors standing behind the Taser booth allowed the curious to handle the latest in the 50,000-volt stun gun technology. On the Taser table a video looped on a monitor: a naked African American man is being chased down by police officers. He is shot once and falls hard to the ground. Tasered again, his body shudders before collapsing altogether. The footage was without any context and was apparently intended to illustrate the efficacy of the stun gun, used by more than six thousand police departments, that had become the leader in the "nonlethal weapons" industry, that is before a spate of negative press, including reports of an SEC investigation, had put the company's stock price into a tailspin, from $33 to $7.59 a share in September 2006.

In November 2004, Amnesty International issued a report that blamed at least 74 deaths since 2001 on Tasers and called for a suspension of their use until further studies could prove just how "nonlethal" these weapons were. Headline business news emerged during the ACA conference: Taser executives were reported to have sold $91.5 million of their own stock, raising suspicions that they sought to maximize their own profits before their product lost ground. The company subsequently announced that sales were projected to slow in the months to come. The stock plunged 30 percent. As if all that weren't bad enough, Taser International president Tom Smith said in an interview that four active-duty police officers had been offered stock options for law enforcement training programs they supervised, which in turn had "led directly to the sale of tasers to a number of police departments." In August 2006, Taser settled a stock and securities fraud lawsuit by paying $20 million in damages to investors and an additional $1.75 million in attorney's fees to their lawyers.

It's a good thing that former Taser spokesman Bernard Kerik cashed in when he did. The former New York City police commissioner and New York City jail chief made more than $6.2 million in pre-tax profits from the sale of Taser stock in the month leading up to his abortive nomination as head of Homeland Security.

Wining, Dining, and Women

Scores of individuals from prison acquisition and purchasing departments, consulting agencies, and the ranks of high-level prison administrators had come to the conference for networking, recruiting and, above all, business. Private contractors, such as food service businesses Aramark and Canteen, discreetly targeted these attendees for their off-site wine-and-dine events, issuing covert invitations to people whose badges indicated their importance in the field.

Following a day of tours at Arizona jails and prisons, about sixty conference-goers headed to the Canteen fete at an upscale Italian restaurant in the nearby Arizona Center. Cocktails and bottles upon bottles of wine were poured out prior to a multicourse meal. Wardens and top-ranking detention facility administrators from Arizona, New Mexico, and Maryland sat in the outdoor patio under heat lamps. Salesmen from Canteen were pressing the flesh and passing out business cards. There were smiles all around.

Like so many other private companies working in prisons, Aramark and Canteen have had their share of problems. Aramark was singled out by "Stop the ACA" union-organized protests outside of the conference. On the third day of the conference, protesters sneaked in and placed informational materials in the toilet seat cover holders of convention center bathrooms.

On the fourth day of the conference, Aramark sought to spruce up its image with a faux New Orleans–style gentlemen's "entertainer," complete with pink top, feather cap, and black fishnets. The heavily made-up young woman knelt before prison administrators giving them free shoe shines.

Aramark's low bids have succeeded in getting contracts in many jails and prisons. The company boasts that it provides more than a million meals a day to prisoners nationwide. Aramark materials also emphasize the company's adherence to ACA standards, but that hasn't stopped the allegations from piling up. In Dauphin County, Pennsylvania, for instance, a grand jury is investigating charges of overbilling and poor food quality. In July 2004, New Mexico prisoners at Los Lunas prison, fed up with Aramark's low food quality and "inedible" meat-type products, organized a hunger strike. Similar problems have been reported in at least a dozen states.

Privatization, Politicians, and Payola

The glossy *GEO World* magazine, distributed at the ACA conference, trumpeted the success of the largest "private-public partnership in the world," a sprawling detention center complex in Pecos, Texas. Known as the Reeves County Detention Center (RCDC), the complex consists of prisons for both Bureau of Prisons and Arizona state prisoners. According to GEO, "the joint venture . . . between GEO Group and Reeves County has been a rewarding challenge."

According to the local *Odessa American* newspaper, however, building RCDC has led to the "near financial ruin of the county." RCDC is currently the subject of an FBI and Texas Ranger investigation over the tampering of government documents. (In addition, two guards resigned in early January 2005 over sexual molestation charges.)

The RCDC is a private-public partnership in more ways than one. Randy DeLay, the brother of House majority leader Tom DeLay, lobbied the Bureau of Prisons to send its prisoners to RCDC, at the behest of county officials. Apparently, Randy DeLay isn't the only member of his family with an interest in detention facilities. In December, 2003, Tom DeLay accepted a $100,000 check from the CCA for the DeLay Foundation for Kids.

CCA has become a leader in securing private prison contracts. In fiscal year 2003, CCA generated more than $268.9 million in revenue from state, federal, and local governments. Greasing the palms of legislators nationwide hasn't hurt: in 2004, CCA's political action committee gave $59,000 to candidates for federal office—92 percent to Republicans.

This is part and parcel of an industry in the business of locking up human beings. As the industry has grown, the ACA has moved away from the ideals of rehabilitation and redemption of the human spirit. Today, human beings behind bars are little more than commodities to be traded on the open market.

Bill Deener, a financial writer for the *Dallas Morning News*, writing about recent gains in the private prison market, put it this way: "Crime may not pay, but prisons sure do."

Three days before the ACA conference, MSN Money's Michael Brush issued a glowing report on the investment potential for the CCA and GEO Group. The children of the baby boomers, he explained, are about to enter the eighteen-to-twenty-four-year-old age group—"the years when people commit the most crimes." He suggested now is the right time to buy in to the trend: "[T]he nation's private prison companies look like solid investments for the next several years."

Author's note: In reporting this story, I did not disclose my identity as a journalist. I believe that operating in undercover fashion allowed me to gain more access to behind-the-scenes information at the American Correctional Association conference without being subjected to increased scrutiny as a member of the media. It also helped me to avoid the possibility of denial of access to certain venues. All quotes are from keynote speakers or workshop leaders.

Jails for Jesus

Samantha M. Shapiro

April 2004

Pastor Don Raymond isn't trained in corrections and is not employed by the government, but he runs a new 140-person wing of the Ellsworth, Kansas, medium-security prison that draws prisoners from throughout the state system.

In the phylum of prison staff, Raymond defies classification. He is not a tight-lipped warden, vindictive guard, or burnt-out social worker. In an industry that thrives on invisibility and resents the media, Raymond drives 140 miles, past newly seeded wheat fields and the rhythmically bowing heads of oil-well pumps, to pick me up from the airport, where he offers prayers of thanksgiving for my visit and "for the ministries of writing He has blessed Samantha with." In a building that hums with hostility, Raymond is attentive, unguarded, gentle. Prison staff are not permitted to share personal information with prisoners, address them by their first names, or socialize in any way; if a prisoner wants to speak privately with a counselor, he has to fill out a Form 9. But these restrictions do not apply to Raymond, who often puts in fourteen-hour days working the cellblocks of the state's prisons, recruiting men to transfer to his wing. In prisoners' marked bodies, averted eyes, and bristling rage, Raymond sees the debts and wounds, not of poverty or addiction, but of sin alone. He believes there is only one cure—Jesus Christ—and that it is a perfect and complete cure.

President Bush wants faith-based programs to take over social services. But what happens when evangelical Christians try their hand at running prisons?

Once at the Ellsworth prison, Raymond and I quickly pass through the general-population area, avoiding the acid attention of men slouched in front of bolted-down TVs, fingering the buttons of their state-issue work shirts. "I seeeeee you," a prisoner coos at me through his window grate as we pass. "Don't think I can't see you." "I got to talk to you, girl! I got to talk to you right now!" another barks.

Raymond's wing, the faith-based InnerChange Freedom Initiative, is identical to the rest of the prison but feels like an entirely different place, an excessively well-lit church basement perhaps. Prisoners have arranged their desks, stacked with Bibles and workbooks, in a tidy circle. One rushes to pull a chair out for me; others reach out for a double-handed shake or a shoulder clap poised to morph into a full-body hug. These prisoners see plenty of women; Raymond keeps a steady flow of church volunteers, mentors, and teachers circulating throughout the wing. They don't behave toxicly, because the InnerChange staff doesn't treat them like they are murderers or rapists, even though some are.

Before Bible study starts, they want to ask me some questions: "Where are you from?" "Have you been saved?" "Do you know Jesus?" After class, perhaps unsatisfied with my answers—I'm Jewish—Raymond presents me with a pocket-size New Testament, "a gift from the guys." He then invites me to spend time alone with a prisoner in his cell to peruse his extensive Scripture library more closely. A passing guard catches a glimpse of us crouched on the prisoner's cot and turns purple. "Don't you know that no one is allowed in cells?" he bellows at Raymond. "Not even me, and I am a guard!"

Raymond is undeterred. Later that evening, after most prison staff have left, he leads InnerChange prisoners across grounds off-limits to them because they are outside the view of security cameras. They set up amplifiers and a drum kit for an evening revival in the mess hall. With a backup band of prisoners chanting, "You are the air I breathe," Raymond preaches until the sun sets and goldfinches circle the indigo sky outside. By the end of the revival, Raymond has achieved his desired effect: the room is still with prayer; prisoners are holding each other; some are crying. At nine-thirty, Raymond can be found in a cellblock, bent at the waist, his face pressed into the food slot of a prisoner on lockdown. When he finally leaves the prison to eat a Dairy Queen dinner in the front seat of his pickup, the night is speckled with stars.

Aided by friends in high places—such as the White House—legislators in Florida, Kansas, Iowa, Texas, and Minnesota have, in the last six years, turned over portions of their prisons, and corrections budgets, to the politically powerful evangelical Christian group Prison Fellowship Ministries (PFM), which pays Raymond's salary. The largest prison ministry in the world, PFM sends more than fifty thousand volunteers into prisons in every state with the goal of "declaring the good news of Jesus Christ to those impacted by crime." The Ministries' "Angel Tree" program has presented more than four million children of prisoners with Christmas presents and evangelistic materials. The goal is clear. As Mark Earley, who was attorney general of Virginia before becoming president of PFM in 2002, writes on its Web site, "I believe God is going to raise up the next generation of leaders for His Church from men and women now behind bars, and from their children."

In 1997, as part of a larger effort to increase funding for faith-based services in Texas, then-governor George W. Bush gave PFM the chance to do more than just visit prisons; he allowed it to run a twenty-four-hour "immersion" program in collaboration with the Department of Corrections. Three other states have since followed suit, and PFM plans to be in five more states by 2005—"God does amazing things!" enthuses InnerChange executive director Jerry Wilger. In June, President Bush held a press conference with InnerChange officials and prisoners, touting a University of Pennsylvania study that he, Majority Leader Tom DeLay, and the *Wall Street Journal* all claimed showed that InnerChange lowered recidivism. Critics later pointed out that the study actually indicated the opposite was true. In any case, InnerChange represents the cutting edge of President Bush's faith-based initiatives, which seek to have religious groups take over social services once provided by state and federal agencies and, in so doing, fulfill two goals dear to many conservatives: bringing more people to Christ and shrinking government.

In Kansas, most prisoners two years away from possible parole are eligible to join InnerChange. Prisoners who choose to live on its wing rise at 5:00 A.M. for morning prayers and bustle purposefully through a day packed with studying Scripture, practicing gospel music, learning life skills, and undergoing "biblically based" therapy designed to transform them through an "instantaneous miracle." Their study regimen includes lessons in creationism and an option to "convert" out of homosexuality. When I asked Alexander Curls, on work release after three years of InnerChange, what he was taught about other faiths, he said emphatically, "I found out that a lot of good people are going straight to hell!"

Many prisoners, however, don't join for the ideology. They do it to transfer from other parts of the prison system, and because completing InnerChange amounts to a get-out-of-jail-free card with the Parole Board: "We have a very positive relationship with the board. Sometimes they just give our inmates a green light and say, 'See you at work release,'" said Larry Furnish, InnerChange program manager at Ellsworth. Kansas has only 298 coveted work-release positions for about 9,000 total prisoners; InnerChange graduates are all but guaranteed a space as well as help finding a job and housing after they get out.

Meanwhile, joining InnerChange brings about a radical

change in lifestyle. The movements of the general population are highly restricted. Those who share a snack or a book will likely be written up for "dealing and trading"; during visiting hours, hugs with family members are timed. But InnerChange "members" have good prison jobs and electric guitars. They are called by their first names, hugged, and told they're loved, and, because the program emphasizes reconciliation with family members, are provided much greater visitation rights—their wives can join them for Bible study and picnics.

And then there is the pizza. When a new class of prisoners joins InnerChange, the staff orders one hundred large pies, a fact that all 800-plus prisoners at Ellsworth appear to be intimately, obsessively, aware of. "We are stretching the local Pizza Hut to its absolute capacity," InnerChange office administrator Gale Soukup told me with a worried look, "and they're the only game in town."

Paid for in part by fees charged to the general population, InnerChange also offers substance abuse treatment and free computer training, hot commodities in a time of budgetary woes. This year, the GED program Ellsworth offers regular prisoners was cut in half, the substance abuse program eliminated. General-population prisoners are still offered a computer class through the local community college, but as it costs $150, and men who are lucky enough to land a prison job make an average of 60 cents a day, the general population's six computers sit under dust covers most days. As Issac Jarowitz, an Ellsworth prisoner who isn't in InnerChange, noted grudgingly, "The Christians do lots of stuff the state used to do, like vocational programs, but now they're only for believers."

"I tell them this is their ticket," Raymond said, gesturing to the InnerChange ID card that prisoners wear on a "What Would Jesus Do?" neck chain, "to everything they need."

Prison Fellowship Ministries, the group that runs Inner-Change, was founded in 1976 by Charles Colson, the "evil genius" of the Nixon administration; one of his unrealized dirty tricks was a proposal to firebomb the Brookings Institution. For his Watergate crimes, Colson served seven months. After being released, he remade himself as a poster boy for the redemptive power Christ can have on criminals and the government, and has since become one of "America's most powerful Christian conservatives," according to the *Weekly Standard*. Still chairman of PFM, Colson is also a prolific writer. In his column for *Christianity Today* or his daily radio address, Colson can be found criticizing PBS for "promoting" evolution, hawking a brochure called "Rick Santorum Is Right," or claiming that the real weapons of mass destruction "are not in Baghdad" but in "the hands of the sexual liberationist lobby." In Colson's first novel, *Gideon's Torch*, the National Institutes of Health plans to harvest brain tissue from partial-birth abortions to treat AIDS patients, a scheme funded by Hollywood galas. Colson even has his anti-abortionist heroes firebomb the NIH. *Gideon's Torch*, like much of Colson's writings, ultimately argues that government without faith is doomed to destruction and corruption.

Colson also drums on the clash between Christianity and Islam, a religion, he told Fox TV, "dedicated toward hatred," but that can be defeated by aggressive evangelizing. Last year, he wrote several op-eds warning that Muslim prisoners present a terrorist threat, a message that's trickled down to InnerChange. Raymond refused to participate in an interfaith conference at Ellsworth last year because he thought the Muslim organizers were trying "to recruit guys." Texas InnerChange prisoners told me they watched an evangelical documentary on a Christian woman who'd been raped by Muslims.

At Ellsworth, Muslim prisoners such as Michael Patterson say that their practices have been restricted since InnerChange arrived. While InnerChange prisoners and their families are treated to a Christmas dinner shared with prison staff, this year the Ramadan feast (which Muslim prisoners must pay for and their families can't attend) was denied. InnerChange prisoners engage in spontaneous prayer throughout the day, but Lakota, Muslim, and other prisoners in the general population need approval to pray together. "If anyone but the Christians gets together for a prayer, security hits the panic button," Patterson said, adding that the prison's chaplain would not order Islamic texts and that a prisoner who started studying Arabic was called into the warden's office. (The warden denies these reports.) To Patterson, this pattern suggests that "through a variety of avenues, the prison is trying to pressure inmates to join InnerChange to turn the whole prison into a Christian place."

That sounds paranoid, and warden Ray Roberts (who's since become warden of another Kansas prison) said prisoners are not pressured, implicitly or explicitly, to join InnerChange. But Roberts, his deputy warden, and the prison's security chief all told me they would like the entire prison turned over to InnerChange. While walking with Raymond, a prisoner suggested airbrushing a giant mural of Jesus on the side of the prison. "The state won't let that fly," Raymond said ruefully. "Wait until we take the place over."

Warden Roberts previously served as director of the Inner-Change unit in Texas, and he did his best to welcome the ministry to Ellsworth. Prisoners in the program repair wheelchairs for an evangelical group that distributes them, and the gospel, in the Third World. When budget cuts affected state funding for InnerChange, Roberts allowed its prisoners to hawk BBQ bacon cheeseburgers to the general population.

The prison's chapel is small, so Roberts raised money for a large "Spiritual Life Center" that he said will make it easier to put on "wholesome entertainment, like gospel concerts." Fund-raising efforts included the sales of his wife's "mop angels" (don't laugh—that's $23,000) and prisoner art, a staff softball tournament, and a civilian-attended prison slumber party. Roberts said he didn't plan to undertake similar efforts to restore the drug abuse or education programs cut this year or to subsidize the $150 that non-InnerChange prisoners must pay for computer training.

Cheeseburgers aren't the most substantial way Kansas' prisoners fund perks for their born-again brethren. Although some state legislatures allocate money for InnerChange (Texas recently set aside $1.5 million), Kansas provides it with only about $200,000 out of the Prisoner Benefit Fund (profits from prison canteens and exorbitant phone rates). Kansas' $4.3 million Inmate Benefit Fund typically buys library books and sports equipment, but Roger Werholtz, secretary of the Department of Corrections, said InnerChange is a fair allocation because it is voluntary and open to everyone. "Not everyone uses the basketball hoops," he added.

In Kansas, the Inmate Benefit Fund covers only about 40 percent of InnerChange's cost; Prison Fellowship Ministries pays the rest, making it attractive to government officials not swayed by the promise of kingdom-building alone. Kansas pays up to $4,000 for each prisoner who participates in a regular group therapy program; InnerChange therapy costs the state only $1,086 per prisoner. What's more, the state saves money when prisoners fulfill their requirements for vocational training or substance abuse counseling through InnerChange. "I know we don't have any good long-term numbers on recidivism with the program," said Werholtz, "but I was willing to suspend judgment because it follows the form, if not the content, of a therapeutic program. I'm interested in any kind of resources we can employ that will be effective on a low-cost or no-cost basis."

Werholtz says, "If you turn down the volume, InnerChange looks like a therapeutic community program." He is right. In their biblically based therapy sessions, InnerChange prisoners break into tears and hugs with a frequency that would exhaust

Oprah. These aren't crocodile tears. Many men are reconciled with estranged family members; all can talk about whatever suffering, neglect, or poverty landed them in prison.

But lest anyone mistake an Inner Change session for group therapy, the program enumerates the differences in a handy page-long chart. For instance, while standard therapy "seeks gradual change of self," the transformation that InnerChange promises "happens through an instantaneous miracle."

InnerChange's substance abuse program is state-accredited, although unlike in the regular state program, addiction isn't presented as a disease to be struggled with for life, but as a sin that can be permanently "cured" through Jesus. This is typical of the faith-based substance abuse programs, such as Teen Challenge, a Southern California–based prototype that President Bush ardently supports. As governor, Bush defended Teen Challenge against charges that it violated state and health-department codes, saying, "I believe that conversion to religion, in this case Christianity, by its very nature promotes sobriety." At Ellsworth, InnerChange staff use Teen Challenge materials whether or not prisoners have a substance-abuse problem. "It's all about discipleship," program manager Larry Furnish explains. "The addiction part is just one component of the materials."

InnerChange is also eager to provide its own faith-based alternative to Kansas' sex offender treatment program. Pastor Raymond doesn't think it would be that hard to develop. "It's all sin," he said, shrugging. Jerry Wilger, head of InnerChange, said the idea is currently under consideration.

I got a taste of what a faith-based sex offender program might look like when I attended an InnerChange support group that Furnish said was "a little like AA for homosexuals." The group was led by Clint Price, 28, who Furnish said "had a reputation across the state for being a flaming homosexual," while the other two members were "former cross-dressers."

Serving out a sentence for burglary, Price showed me pictures of his pre-InnerChange days when he plucked his eyebrows and had long hair. "At one point, I had the Bloods and the Crips fighting over me," he said with a trace of pride. Price joined InnerChange because he had "some bad relationships and got let down and hurt so much. I was sick of competing with other queens in the system. In the prison environment, people are just not faithful and I was taking a lot of abuse." At InnerChange, Price was encouraged to grow out his facial hair, lift weights, stop shaving his legs, and abandon "the lifestyle." The group Price leads—InnerChange plans to have him minister to those "in the lifestyle" when he's released—is supposed to affect a similar change in the others.

I entered the InnerChange library unattended by any guard or staff. Sitting in the darkened room with Price's group as he read evangelical texts on homosexuality off a slide projector in a monotone—"Start your life moving." Click. "In a new direction towards complete manhood." Click—was a profoundly unsettling experience. It quickly became clear that the other members, Terry Hoffman and James Gavin, were not simply "cross-dressers" but serious sex offenders; Hoffman said he'd attempted to sodomize a blind man, and Gavin had sodomized his four-year-old daughter. Hoffman attended InnerChange because he'd been thrown out of the state-run sex offender program, which Gavin had completed. As Price shared the trials of growing up gay, Asian, and uncoordinated in "a town smaller than Ellsworth, where sports are everything," it was clear he was out of his depth.

Privately, Price acknowledged that he's "really not for sure on how to deal with someone who has a sex crime. Some of the things they bring up from their past—real, real dysfunctional things—go beyond my experience," he said uneasily. "I don't know what to say, so I just have us pray together."

Letting Christ-based programs "cure" sex offenders—

exempting them from state programs that employ aversion therapy and normative counseling, and releasing them into society armed primarily with polemics about sin—seems risky, to say the least, but Furnish is confident the state will go for it. "We already offer GED, substance abuse, and pre-release programs. If we get sex offender treatment, we'll have the whole ball of wax for the state at a bargain-basement price," he said.

InnerChange is the sort of program President Bush is promoting with faith-based initiatives, appointments, executive orders, and (so far failed) legislative attempts. The director of the White House Office for Faith-Based Initiatives says Bush has asked Attorney General John Ashcroft to investigate using InnerChange in federal prisons. Former PFM officials also lead Dare Mighty Things, which, thanks to a $2.2 million grant by the Department of Health and Human Services, now serves as a clearinghouse for faith-based and community groups applying for federal money.

It was already possible for faith groups to receive government funding to work in prisons; they simply have to separate their charity from their sermons and are forbidden to proselytize. But Bush's faith-based initiatives promote a very different theology of social action—one that he and Colson have personally experienced—that claims religion itself is the cure for social ills. PFM can receive state funds because InnerChange members enroll voluntarily, though it's hard to see the program as entirely voluntary when lifestyle and parole benefits serve as both carrot and stick. Furthermore, lifers who graduate from the InnerChange "God pod" return to cellblocks as "disciples" and are encouraged to proselytize.

Bush's faith-based initiatives are also part of a larger effort to privatize social services. As Robert Boston, a spokesman for Americans United for Separation of Church and State, says, "This is really about making dramatic changes in the structure of the social safety net." Boston's group is suing InnerChange in an effort to challenge faith-based initiatives on constitutional grounds.

Colson, in a recent radio address, said, "What's at stake [in the suit] is not just a prison program, but how we deal with social problems in our country. Do we do it through grassroots organizations or big government? We know what works."

In fact, there's no conclusive research about whether the treatments InnerChange is experimenting with do work. The Texas Freedom Network recently reported on how Bush's faith-based initiatives have fared in that state, where they've existed the longest. It documents rampant safety violations at deregulated faith-based child-care centers and alcohol treatment programs. Data compiled by Texas' Criminal Justice Policy Council suggests InnerChange graduates have lower rates of recidivism. But as University of Arizona sociologist Mark Chaves notes, "Prison Fellowship claims amazing success rates, but in prisons where it exists, it's often the only rehab program. We don't have comparisons between PFM and secular programs; we have comparisons between PFM and nothing."

Faith-based programs have a synergetic relationship with government cutbacks; InnerChange derives its transformational force from the stark neediness of prisoners. It's hard—even for Muslim prisoners such as Patterson—to be overly critical of InnerChange, because the services its prisoners receive are such an improvement on what is offered in regular prison. Amy Fettig of the ACLU National Prison Project says InnerChange is "potentially problematic," but "we haven't had any complaints from inmates. It may be that folks are just desperate to get any services with states cutting back their budgets so much." Meanwhile, she adds, "we have to focus on other conditions, like deprivation of food, crowding, and violence."

Those are some of the conditions that Rodney Woods, thirty-one, said drove him to enroll in InnerChange. Previously, Woods was serving time in the Hutchinson, Kansas, maximum-security prison, where he shared a cell with four other men and was let out to exercise for an hour a day.

Woods, who has wide almond eyes and rows of neat braids knotted behind his ears, said he was angry all the time, frustrated, and scared of what he might do. "My homeboy got jumped and I knew when he got out of the hole we were going to take care of it. I was going to end up fighting, kill the guy if need be. I was going to do something I was gonna regret." When Raymond came to speak at Hutchinson about the faith-based prison wing, Woods said, "I was attracted to the aspect of change. I wanted to be around positive people with a message of love."

Woods belongs to a Black Muslim sect and said he wasn't interested in finding Jesus. "All I knew," he said, rolling his WWJD neck chain around his index finger, "is I had to get out of Hutch."

Florida's Private Prison Industry Corporation Under Siege

David M. Reutter

January 2005

In 1980, drugstore mogul Jack Eckerd was struck with a business epiphany: there was a heap of profit to be made by private industry in prisons. This was a cutting-edge notion with few models at the time; nevertheless, Eckerd went straight to the Florida legislature and lobbied his dream into reality. In 1981 the Florida legislature enacted a statute creating the Prison Rehabilitative Industries and Diversified Enterprises (PRIDE), a private, nonprofit corporation, to lease and manage the state prison industries program (Florida Statutes, Title XLVII, 946.501 et seq.). Eckerd then installed himself as PRIDE's first chairman, a position he held from 1981 through 1990.

Per the new Florida law, PRIDE's mission was to provide education, training, and post-release job placement to prisoners to help reduce recommitment; enhance security by reducing prisoner idleness and providing an incentive for good behavior in prison; reduce costs to the state by operating enterprises primarily with prisoner labor while not unreasonably competing with private enterprise; and rehabilitate prisoners by duplicating, as nearly as possible, the activities of a profit-making enterprise.

PRIDE was also granted a number of remarkable protections for a private entity: it was allowed sovereign immunity, which shielded it from liability from lawsuits for its actions in the same manner as the state, and it was exempted from unemployment compensation or workers' compensation, in most cases, to prisoner workers. Most significantly, PRIDE is not subject to the authority of any state agency, except the auditing and investigatory powers of the legislature and governor. This level of liability would protect PRIDE from years of corporate malfeasance but would not be quite enough to shield it entirely in the end.

Anatomy of a Prison Industry

PRIDE chugged along—growing in size and influence—for a couple of decades. By fiscal year 2002–03, PRIDE operated thirty-eight industries in 21 of Florida's 121 prisons and facilities. Those industries included businesses as diverse as dairy calves, office furniture, heavy vehicle refurbishing, printing, digital information services, and citrus processing. By 2003, PRIDE provided 1,995 jobs to Florida's 80,000 prisoners. Though a fairly low percentage of the prisoner population were employed by PRIDE, the company nevertheless generated $60.9 million in sales that year.

The criteria for PRIDE jobs are selective: to be placed in PRIDE jobs, prisoners have to be free of disciplinary reports for six months prior to placement, and they are removed from that job if they receive a disciplinary report for any offense. In return for their labor, prisoners are paid between 20 cents and 55 cents per hour, depending on their skill level and length of service. These low-paying jobs are highly coveted in Florida's prisons, where the only other paying jobs available are a handful of positions as canteen operators or staff barbers.

PRIDE is also certified under the federal Prison Industries Enhancement (PIE) program, which was enacted in 1979. The PIE program is a federally certified program created to encourage state and local governments to develop prisoner employment opportunities that approximate private work sector opportunities. PRIDE reports 10 active PIE programs that in turn employ 249 prisoners.

Under the federal certification program, tax or other deductions from prisoner pay cannot exceed 80 percent of prisoner gross wages. Permissible deductions are limited to crime victim compensation fund, taxes required under federal law, costs of incarceration, and family support. (Additional deductions may be made for a savings account for release purposes.) Under the PIE program, private, for-profit businesses are allowed to employ prisoner labor directly, provided that the prisoners are nominally paid the minimum wage or prevailing wage for the work they perform, whichever is higher.

While PRIDE's normal operations provided only $249,991 to victim restitution for fiscal 2002–03, its PIE program, with only about 15 percent of PRIDE's prisoner workforce, generated $125,043 in total deductions from prisoner wages. Those deductions amounted to $28,785 for victim restitution, $18,624 in taxes, $73,353 room and board, and $4,282 in family support. To the extent that restitution and similar deductions rely on the prisoners' meager wages, it is obvious that the less the prisoners are paid, the lower the deductions. However, the low prisoner wages do not translate into lower prices for the products sold by PRIDE nor lower profit margins for the private businesses using the PIE program.

The state is entitled to a 50 percent share of PRIDE's profits, but that provision of state law has not been exercised in years. PRIDE has opted to use proceeds for capital improvements and expansion. If PRIDE fails, the state is the beneficiary as it is slated under Florida law to receive all PRIDE assets.

A Declining Industry

Between 2000 and 2005, PRIDE's sales fell by 25 percent. A number of factors contributed to this decline, including federal limitations on the sale of interstate goods manufactured by prisoners, general economic conditions and state spending, state agency resistance to using PRIDE products and services, and private sector concerns about using products manufactured by prisoner labor. PRIDE has taken steps to increase its sales in recent years, but its effects have had limited success.

In 1934, Congress enacted the Ashurst-Summers Act (18 U.S.C. § 1761), which banned the interstate transportation of prison-manufactured goods. The law applies only to manufactured goods, and PRIDE has established industries such as data entry, calf raising, and vehicle restoration that are specifically exempted from the ban. PRIDE takes advantage of such statutory exemptions, building its industries around just these types of industries to sidestep federal law. Nonetheless, federal law restricts PRIDE's potential markets by requiring that prisoners making goods transported in interstate commerce be paid the minimum wage or prevailing wage, whichever is higher. The law also requires that goods made with prisoner labor be plainly marked as such. These restrictions do not apply if the prisoner-made goods are exported, and PRIDE exports items such as shoes and clothes to Nicaragua, Mexico, and the Dominican Republic, among other countries.

The United States, however, prohibits the importation of prisoner-made goods from overseas. In addition to the numerous benefits provided PRIDE under Florida law, the state actually mandates that state agencies prioritize business with PRIDE when their products are of similar quality and price to those offered by other vendors. As a result, in 1995, for example, purchases by state agencies accounted for 83 percent of PRIDE sales. Though this statutory preference was by no means a guarantee of business with this corner of the market, it certainly elevated PRIDE's chances of success far beyond its counterparts.

When the Florida Department of Corrections (FDOC) entered into a contract with Aramark to privatize its prison food services, the new contract required a corresponding increase in the warehousing and delivery of produce and goods, which PRIDE was unable to provide. FDOC canceled its contract with PRIDE, and PRIDE's revenue dropped $30 million.

PRIDE faced additional problems: Florida's Department of Management Services reported that the statutory preference clause requiring that state agencies purchase from PRIDE generated resentment, and that some agencies refused to comply with the requirement. There was also some resistance to prisoner-produced goods in the private sector. Coca-Cola and Wal-Mart, for example, have internal company policies that prohibit using goods produced by forced or prison labor. The public relations factor is significant in that few companies want to be linked in the public mind with prisoner labor. Private companies also resisted PRIDE's efforts to expand operations into new industries, rightly asserting that PRIDE has an unfair competitive advantage due to the low wages it pays prisoners.

For example, when a federal prison industry won a contract to produce missile-shipping containers, Tim Graves' eighteen-year-old company in Marietta, Georgia, was promptly driven out of business. "It's hard for me to accept that the government would put the welfare and benefit of convicted felons above the interests of its taxpayers," said Graves.

This setup, which pits convicted felons against taxpayers for jobs, is a kind of smoke-and-mirrors trick of the industry. The average worker who loses his or her factory job to a convict is justifiably angry; but often the anger is misdirected back at prisoners, when the real problem is the industry that profits from paying pennies on the dollar to their captive employees. Prisoners—for whom such jobs are fiercely sought after—are a great deal for their employers, requiring no health care, L&I, workers' compensation, or a penny above minimum wage.

Mike Harrell, vice president of business development for PRIDE, says PRIDE "will not enter into a relationship with a company if there's a displacement of workers." But with sales declining and its market limited, PRIDE had to take action to survive. In order to increase its revenue, PRIDE has become a conglomerate that easily masks its industries and encroachment into the private sector.

Expanding PRIDE's Umbrella

"We knew looking down the road that PRIDE couldn't continue to do business the way it always had, relying on state agencies as its primary customer," said PRIDE CEO Pamela Jo Davis, a former jail warden in Miami-Dade County and former deputy state corrections secretary.

In light of the negative PR generated by the statutory reference clause, and declining profits that resulted, PRIDE took a new angle: it began creating spin-off companies, some nonprofit, some for-profit. The spin-off companies would allow more aggressive business practices unhampered by the restrictions of PRIDE's mission or by federal wage requirements. Post-release services for prisoners were now housed within the new entity, such as Industries Training Corporation (ITC), a nonprofit corporation. ITC in turn created Labor Line Services, Labor Line, Inc., and Global Outsourcing, Inc., and formed private partnerships to create Florida Citrus Partners and Diversified Supply Management—all technically new business entities no longer confined by PRIDE's former restrictions under state and federal law.

The apparent purpose of ITC was to manage prison work programs for PRIDE by entering into various business relationships and providing administrative and managerial support. The companies were plainly interrelated, if not entirely in union. ITC's fee was based on PRIDE's budget, although the services contracted to ITC were not offered for general or public bid to comply with the statutory preference requirements. PRIDE and ITC have common managers and common board members, and use the same offices. The phones are even answered with "ITC/PRIDE." All of ITC's current board members are either current or former board members of PRIDE. The two companies appear to be one.

ITC wholly owns Labor Line Services (LLS), a nonprofit corporation. LLS offers transitional support and job training to PRIDE prisoners upon their release from prison. PRIDE pays LLS to assist released prisoners, at no charge, with finding housing, transportation, and employment, as well as general encouragement and support.

Another company ITC owns is Labor Line, Inc. (LLI), a for-profit corporation. LLI is a temp-to-hire staffing company that provides jobs for former PRIDE prisoners and other under-employed individuals. LLI provides labor to several companies throughout Florida.

Global Outsourcing also does business as Global Digital Services, a company that uses PRIDE labor to provide various digital services to the private sector. Many government agencies have an excess of records in need of electronic storage and retrieval. To help alleviate this problem, prisoners at Florida's Liberty Correctional digitally scan records, and then index them.

PRIDE and/or ITC created another significant entity: Florida Citrus Partners, a limited liability corporation with split ownership between ITC and South Florida citrus grower Bernard Egan. The split venture with Egan fractured following a failed investment of Egan's that became mired in litigation. ITC owes PRIDE $3.5 million in operating costs, supposedly to be paid from future ITC revenue.

Corporate Nepotism at Work

To fund the spin-off entities, PRIDE invested more than $10 million by providing loans to its fledgling companies.

As of December 31, 2002, ITC owed PRIDE $9.7 million. According to PRIDE officials, the debt had been reduced to $8.7 million as of December 1, 2003. At that time, PRIDE had not established formal terms for repayment of these loans.

It is questionable if repayment was ever expected. PRIDE's 2002 annual report noted that PRIDE had advanced funds to "certain parties," but did not disclose who the recipients were, PRIDE's purpose in advancing such funds, or why over $5 million was forgiven for debt to the undisclosed parties.

When Diversified Supply Management (one of the several spin-off companies) was created, ITC did so with three private investment partners: PRIDE's CEO Davis, former PRIDE board member and former president of Florida A&M University Frederick Humphries, and Maria Camila Leiva, a PRIDE board member's spouse. Davis also serves as ITC's president.

In this cozy formalization of the union between the companies, the bylaws of ITC provided that if it somehow terminated as a business, PRIDE would inherit its assets. (A future ITC board could, however, change the bylaws and sever its relationship with PRIDE.) With no formal contract governing any of the terms of repayment for PRIDE loans to ITC, PRIDE was free to gift ITC with expensive assets, including a cold storage facility valued at $2.5 million—a significant asset PRIDE would have no ability to regain if it ever became necessary.

While PRIDE's prisoners earned just pennies an hour, its CEO's annual salary was increased by $236,000 to act as ITC's president. CEO Davis' salary has increased 35 percent since 2000. That salary is more than double what Florida's secretary of corrections earns to run the entire prison system, which houses 80,000 prisoners with a $1.7 billion yearly budget. For a time, the formula of low wages and payroll deductions for the prisoners reliably resulted in high wages and lavish living for the corporate CEOs. The state of Florida has succeeded in creating a for-profit business atmosphere to prepare prisoners for the reality of wage slavery that faces them upon release. PRIDE's prisoner workers are also prohibited from unionizing or otherwise seeking better wages or work conditions, as is the case generally, in prisons.

Investigating the PRIDE Conglomerate

In 2002, Florida's Corrections Commission (FCC) requested additional financial information from PRIDE following its disclosure of ITC and its related corporations. Initially, PRIDE balked and vociferously challenged the FCC's authority to review its books. The FCC reported PRIDE's unwillingness to document its activities, and recommended an audit by the auditor general, or the Florida Office of Program Policy Analysis and Government Accountability (OPPAGA).

The resulting review was highly critical of the cozy relationship within the conglomerate that PRIDE has birthed. In its audit, OPPAGA highlighted PRIDE's failure to communicate clearly with its key stakeholders, namely, the taxpayers of Florida. Specifically, PRIDE had neglected to fulfill its requirement under Florida statute to report annually the status of proposed profit use, amount of nonprisoner labor employed, work subcontracted to other vendors, use of consultants, finished goods purchased for resale, and the number of prisoners it currently employs.

OPPAGA found that PRIDE's reports provide only cursory information about its evolving structure, and noted that PRIDE misleadingly referred to ITC and other corporations only as "related parties" without further identification or explanation. PRIDE's reports also failed to include information about profit use, the amount of work subcontracted to ITC and Labor Line Services, Inc., and the amount of finished goods purchased for resale

The auditor's report made a number of substantive recommendations, including that PRIDE revise its financial reports to include definitions of the fiscal relationships between its various corporate entities, including the amount and status of and rationale for the loans and gifts exchanged between the corporate entities. The revised reports were also to include descriptions of the costs the state incurs to support PRIDE. "In 2001–02, the Division of Risk Management reported that the state paid 12 liability claims related to PRIDE for a total of $128,888." As the state pays the medical bills of prisoners injured on the job, the cost of accidents—such as a prisoner who lost a portion of a leg working in a PRIDE industry—was borne by the state, and therefore also are of interest for inclusion in the revised PRIDE reports.

When PRIDE was created, the state donated property to ITC because Florida law does not speak to the state's interest in this property, or PRIDE's liabilities, should it fail. OPPAGA therefore also recommended clarification of relevant state law to better define the state's interest in PRIDE.

Regarding its lack of transparency, OPPAGA wrote: "PRIDE needs to recognize that as a state created entity it has a fundamental responsibility to provide accountability information on its operations, including those conducted by closely related corporations."

After OPPAGA's report was issued in December 2003, then-governor Jeb Bush made motions to shake up PRIDE. Minutes of PRIDE's April 2004 board meeting show that a member of Bush's senior staff directed PRIDE's entire board to voluntarily resign and apply for reappointment. Governor Bush's people also requested that PRIDE revise its bylaws so that the governor, not the board, would select the chairman. PRIDE's fourteen-member board refused the requests. While most of PRIDE's board members were appointed by the governor, each was vetted by PRIDE's CEO Davis prior to submission of names to Bush.

By June 2, 2004, Foster Harbin, governmental relations director for PRIDE, wrote Bush an e-mail voicing concerns about Davis' leadership. Harbin wrote that "the current Board of your appointees have fully abdicated their fiduciary responsibility to the state in what may be ultimately prove[d] to be a criminal act. . . . I'm not sure anyone is paying attention."

Bush then called in his inspector general, Derry Harper, who wrote CEO Davis on June 8, 2004, requesting the board postpone a meeting scheduled for the next day, which had on the agenda a new agreement between PRIDE and ITC. The board held its meeting and suspended Davis and president John F. Bruels for sixty days. While a firm move in appearance, the decision had little or no negative effect on Davis, who continued to hold her position as CEO. She was not even financially impacted, either, as the PRIDE post was unpaid. Her $236,000 yearly ITC salary unaffected, the suspension was an empty gesture.

Then, on July 22, 2004, PRIDE asked Davis and Bruels to resign. A consultant hired by PRIDE during the suspensions and subsequent resignations found nothing amiss between PRIDE and its spin-offs. "There is no wrongdoing," said Leiva. "There was just a feeling that people needed new leadership." Of the resignations of Bruels and Davis, Leiva said: "They were not working well together and neither could take the full load. . . . We will look for one person to do both jobs." Davis's position at ITC was unaffected by the PRIDE maneuvers, and she stayed on as ITC's CEO.

In September 2005, PRIDE filed suit against ITC seeking repayment of the $19.2 million it lost in its dealings with the ITC. In August 2006, PRIDE and ITC entered into an undisclosed settlement agreement dismissing the lawsuit. According to the OPPAGA, "PRIDE's management indicated that ITC and affiliates had minimal assets and could repay at best a small fraction of the money owed." *Prison Legal News* obtained the secret settlement using Florida's Public Records law. The settlement showed that ITC board members bilked PRIDE for $19 million and agreed to repay $537,000. Taxpayers took a loss on the rest.

Defining PRIDE's Mission

Despite its problems, PRIDE has its supporters. "In juvenile justice we have so many programs that absolutely do not work, yet we spend millions on them," says Daniel Webster, a former Speaker of the Florida House and chairman of the state's governmental oversight and productivity committee. "PRIDE is working, and we're not even paying for it. I would be willing to do it even if we had to pay for it."

"The benefit to the public is awesome because those people are not going back to the correctional facility, or causing more havoc—whether it's murder, rape, burglary, destroying property. Those things cost the private sector lots of money. If you look at the recidivism statistics—even over an extended period of time—those prisoners in PRIDE usually don't come back. They have a skill that is marketable, and their supervisors know what they can do. We have employers who are signed up to hire them," said Webster.

At first glance, PRIDE's recidivism statistics are impressive. The OPPAGA report, however, said, "PRIDE's effect on recidivism cannot be confirmed." PRIDE reports a recidivism rate of 18.1 percent for prisoner workers released in fiscal year 2001, which compares favorably to FDOC's reported recidivism rate of 33.8 percent for all prisoners since 1993.

PRIDE's analysis does not take into account the fact that it uses prisoners who tend to be older, to have been incarcerated longer, to be white, and to be more educated, as well as prisoners serving life or otherwise lengthy sentences that makes their release from prison unlikely. These factors make PRIDE's prisoner workers less likely to return to prison even before they enter the program, assuming they get out. Once those factors were removed, the OPPAGA found no net impact on recidivism by PRIDE.

"You've got the question of, what is the mission of PRIDE?" Governor Bush said he sees PRIDE's mission as training Florida's prisoners "to have a skill so they can live a productive life beyond when they're finished." Going beyond that "may not be appropriate," says Bush. While much has been complained of regarding PRIDE's structure, Davis and her cronies are still in positions to reap a profit from a seriously questionable source. Significantly, no one has demanded PRIDE's structure be altered, only that it be more transparent in its actions.

As a successful businessman, pharmacy mogul Jack Eckerd was prescient in his ability to spot a lucrative industry in prisons. His successors at PRIDE have followed his lead, with no real consequences for corporate wrongdoing and acts of malfeasance committed along the way.

Part III

Making Out Like Bandits

Behind Closed Doors:
Privatized Prisons for Youth
Tara Herivel

March 2007

When attorney David Utter co-founded the Juvenile Justice Project of Louisiana (JJPL) in 1998, the group's mandate was broad: to decrease the numbers of incarcerated youth in Louisiana and improve conditions in the state's juvenile detention facilities. The mandate did not specifically include waging war against the state's privatized juvenile facilities[1] and their owners, but contemporaneous with opening JJPL, Utter and his colleagues began receiving a flood of calls from parents of children incarcerated in the state's privately owned prison for youth, the Swanson Correctional Center for Youth—Madison Parish Unit, better known as Tallulah. Nearly all of the reports involved an undeniable pattern of significant abuse and neglect, which propelled a six-year battle against Louisiana's entrenched system of violence and corruption in its private facilities for children.

JJPL's follow-up visits to the Tallulah facility unearthed a pattern of violence that was remarkable in its pervasiveness and randomness, said Utter. Of the seven or eight children interviewed on JJPL's first visit, half exhibited serious injuries, such as black eyes or broken limbs and noses—injuries the children all complained of having received no or little medical treatment for. The violence, says Utter, was largely based upon where a child was from, and was not necessarily race-based when inflicted by other children: with a population that was about two-thirds African American, the issue of racial animus was less central than it would have been in another locale.

Guards, however, were another matter. JJPL staff also heard multiple reports of children beaten and sexually assaulted by guards who routinely hurled racial epithets along with fists.

While the problems at Tallulah were multiple and complex, one central problem was the inadequate training received by prison staff, who were untrained or trained entirely in adult facilities such as Angola, the state's infamously brutal adult prison. Tallulah was "an adult prison with teenage kids in it," said Utter. But it's difficult to find skilled employees when the pay offered is $5.77 an hour, the going wage for guards at Tallulah.

Services and programs of particular importance for incarcerated children—including mental health, education, and medical care—were also appallingly substandard. The education and special education services provided at the time of the suit did not exceed 2 hours per day, and mental health and medical care were even less of a priority, as demonstrated by the injuries children displayed to attorneys during their visits. The most basic of services were withheld, such as adequate food and clothes, as the facility's owners cut costs and trimmed corners.

Louisiana has a heavily privatized corrections system, where private facilities outnumber public ones by two to one. Louisiana also has a long and seemingly intractable history of political corruption, and it is a painfully poor state—all factors at play in Tallulah's inception and brief history. The behind-the-scenes machinations displayed in facilities such as Tallulah provide a stark depiction of the results of pitting profit motive and cronyism against the inherently conflicted interests of the well-being of incarcerated children.

"Born of Parents Named Avarice and Greed"

Tallulah opened in 1994 and was owned by a clutch of political allies of former four-term Governor Edwin Edwards, who was sentenced in 2001 to ten years in a federal prison in Fort Worth, Texas, for racketeering.[2] The Tallulah gang of owners—calling themselves the Trans-American Development Association (TADA)—finessed a deal with Edwards to build the 700-bed facility for $122.5 million, backed by state-insured and financed bonds. TADA was helmed by people with no experience in juvenile justice. "Their only strength," said David Utter, "was their friendship with Edwards."

Assisted by Louisiana's Secretary of the Department of Corrections, Richard Stalder, TADA easily finessed the contract to purchase development rights for Tallulah; no apparent thought was given to TADA's background, interests, or ability to run a detention facility for children. By 1997, it should have been clear to the state that TADA was incapable of responsibly running the facility: in the company's 1996–97 budget provided to the state, no money was slated for children's treatment, post-release services, or recreation (federal law requires a minimal amount of recreation per day for health reasons). Instead, a full 29 percent of the budget was earmarked for construction loans financed by the state.[3] This should have tipped the state off to the serious problems that loomed in Tallulah's very near future.

By the time JJPL filed suit in 1998, the extreme violence and corruption of Tallulah drew the attention of the federal Department of Justice (which joined JJPL as a party to the suit), human rights organizations including Human Rights Watch, and journalists across the country, who dubbed Tallulah the "nation's worst gladiator school."

Children at Tallulah were kept in solitary confinement for extended periods of time, abused and beaten by staff, pitted against each other as entertainment for staff, and deprived of adequate clothing, shoes, blankets, and food.[4] The situation was so grim and the youth so desperate that during a visit by the late Senator Paul Wellstone of Minnesota, children caught his attention by escaping to the roof and yelling their complaints down to him.[5]

In a remarkable display of fortune, many of the key players who orchestrated the backdoor dealings emerged from the scandal largely unscathed. Following the revelations about Tallulah, TADA partnered with the private firm FBA LLC, taking the latter's name, and converted Tallulah to an adult substance abuse center run by the state DOC but still owned by FBA. FBA then began collecting payments from the state of over $3.4 million per year for the state-backed and -insured construction bonds orchestrated for the TADA group by now-imprisoned federal convict and former Governor Edwards, an arrangement slated to end in the year 2020. The state was unable to gain release from the bonds it had provided TADA to finance Tallulah's construction, as doing so would send the entire state's credit rating plummeting: a nice trick achieved by former Governor Edwards and TADA partners.

The state recently reached an agreement with the TADA players to "purchase" Tallulah, but the agreement would relieve only some of the state's tax burden and expenses for Tallulah: it will not unburden the state of its bond payments to FBA. In fact, the deal puts the state deeper in debt: to enter into the deal with FBA, the state borrowed another $30 million from the State Bond Commission, whose approval of the deal craftily secured indemnity for the state from a pending lawsuit between the City of Tallulah and FBA.[6]

With the exception of former Governor Edwards, in the end, despite the considerable level of attention drawn by the horror stories at Tallulah, neither TADA nor those who facilitated TADA's creation, like DOC Secretary Richard Stalder, suffered any real consequences. As Republican Senate president John Hainkel told DOC Secretary Stalder: "I think there is a general agreement that Tallulah was born of parents named avarice and greed."

The Hydra Sprouts Another Head:
Jena Juvenile Facility

"We're not going to have another Tallulah at Jena," said Louisiana federal district court judge Frank J. Polozola. But at the same time that attorneys at JJPL battled Tallulah, identical problems arose at Jena, a privatized juvenile detention facility managed by Wackenhut (now called Geo), the world's largest operator of private prisons. The problems at Jena surfaced with a bang: riots erupted only fifteen days following its opening in December 1998. JJPL attorneys would discover that the riot began when a hungry youth charged a food cart. Panicked, untrained guards responded by launching tear-gas grenades and illegally gassing the youth inside the prison, setting off a full-scale riot. Ordered to cut costs, Jena's administrators had minimized food rations, among other nonexpendable essentials.

Jena presented a web of familiar problems—including financial misdealings and nepotism among contracts facilitated by Governor Edwards' office—that were apparent nine full months prior to Jena's opening. The opening was delayed by court order until Jena's administrators and contractors made sufficient attempts to avoid the pitfalls of Tallulah. Though the very foundation upon which Jena was laid was irrevocably corrupted, the facility's opening charged on.

Jena was a failed effort before it ever opened its doors, and the stories that emerged were entirely predictable, particularly in the stark light of the havoc unfolding just down the road at Tallulah. Substantiated reports of abuses at Jena included physical abuse by guards and excessive use of restraints due to poor training and supervision of staff, routine deprivation of adequate food and clothing, use of racial epithets by guards against African American youth, and overuse of isolation. One particularly disturbing example involved a seventeen-year-old who was repeatedly kicked in the stomach by guards while he was wearing a colostomy bag, having just undergone abdominal surgery.

JJPL brought a suit against Jena containing identical claims to those filed against Tallulah. Jena also was similarly embroiled in political scandal. In later criminal proceedings against Governor Edwards, an FBI agent testified that in 1996 Edwards received a million-dollar bribe from developer and crony, Fred Hofheinz, a former mayor of Houston, to purchase the contract to build Jena. Hofheinz and Edward's business partner Cecil Brown would be federally indicted on charges of corruption including conspiracy, extortion, and bribery in 1999.[7] When the deal with Hofheinz fell through due to the group's failure to secure financing, Edwards tapped his own niece to lobby Wackenhut to purchase Jena. Wackenhut eagerly stepped into the deal.

Public opprobrium followed in the wake of the JJPL suit against the miserable conditions of confinement at Jena, and in reaction to the Edwards gang's acts of criminal malfeasance in securing the facility's contract. Wackenhut would do its best to dump its interest in Jena, but was unable to, and the facility now stands empty.

JJPL reached settlements and obtained a consent decree from the court in the two cases that impacted the state's five juvenile prisons. The settlements and consent decree brought with it tens of millions of dollars for improved services such as mental health services, medical care, and education for the children, and training for staff. Former governor Edwards went to prison, and Kathleen Babineaux Blanco was voted into the governor's office on a platform that included repair of the state's crumbling juvenile justice system.

Governor Blanco is widely viewed as a true advocate for children: one of her first steps following election was to separate the juvenile justice department from its previous home within the adult Department of Corrections. This was a significant move, in that it not only created a much-needed, specifically tailored department to address the particularized needs of incarcerated children but also removed oversight by Secretary Richard Stalder of the juvenile department, though he would still head the adult department. This shift in Stalder's authority may have been a consequence of his prominent role in brokering the Tallulah deal for the now-indicted Edwards gang—but it would be Stalder's only apparent repercussion for compromising his state's credibility, both financial and otherwise.

Drawn by the firestorm fueled by the Tallulah and Jena scandals, the philanthropic Casey Foundation descended upon Louisiana armed with substantial resources and aligned with Governor Blanco to rebuild Louisiana's fractured juvenile justice system. The children who survived this period, however, are largely left to their own devices to repair the damage done to them.

Growth of the Industry

The first high-security entirely privatized facility under contract to a state was a boys' detention facility: the Weaversville Intensive Treatment Unit for Juvenile Delinquents, opened in 1976 by RCA Services in Northampton, Pennsylvania.[8] The next private facility opened in 1982 in Florida, but privatization didn't pick up speed until the early 1990s, when the myth of the "superpredator" first appeared and forever altered juvenile justice philosophy.

Within the past fifteen years, a sea change has occurred in juvenile justice philosophy: children once widely viewed as malleable, largely victims of familial instability, and capable of being rehabilitated instead became widely viewed as "superpredators" beginning in the 1980s and 1990s. Thanks to the hysterics whipped up by fear-mongers such as Princeton professor John DiIulio (who infamously forecasted in the 1990s that 270,000 juvenile superpredators would be out on the streets by 2010, a prediction based neither on reason or fact), a hundred years of rehabilitative juvenile justice philosophy was turned on its head.

Overeager legislators jumped on the "superpredator" bandwagon, and an epidemic of new legislation spread across the states. State prosecutors champed at the bit for legislation that would facilitate prosecuting children as adults, and legislators in nearly every state obliged. But the predicted crime wave never came: in fact, by 1997, juvenile crime began a steady decline that hasn't deviated much since. At present, adolescent crime rates have fallen by 50 percent, a thirty-year low.[9] But the laws set in motion across the country nevertheless created a whole new class of child criminals who, once sentenced, would have to be housed in a detention facility somewhere. In anticipation of a "baby boomlet" of child criminals-to-be, the private juvenile detention industry raced to pick up the slack: between 1991 and 1999, the number of children held in private detention facilities grew by 95 percent, with only the most minimal decline since (4 percent).[10] Despite an indisputable current decline in crime committed by youth, the private youth detention industry nevertheless managed to carve out its niche based largely upon a phantom child criminal. As in the adult private prison industry, the philosophy of "If we build it, they will come" pervades.

The Business of Kiddie Lock-up

Nationally, about 92,000 children are held in juvenile detention facilities, 30,000 of whom are confined in private detention facilities. According to the most recent census of juvenile facilities analyzed by the Department of Justice, 60 percent of all juvenile facilities are privately operated, accounting for about 30 percent of the total juvenile population.[11]

The private sector's interest in building and maintaining juvenile facilities currently enjoys a vibrant, upwardly inclined growth curve. In the past decade, the annual growth rate of increased private facilities has steadily risen by about 45 percent, with a bustling $33 billion annual profit.[12]

Seven major privately owned corporations possess the most significant interests in juvenile facilities: Youth Services International (YSI), Children's Comprehensive Services (now Ameris), Cornell, Res-Care, Wackenhut, Ramsey Youth Services (now Premier), and Correctional Corporation of America (CCA). In recent years, the companies have changed hands frequently, usually amidst erupting scandal: YSI was purchased by Correctional Services in 2000 following cancellation of multiple contracts in states like Louisiana and Florida where reports of severe problems surfaced. In 2002 Children's Comprehensive Services was acquired in a hostile takeover by Ameris Acquisition, a KeyCorp/Key Bank affiliate, and in 2003 Wackenhut created a spin-off company and renamed itself the GEO Group following a rash of problems, including youth deaths and rioting in facilities such as Jena.

Of the big seven, all have lost contracts in the past several years due to a spate of lawsuits regarding abusive and substandard conditions and scandals such as Tallulah and Jena. But even with a hit to business, the bottom line is still very good, particularly for companies adept at changing identities through mergers and acquisitions when necessary. In 2000, YSI, or Correctional Services Corporation, led the pack with revenue of $150 million; Ramsay Youth/Premier made the least, taking in $20 million in revenue for its shareholders that year.[13]

Success at a Price

The industry's success comes at a cost for children incarcerated in such facilities. Only 10 percent of all privatized juvenile facilities are accredited by any professional organizations,[14] and governmental oversight that is critical to protect this particularly sensitive population is severely compromised by the very nature of turning juvenile justice into a business.

The youth who land in juvenile detention share distinct social and cultural disadvantages: they are disproportionately poor, of color, with mental illness and other disabilities, and have significant histories of familial trauma, abuse, and substance abuse. As a population, they require careful attention to address the complexity of issues they face, issues exacerbated by the immediate predicament of being a teen now seriously entangled with the criminal system and removed from all support systems. Cost cutting in this arena inflicts a heavy price upon one of society's most vulnerable populations, and ultimately on society itself.

The percentage of children in juvenile justice system with mental illness and/or learning disabilities ranges from 25 percent to 60 percent of the population, depending upon the study. With a minimum of a quarter of the population of any juvenile facility so impacted, these children become easy marks for abuse by other children and guards.

This distinctly disadvantaged population has the added misfortune of placement in a setting that appears to have neither the ability nor the motivation to care for them. The National Mental Health Association (NMHA) produced a comprehensive report that addressed privatization and managed mental health care in juvenile systems. Noting that the corrections system presents unique challenges to privatization (including overrepresentation of youth of color, family abuse, and the propensity of mental health issues), the report found wide-ranging inadequacies among privatized facilities. The report found, for example, that despite a well-documented need for mental health treatment in juvenile facilities, only half of all privatized juvenile facilities interviewed provided in-house mental health care.

Private facilities are also far less likely to perform adequate suicide screening of youth, as compared with their publicly run counterparts, and staff training is likely to be substandard overall. Most significantly, the report's authors found that when services are privatized—either wholesale or by contracting out services such as education or health care—government management and oversight of services are necessarily hampered.

The impact upon children with mental illness or disability who are placed in a private setting is difficult to quantify. While there are data that record the number of suicides per year in private versus public settings (in both settings the numbers are surprisingly low), there are more subtle issues at play that research has yet to capture, such as victimization of children with disabilities by other youth or staff. Anecdotally, it is no leap to conclude that this group of children will encounter more frequent acts of harassment or victimization when placed in a private setting where there is substandard mental health care or a lack of practitioners and the staff is underpaid and poorly trained.

Youth who exhibit symptoms of mental illness but are not yet diagnosed are extremely difficult to identify by anyone other than trained professionals. It is especially critical that this population receive professional care, including rigorous screening at entry points to the juvenile system, as youth are more likely than their adult counterparts to be at the initial stages of the onset of mental illness: they are therefore likely to exhibit symptoms that to the untrained eye appear merely to be "problem behavior." Manifestation of such symptoms may, in fact, be the causal factor that brought them into the juvenile system in the first place.

Given the complicated interplay of factors such as mental illness and developmental or learning disabilities that disproportionately impact the juvenile population, the need for highly skilled, well-trained, and adequately paid staff is critical. The repeated failure of private facilities to provide adequate care for such children raises the question of whether private juvenile facilities are intrinsically inappropriate to carry out what are, or should be, functions of the public domain.

The Exception? Or the Rule?

The exceptional growth of privatized children's detention facilities—with their lack of oversight or serious standards of care—too often results in direct damage to this fragile population. Though the examples of Tallulah and Jena highlighted above might seem like aberrant displays of violence and corruption with problems specific to Louisiana, a review of other jurisdictions shows otherwise.

Florida Leads the Privatized Pack

Florida's juvenile justice system is the most highly privatized system per capita in the country. Florida provides about $400 million per year to around two hundred private entities to house and service its juvenile population. Florida is unabashedly proud of this private venture: Department of Justice Secretary Bill Bankhead stated to the *Palm Beach Post* that the state had made a "philosophical commitment" to privatize juvenile justice. By privatizing, a state may wash its hands of political minefields such as layoffs of state employees and cutbacks. For the state considering privatization, the accelerated pace of private companies in implementing programs is appealing as compared with a public system that is a quagmire of complicated policy requirements, oversight mechanisms, and multiple levels of administrative detail. But in delegating the well-being and safety of its juvenile population to private interests, Florida, like Louisiana, places one of its most vulnerable populations directly in harm's way.

With a particular penchant for boot camps, the state's privatized juvenile facilities have produced a familiar litany of complaints: excessive use of force; inadequate education, medical care, and mental health treatment; poor training; and cost cutting at the immediate expense of child welfare and safety. One company seems to produce more horror stories than any other: boot camps run by Premier Behavioral Solutions (PBS, formerly Ramsay Youth Services). In 2003, staff at the Florida Institute for Girls in West Palm Beach slammed one girl's head into a wall and struck her in the mouth, leaving her covered in welts and bruises. At the Okaloosa Youth Academy that same year, a sixteen-year-old in isolation was tossed by a guard against the wall and sink of his isolation chamber, leaving him with a gash that required six stitches. Also during 2003, three teens suffered broken arms while restrained by staff at the Southern Glades Youth Camp in Florida City. In other PBS facilities across the state, reports emerged that staff used banned restraint techniques against children, such as hammerlocks (twisting the child's arm up behind her back), and would routinely head-butt and choke youth as forms of punishment.

In its defense, PBS spokeswoman Isa Diaz told a local Florida paper: "Our organization has taken on the challenge of dealing with the most difficult juvenile offenders in the state, currently servicing roughly 1,100 juveniles, many of them suffering from serious emotional and behavioral problems."

Despite abuses in its facilities serious enough to trigger legal action, PBS managed to escape any real consequences and earned $35 million on its juvenile facilities' contracts in the same year its staff answered grand jury inquiries regarding rampant abuse in its Florida facilities.

Florida has a long-established history of privatization under former Governor Jeb Bush, whose preference was to privatize as many industries as possible. Such privatization efforts undercut not only the quality of services provided but also the quality of staff employed. For example, per diem rates accorded by the state to contract out its juvenile services had not increased in many years. By 2004, industry lobbyists for the state's more than two hundred private providers caught the ear of the Florida legislature with aggressive lobbying efforts to increase its per diem pay rates. At the legislature's request, the Office of Program Policy Analysis and Government Accountability initiated an investigation of qualifications, salaries, training, and turnover rates among Florida's juvenile justice employees. While the report was not focused on the abuses emerging from various private facilities, its findings exposed key issues that engender a setting prone to abuses.

The OPPAGA report found that the central problem in private sector facilities was their cost-cutting, profit-oriented model: private facilities uniformly underpaid their staff and failed to train staff adequately to manage the daily trials endemic to the job. OPPAGA found that with a median income of only $18,663 for full-time private facility employees, the typical juvenile facility staff was of the growing class of American working poor, or those whose full-time employment does not raise them out of poverty. The report found, for instance, that the typical full-time employee in a privatized juvenile facility was eligible for government assistance for the poor, such as food stamps. In contrast, the state's median income for the equivalent position in a public youth facility was a good $2,000 more. (This trend reversed itself when comparing the salaries of state and private administrators, the latter gathering a whopping $13,000 more per year than their counterparts employed in the state setting.)

The report also found that the education and experience requirements for employees in the private facilities were significantly lower than those required of their state-employed counterparts. Thus poorly paid, inadequately trained staff are turned loose in an extremely high-stress environment without the necessary skills or education to mediate their surroundings—an entirely foreseeable setup for failure. The OPPAGA report was somewhat critical of the state's failure to retain, train, supervise, or adequately pay staff in private facilities. But while the OPPAGA report's findings were important on a theoretical level, they appear to have had little practical impact. When asked if the report produced any changes in the industry, OPPAGA deputy director and report supervisor Kathy McGuire replied that she "wouldn't say there were too many direct changes as a result of the report." She also noted that Florida's funding of its private youth facilities, which does not require specific designation for monies provided to the facilities, would remain unchanged despite acknowledged problems such as failure to provide adequate training for staff in such facilities. Florida's private facilities are left entirely to their own devices to spend down state funds as they see fit.

An investigation alone—no matter how thorough, well-intended, or critical—is not enough to produce change, especially when faced with the formidable resources of an enormously profitable industry intimately intertwined with Florida's powers that be. PBS and its predecessor, Ramsay Youth, secured its position as the state's largest for-profit juvenile manager by contributing substantially to both the Florida Republican Party and GOP lawmakers. Former juvenile judge Frank A. Orlando commented, "If it wasn't for the contributions, I don't think [Premier] would be trusted with the lives of the kids they are trusted with."[15]

The Maryland Example

In Maryland, the state was forced to close its largest private juvenile detention facility, the Charles H. Hickey Jr. School, after months of bloodshed and abuse against the children held there. With no real government oversight, staff at the Youth Services International–managed Hickey School abused youth to such a degree that in 2004 youth rioted, using chairs and mops as weapons against each other and guards. Before the disturbance was subdued, guards inflamed the riot by deliberately pitting rival youths against each other to orchestrate gladiator battles for the guards' apparent entertainment.

As in Louisiana and Florida, staff at Hickey were underpaid and poorly trained. One guard failed to supervise one of his charges, who was subsequently involved in a rape of another youth. The guard, who was paid $7 an hour, had an employment background as a dishwasher. A setup like this compromises all involved: the child, the child's victim, and the guard, who plays the scapegoat when the inevitable harm occurs.

Youth Services International's five-year contract with Hickey expired in the midst of public outrage over the brutality at the facility. While the state did not renew the contract, it took immediate steps to contract with another private company to operate Hickey—an attempt that was quashed by an outpouring of public sentiment in opposition.

Maryland Juvenile Services Secretary Kenneth C. Montague Jr. sought a refund from YSI of $1.5 million for "poor performance," citing weekly incidents of child abuse at Hickey under the mismanagement of the company. A later state report found that an additional 2.5 assaults occurred daily (as the report rightly notes, this is a low estimate, as many youth do not report such incidents for fear of retaliation.)[16]

In 2002 the State of Maryland entered into a settlement with YSI and recovered close to $800,000 in reimbursement for services YSI failed to provide at Hickey, mostly in the area of employee training (or lack thereof): under YSI, of 108 employees, only 1 received full training and 34 received no training at all.

"A Pure Matter of Money":
New York, Arkansas, South Carolina

In New York City, the juvenile justice department farmed out nineteen facilities' health care services to Prison Health Services. With only one full-time doctor serving the nineteen facilities, the move meant a sharp reduction in care received in those facilities for the 5,000 youth who would pass through the facilities each year.

Following a series of missteps in medication, treatment, and overall demonstration of incompetence by PHS staff, in 2000 a Brooklyn judge held a juvenile justice commissioner in contempt for PHS staff's failure to provide AIDS medication to a thirteen-year-old in its care. PHS would eventually lose its contract with New York in 2003, but only after being paid $15 million.[17]

In Arkansas, the Division of Youth Facilities contracted with Cornell Companies, Inc., in the late 1990s to run its Alexander Youth Facility. By 2002, the Attorney General intervened following a series of escapes, injuries, and reports of abuse, including routine use of psychotropic drugs to restrain youth. Cornell's management of the facility painted a familiar picture of overall failure to provide for the well-being, treatment, and education of the youth housed at Alexander.

Cornell entered into a settlement agreement with the state, and its contract was eventually terminated in 2006. The state was apparently unfazed by its poor experience with privatization in the juvenile arena, and promptly secured a multimillion-dollar contract with another private company, G4S Youth Services of Virginia, to fill Cornell's place.

A surprising advocate spoke out against the new contract. Following the state's move to contract with G4S, former Youth Services Director Russell Rigsby warned in a statement provided to an online business news site: "Private contracting is not a long-term solution and the Alexander youth lock-up, together with the entire philosophy of large-scale youth detention centers, should be abandoned for good." Rigsby went on to note: "The history of such centers alone stands as immutable evidence that they are not successful and represent a breeding ground for attenuated safety and lack of successful treatment programs. As a direct consequence of the size and capacity of such centers, children placed in such centers become exposed to a mentality garnered by both children and oversight staff that does not equate with either safety or positive treatment."

Rigsby also stated that the problems present at Alexander under Cornell would be replicated by G4S, in part because the size of the institution necessarily places children in jeopardy. "It will never change until the doors are closed and a change is implemented to create smaller centers with no more than 40 children maximum . . . [so that] *all* children in the community [are treated] rather than those they 'select' for treatment." But, he said, "it's always been a pure matter of money."

Other jurisdictions that privatize juvenile facilities fare much the same. In Columbia, South Carolina, the CCA-operated Columbia Training Center for Boys was sued multiple times for terrorizing the children unfortunate enough to be held there. In one federal claim, brought in 1998 on behalf of a youth referred to in court papers as William P., claims against CCA staff included inappropriate use of chemical restraints (Mace) used against him, hog-tying, and placement of William—who stood just five feet tall and weighed ninety pounds—in a cell with a youth who was six foot four and a known aggressor, "with the knowledge and expectation" that William would be assaulted.[18] By the time William left the CCA facility, after a year, he had been attacked by his cellmate and hog-tied by staff more than 30 times.

After a jury awarded a $3 million verdict against CCA on the basis that the facility evidenced a policy or practice of abusing youth, the state of South Carolina terminated the CCA contract.

After William P.'s year at the Columbia Training School, he was committed to the acute-care psychiatric unit of a state hospital, where he was treated for post-traumatic stress disorder and other severe psychological damages as a result of his time in the CCA lockup.

Conflicting Interests

There is an inherent conflict between acquiring profit and providing effective care, education, and treatment for incarcerated children. Even the for-profit industry complains openly of this conflict (though for entirely different reasons than child advocates: the particularized services—such as mental health treatment and education—that are required for effective care of children in detention are very costly).

In a report produced for the private prison industry by investment analysts First Analysis Securities Corporation, the report's authors make no attempt to disguise the nature of their interests in the juvenile privatization industry. This report back to the major syndicates of privatization baldly unveils the industry's motivations:

> Positive: With the baby boomlet demographics, we foresee increasing demand for juvenile services. This market has a longer history of privatization and expected higher rates of outsourcing new beds. . . .
> Negative: With high inmate turnover (the average stay is only six months) and specialized facilities for each category of offender, it is often difficult to maintain the occupancy rates required for profitability. Further, filling facilities with out-of-state juveniles is not as acceptable as for adults. This sector is also very susceptible to negative news and events

given the media's placement of high news value on issues related to incarcerated children.[19]

In addition to the "obstacles" noted above, the leading obstacle to profits would seem to be a downturn in juvenile crime. But, as noted, juvenile crime has substantially declined in recent years, with no apparent impact upon the numbers of for-profit beds created in private juvenile facilities in some jurisdictions.

Despite reductions in juvenile crime and corresponding populations in twenty-three states, in some jurisdictions juvenile populations inexplicably rose in private facilities.[20] In New Mexico, from 2002 to 2003 the number of juveniles in custody declined overall by 9 percent with a corresponding decrease in public facilities by 17 percent, but the percent number of juveniles in private facilities skyrocketed by 123 percent.[21]

This profound discrepancy cannot be easily explained, particularly given the difficulty in obtaining responses to difficult questions from private entities not bound by public duty or governmental scrutiny. But the growth rate of the industry in New Mexico and other states may speak for itself: where the private detention industry is unhindered by dramatic downturns in juvenile crime, it must be driven by other factors. Regardless of whether those factors can be agreed upon, most would concede that detention beds should not be created for children based on any factor other than actual need.

An Absence of Federal Guidance or Oversight

A central problem with both privatized and public juvenile facilities is the absence of sufficient governmental oversight or relevant federal standards. Patricia Arthur, senior attorney with the National Center for Youth Law, noted, "Oftentimes, states that use private providers provide very little oversight themselves, and by using these providers are distancing themselves from liability."

There are only the most minimal of federal standards for youth facilities that accept federal funding, such as public state juvenile facilities, but the relevant legislation allows a wide berth for private facilities to escape its already minimal mandates. The Justice and Delinquency Prevention Act of 2002[22] set forth some standards for states whose juvenile facilities are federally funded—that is, all public juvenile facilities. The main consequence under the Justice and Delinquency Prevention Act for noncompliance is the withholding of federal funds, but because privately funded for-profit facilities are less tethered to receipt of federal grants, they are largely unaffected by such financial consequences.

Compliance monitoring and data collection, which are mandatory for public facilities dependent upon federal funding, also do not apply to primarily for-profit facilities. Independent monitoring is then left to the states to install and oversee, which most states do not pursue with commitment.[23]

Juvenile standards are instead determined state by state, by local and state statute or administrative code that changes in form and substance depending upon the vagaries of the locale. In the absence of guiding federal legislation that specifically addresses privatized settings and provides for governmental oversight in this context, private juvenile facilities are allowed far too much discretion to self-monitor, usually with tragic results, as seen by the examples highlighted here.

The Heart of the Matter

Conflicting aims in juvenile justice lead policy goals in divergent directions. Is the goal of juvenile justice to punish, rehabilitate, provide diversion opportunities, serve public safety, provide treatment, and reduce recidivism? Or is the goal to turn a profit? If the underlying philosophy of the juvenile justice system is, or at least should be, rehabilitative in nature, then a population with such a complicated weave of issues—trauma, mental illness and other disabilities, substance abuse, cultural and economic disadvantage—must have a well-trained, well-educated, culturally competent staff to support the youths' recovery and return to society. The underlying philosophy of privatization, however—making a buck at the least cost possible—stands in essential conflict with the philosophy of rehabilitation in juvenile facilities.

Yet it would be unrealistic to pursue a plan of total public reappropriation of privatized facilities. Considering how effectively private interests have insinuated themselves within the corrections system, it is unlikely that privatization of juvenile facilities will end anytime soon; this does not, however, mean that the public sector does not have a corresponding duty to provide increased protections for children housed in such facilities. Given the profoundly limited access for this population to any form of recourse, including legal counsel when abuses arise, the need for dedicated governmental oversight for all juvenile facilities could not be more urgent.

Though the speeding train of privatization appears unhindered by the outrage provoked by its many failings in this context, what may impress agents of privatization are the escalating costs of liability incurred. Perhaps when the industry becomes less profitable to run—with an increase in critical news stories, public outcry, and an ever-extending queue at the courthouse—the industry powers might be motivated to divest at least some of their dubious interests in children's detention. As an attorney for Wackenhut complained during the Jena debacle in New Orleans, "Every time [children's attorney] David Utter opens his mouth, our stock drops a million."

Sick on the Inside:
Correctional HMOs and
the Coming Prison Plague

Wil S. Hylton

August 2003

When David Hannah walked into a small office on the second floor of the Moberly Correctional Facility in Moberly, Missouri, last fall, carrying his belly like a hundred-pound sack of sand, the staff knew him well enough not to worry about what he might break or steal or soil in their private offices, which were normally not accessible to inmates, so I was able to close the door behind him and we sat together and talked about what was happening to his body. He was a pale, fifty-seven-year-old white male, serving a sentence of life plus three years for rape, and his gray hair was matted to his head. His face was as worn and gaunt as a much older man's.

Hannah was angry. "Look at it," he said, glaring at his gut. "Do you want to see it?"

I didn't want to see it, but I nodded anyway. I had come precisely to see it, to witness Hannah's disfigurement, the fruit of a long series of medical miscalculations. It had begun in the 1980s with two kinds of hepatitis, B and C, a condition that prison doctors had largely ignored for a decade, then treated with a series of botched, questionable procedures that caused David's cells to cease performing osmosis properly, so that over time his natural body fluids began to collect, trapped inside his gut with no way to evacuate, his midsection swelling to accommodate those fluids, expanding to such a size and weight that the mere act of walking around had given David, by December 2000, a pair of hernias, neither of which the prison doctors had bothered to treat. David stood now to show me the belly and the hernias, the condition his body had arrived at through an utter lack of attention. He pulled his flannel shirt to the side of his waist and lifted his gray T-shirt, and, in spite of myself, I winced. His belly was enormous, taut and pasty, seemingly glued to his gaunt frame. At the front of it, a hot-pink hernia, about the size of a grapefruit, seemed barely attached where the belly button should have been, giving David's midsection the overall contour of a giant breast and nipple. Bracing myself, I asked him where the other hernia had emerged. He studied me, obviously not fond of baring his physique. After a moment, he shrugged and unbuttoned his pants.

To describe David's scrotum as swollen and red would be a failure of language. It was about the size of a rugby ball, so raw and irritated, shiny and crimson, that it almost seemed to be covered with blood. David hung his head. "They give me aspirin," he said.

Later, when I heard that David had died of indeterminate causes and that his body had been cremated, I realized that I had probably been the last person outside of the prison staff to see David alive, to see what his body had become from all those years of mistreatment, and I wondered: can such a secret be kept?

It occurs to me now that prisons are designed for keeping secrets, for holding inside not just men but also their lives and the details of those lives. In prison, social isolation is a matter of policy, and inmates are neither expected nor encouraged to have more than a modicum of contact with the outside world. This is not necessarily, or at least not ostensibly, vindictive. In many cases, isolation is the prison's approach to rehabilitation. As Alexis de Tocqueville observed nearly two centuries ago, "Thrown into solitude [the convict] reflects. Placed alone, in view of his crime, he learns to hate it; and if his soul be not yet surfeited with crime, and thus have lost all taste for any-

thing better, it is in solitude, where remorse will come to as-
sail him."

Still, the social isolation of prisoners creates a host of difficulties, not least of which is that of monitoring their treatment,
of ensuring that they are assailed only by their own remorse
and not by anything else—by, say, other prisoners, or by those
who keep the watch. Opacity, after all, runs both ways, and if
the prison walls keep convicts in, they work just as effectively
to keep observers out.

This problem is only made worse inside the prison infirmary. By its very nature, medicine is a private matter, and a
prisoner's medical records are protected by the same confiden-
tiality laws that protect free citizens. This means that a prisoner's medical chart is both locked inside a physical fortress and
shielded by a battery of privacy restrictions, all of which leaves
the field of prison medicine cloistered and nearly impossible to
survey. Compounding this is the fact that prison medicine and,
indeed, the principles of medicine itself are fundamentally at
odds with all other facets of prison life. Even the term "prison
medicine" borders on oxymoron: whereas prison is designed
to alienate and punish, medicine exists to nurture and soothe.
So where is the boundary between care and punishment? At
what point do they meet?

Until the 1970s, which is to say for the first two centuries
of American life, these were not questions that anyone felt
compelled to ask, let alone answer. As a matter of law, prison
medicine had always been considered a privilege, not a right,
and the final authority on treatment was not a doctor or even
a court but the local warden. Prisoners whose medical needs
were not being met, whose broken noses and diabetes were left
untreated, who were stabbed and not sewn, feverish and not
medicated, prisoners who had cancer but no treatment, who
had prescriptions that wardens refused to fill, whose mental
health teetered at the edge of self-destruction—those prisoners

had no recourse, nor reason to expect it. In the early 1970s, a survey of jails by the American Medical Association found that fewer than 30 percent had medical facilities and only about one in five had a formal arrangement with any medical provider.

Things began to change in 1971, when an uprising at the Attica penitentiary in New York forced the subject of prison conditions into the national conversation. Amid a flurry of laws enacted in response to Attica, state and federal legislators began crafting measures to guarantee basic health care to prisoners. Although the laws have changed over the past thirty years, little else has. If anything, prison health care is in further decline now than ever. Most departments of correction have chosen not to invest in medical infrastructure but rather to farm out the business to subcontractors, and these days a single, private corporation controls the health care of all prisoners in ten states and manages a portion of inmate health care in another seventeen, having underbid competitors everywhere it exists. Correctional Medical Services is not merely the nation's largest provider of prison medicine; it is also the nation's cheapest provider, a perfect convergence of big business and low budgets. But unlike the traditional HMO, whose risk of a malpractice suit is real, and is felt, and is reflected to at least some degree in the quality of medical care, companies such as CMS have little or no reason to protect themselves. Most juries are reluctant to decide in favor of a convict, and those juries that do favor the convict are often reluctant to award money. Cost-benefit analysis takes on special, human overtones behind bars.

Perhaps even more significantly, private companies such as CMS feel no responsibility, and have no legal obligation, to account to the public for what goes on inside their facilities. So, while CMS receives about $550 million of taxpayer money each year, the company chooses not to provide any accounting of how that money is spent or even how much of it is spent—and how much unspent, to be pocketed as profit. And although lawsuits over the years have revealed discredited health care professionals working in CMS facilities, the company refuses to reveal the names of its doctors and nurses for verification or to provide any account of how many have been disciplined or had their licenses revoked in other states. With CMS responsible for so many patients nationwide, it is fair to say that the practice of medicine in prison has reached an unprecedented level of inscrutability—indeed, secrecy—and if this fact seems abstract or unlikely to affect regular folks in the general population, well, just wait until the hepatitis epidemic comes flooding out of the gates.

For those of you who have never been personally acquainted with the hepatitis virus, allow me to describe it briefly. In the spring of 1995, I downed the wrong glass of frozen margarita somewhere in the Chihuahua desert and unleashed the disease on my insides. Unaware, I took a bus back to Juárez a few days later, walked across the border, drove home to Albuquerque, and, when the travel itch returned a few weeks later, set out for Glacier National Park, where I intended to spend thirty days in the backcountry, mountaineering. By the time I arrived in Montana, however, the virus had begun to set in, and I found myself overwhelmed by fatigue. Deciding to get some rest before starting out, I found an empty cabin near the boundary of the park, crawled down to the basement, settled into a bed, and, with one last glance at my backpack by the door, passed out. When I woke up several days later, I was lying on my back in a medical facility 120 miles away with an IV in my arm and a sign on the door that said, "Warning: Take Enteric Precautions Before Entering." Asking around, I learned that I had been delivered to the medical center by a friend who worked in the park. My liver-enzyme levels, upon check-in, had been gauged at more than a hundred times the normal level. The first time I looked in the mirror, I saw that my jaundiced skin was roughly the same color and texture as a dried tangerine. I spent several days lying in place, flitting in and out of consciousness, playing host to an array of curious physician's assistants, nurses, and certified nursing assistants, some of whom ran tests on my urine and blood while the rest mostly stood around marveling at how odd I looked. That was the beginning. For the next six months, I was forced to live at my parents' house, where my daily priorities became eating healthy food, sleeping at least half of each day, and wishing that my perpetual headache would relent. This was the face of hepatitis A, the least virulent strain of the virus.

The difference between the type of hepatitis I contracted and, say, hepatitis C, which is the most severe strain, is mostly a matter of intensity. My hepatitis eventually went away; hepatitis C, in most cases, does not. It keeps on attacking your liver for the rest of your natural life. That means people with acute hepatitis C can essentially forget about all the wonderful things that livers do, such as fighting infections, filtering toxins, and storing energy. To make matters worse, people with hepatitis C are contagious for the rest of their lives. Even twenty years after their initial infection, even if the virus is in remission and they feel pretty good, they still constitute a walking weapon and had better be careful where they bleed. It is worth noting, then, that somewhere between 20 and 40 percent of American prisoners are, at this very moment, infected with hepatitis C, and therefore quite contagious. It is also worth noting that most of them will eventually be released back into the general population, where the infection rate is, for now, only about 2 percent. The Association of State and Territorial Health Officials noted in a 2000 report that "an estimated 1.4 million HCV-infected persons pass through the correctional system each year." And although the virus is most pervasive in prison because of the high incidence of injected drugs there, it can be transmitted just as easily on the outside through sex, blood, transfusion, or even a nasty fistfight.

With a scourge like this roiling on the inside, threatening

to boil over to the outside, you might expect prisons to adopt some kind of screening policy for inmates and to institute a treatment offensive for the afflicted. Unfortunately, no such national program exists. Although the cost of a hepatitis test is only a couple hundred dollars, very few facilities volunteer to provide them, and there has been no federal legislation to require the measure. "It's a missed opportunity," says Dr. Cindy Weinbaum of the Centers for Disease Control and Prevention. "The number of prisoners with hepatitis C is incredibly high. It's unbelievable."

The fact that most prison doctors have not seized this opportunity doesn't reflect any inherent challenge to their doing so. On the contrary, a couple of states have developed simple and effective hepatitis programs that test all prisoners upon intake, making the disease relatively easy to track and monitor. One of those states is Texas, and there, not surprisingly, prison health care is managed not by a private company like CMS but by two universities, the University of Texas and Texas Tech University. Dr. David Smith, who is the chancellor of Texas Tech and who led the battle to make hepatitis screening mandatory in Texas, assured me that the hepatitis program he created is not very special at all, or anyway that it shouldn't be. "It's just the smart thing to do," he said. "We have almost 30 percent of our prison population in Texas infected with hepatitis. That's not so different from the numbers you see in the Dark Ages with the plague."

When I visited a handful of CMS facilities last fall, I found a very different attitude. Under CMS care, 214,000 inmates are expected to petition for any hepatitis tests they want, and even if those petitions are granted, and the tests given, and the results positive, the chances of getting any kind of treatment are only slightly better than of getting a presidential pardon. This became most obvious to me when I heard the story of Larry Frazee.

I met Larry at the Western Missouri Correctional Center in Cameron, about four hours west of St. Louis. He was a gaunt little man with a circular face surrounded by brownish gray hair, and his thin mustache seemed to weigh on his lips when he spoke. He walked with a silent shuffle, and from the black bruises under his eyes you could see that he hadn't slept well in months, if not years. When I began reading through his medical record, it was easy to see why. Larry had first been diagnosed with hepatitis in the early 1990s, when a prison plasma center rejected him as a donor. The diagnosis had been confirmed by a prison infirmary in June 1994, but even so, between then and the end of 1997, he had managed to wrangle only a half dozen doctor's visits. It wasn't until January 2000, a full five and a half years after his diagnosis, that CMS doctors began formally monitoring his condition. Even then, treatment was not forthcoming. As Larry discovered, CMS doctors required him to meet a long checklist of conditions, known as a "protocol pathway," before he could receive any treatment for his disease. Some of those items required off-site consultations. One of the things he needed, if he wanted treatment, was a liver biopsy. But when Larry went to the prison infirmary to ask for one, he learned that he had to have a psychological evaluation first, then enroll in a drug-abuse awareness class and sign a slew of forms releasing CMS from liability for anything that might happen during the biopsy. So Larry did those things one by one, and he signed the papers, and he went to see the biopsy specialist, who promptly sent him back to his cell because he didn't know his virus genotype. Larry couldn't find anything in the protocol pathway that required him to know his genotype, but to be a good sport he put in a request at the infirmary for a genotype test. A few weeks later, he got the test, but the laboratory somehow screwed up his results, so he had to file for a second test and wait for a second appointment and a second set of results before, in February of last year, he finally returned to see the biopsy specialist, who sent him away again, this time saying that Larry shouldn't bother getting treatment anyway, because it can be somewhat dangerous. Larry argued that it was his decision to make, and that he wanted the treatment, or at least the biopsy that he was entitled to, and maybe afterward, when he had the biopsy results and could take an informed look at them, he would be willing to discuss the risks of treatment, but the doctor just shook his head. The decision was final, he said. No biopsy. He sent Larry back to his cell, where Larry has been ever since, without a biopsy, without any treatment, feeling sick and tired and a bit like he failed himself.

But what Larry didn't realize, and what he's only now beginning to grasp, is that he never had much of a chance in the first place. As a matter of formal company policy, CMS discourages treatment for hepatitis, and the protocol pathway is just a way of making it harder for prisoners to demand it. Although a CMS spokesman insisted that CMS doctors are private contractors and that "it is the individual physician's responsibility to make sure care is given to patients," an internal memo from CMS regional medical director Gary Campbell to his fellow directors in February 1999 reveals just how much authority the doctors really have at CMS. "I am not encouraging anyone to undergo therapy," the medical director wrote. "However, if you have someone that is insistent, then this pathway is to be followed." Campbell added, "Unless I have given you specific approval to do Hep C testing, do not do so unless the patient has obvious moderate to severe liver disease or has exposure as described by the exposure policy of the DOC. Remember, all Hep C testing has to be approved by me."

And so, for the 214,000 prisoners whose health is supervised by CMS, the hepatitis epidemic continues to grow, untested and untreated, virtually unencumbered by the forces of modern medicine, while people like Larry Frazee remain right where the company wants them: stalled along the protocol pathway. Whether or not this is legal remains to be decided. In January of 2003, the University of Michigan law program filed suit against CMS for failure to address the hepatitis problem in that state. If their case is successful, similar lawsuits may follow in other states.* Until then, however, the policy stands: No testing, no treatment.

"CMS is an HMO with a captive audience," says David Santacroce, the professor who is spearheading the Michigan lawsuit. "The fewer patients they treat, the more money they make."

"This is deliberate indifference," adds Michael Steinberg, legal director of the Michigan ACLU. "There is a standard for testing and treatment of Hep C that the Centers for Disease Control came out with, and CMS simply is not heeding it. It's not just hepatitis, either. You talk about the tip of the iceberg! There is a systemic problem of not providing good health care to prisoners. Hepatitis is the tip of it, but there's a long list of issues below the surface that we haven't even begun to address."

Some of those issues have been addressed in other courtrooms, however, in other states, by other groups, and taken as a whole, the litany of malpractice crimes committed by CMS doctors begins to read like a horror novel. Take the inmate in Alabama who died of dehydration and starvation in a CMS infirmary after receiving care that one medical director described as "non-existent" and "a gross departure from medical community standards." Or the inmate in the same state who died when CMS staffers injected him with the wrong medicine. Or the CMS doctor in New Mexico who testified that he was required by the company to prevent off-site referrals.

---

*The Michigan suit was dismissed by the district court six months after it was filed due, in part, to the plaintiffs' alleged failure to exhaust administrative remedies. The suit has not been refiled.

Or the district judge in Idaho who found that an inmate's care in the state prison "more closely resemble[s] physical torture than incarceration." Or the inmate in Nevada who died because a CMS doctor canceled her prescription for insulin. Or the federal judge in Michigan who described CMS follow-up care as "bureaucratic purgatory." Or a U.S. Justice Department inquiry in Virginia, which found that CMS medical records "failed to meet any known professional standard." Or the district court monitor in Georgia who found that CMS ran a "medical gulag" in the state prisons, giving one prisoner ibuprofen for his lung cancer and making another wait ten months to see a doctor for a broken arm.

Yet, perhaps because juries so rarely award money to convicts, there is essentially no incentive for lawyers to bring these crimes together into a comprehensive, class-action lawsuit. Without the lure of a large settlement, most trial attorneys are unwilling to fork out millions of dollars in research and lost wages to fund such a massive endeavor. As a result, the central figure in the movement against CMS is not a major national law firm or even a renegade lawyer, but an aging, confrontational activist named Karen Russo.

I met with Karen, who runs a prisoner-advocacy group called the Wrongful Death Institute, one evening last winter at her home in the suburbs of Kansas City, and she invited me inside to sit at the small wooden table in her dining room, where we ate meat loaf and potatoes while her three dogs scurried around and her teenage kids and their friends traipsed up and down the stairs. Karen was undaunted by the chaos around her. When she had finished eating, she smoothed her dark brown hair behind her ears, sat back in her chair, and, as if she were in an office or behind a podium, she cleared her throat, blinked her heavily painted eyes, and launched into a tirade against CMS, her voice ringing through the house fervently, sometimes furiously.

"They don't want anyone to know what's going on in these facilities," she said. "Getting medical records and company documents is like going up against Fort Knox. We have to resort to all sorts of methods. We have a network of prisoners across the country who have ways of getting paperwork out to us, a couple of pages at a time. We have nuns who go in and bring documents out with them. We have nurses, doctors, whistle-blowers. It's a war for information, and CMS knows it. They're just waiting to take me out. They hate me. Every Monday at noon I do a radio show on a local station, and it's like a fireside chat. The CMS headquarters is just over in St. Louis, so they have people listening. Everybody wants to know, 'Who's she going to get today?' And it could be anyone. I could go after a nurse, I could go after a doctor, I could go after the corrections staff. And I've gone after all of them. I'm putting together a file on every one of them. I call out their names on the air. 'Nurse so and so, I want you to know that I'm on to you.' And the prisoners are listening too. This thing is growing like wildfire. A couple of years ago I was getting maybe two or three letters a week; now it's anywhere from twenty to thirty letters a day, from all over the country. Of course, some of those are from CMS decoys. That's why they're doing now—they get offenders to write me letters that say, 'I'm not sick, but I heard about what you're doing and I was just wondering how you got started,' and so on. You know, just dripping with it. They want to know what I've got. But I'm not naive: I can see right through that; I can smell it. They're scared, and they should be. We've got them. I know what they're doing."

Karen's invective seemed over the top, but she was the genuine article: a nearly obsessive crusader who had long ago discarded any semblance of a normal life in favor of late-night phone calls with sick inmates and interminable afternoons poring over their medical records. The dust on her antique piano had become so thick and sticky that it made my eyes itch after only a few bars, and the ceiling in her bathroom was crumbling to the floor. Yet Karen's memory was immaculate; she had converted herself into a database of detail, packed with accounts of prisoners met, their medical histories, life stories, and extraneous personal minutiae. To reinforce this glut of information, the back rooms of her house were stuffed with thousands of papers, most of which she could locate and produce within a few frenzied moments. When pressed, she could also furnish names and numbers for a whole range of sources, including guards and activists and prisoners' family members (though she was more reluctant to reveal others, such as the nuns and nurses she claims to consult). In her utter submersion into the topic, Karen had even developed a personal bond with one of the prisoners, a man named Raymond Young, who was locked up nearby on drug charges and whose persistent back problems and hernias kept him in a wheelchair, but who gave off an almost eerie radiance on the day I met him, with a great, black, bald head that shone like an eclipsed sun and a grin full of golden teeth inscribed with the numbers 3, 3, and ⅓. ("Thirty-three and a third," he said in a gravelly whisper. "I'm a traveler. A lone traveler.")

On the night I visited Karen, however, she took me to meet a different friend, Leland Hunley, who had only recently been released from the prison where Raymond is housed. When I saw Leland's apartment, it was hard for me to imagine that he was any more comfortable than he had been on the inside. His building, an indistinct brick high-rise, was in the kind of neighborhood that most middle-class people choose not to know about. There were crack dealers selling openly and loudly on the corner and drunks fighting in the street. The Plexiglas front doors were smeared with random crud and old graffiti, and the spun-polymer carpeting of the lobby seemed almost melted across the floor. Up the clattering elevator a few floors, down the narrow, echoing hallway, Leland's door opened into a single shabby room where he sat in a wheelchair watching a fuzzy television set that was on top of a little table above a small collection of right-footed shoes. Leland's left leg was missing.

"Come on in," he mumbled to us, pointing toward a couple of chairs and wheeling himself around beside them. I sat down, and we made small talk for a minute, then Leland cut to the story. "Basically, what happened was, I was living on the bay," he said. "That's the common area. It wasn't meant to be a living quarters, but the rooms were all full, so they had about thirty or forty cots in the bay, and I lived on one of them. I was there for about a year. The whole time, they never turned out the lights. But anyway, I was getting up for breakfast one morning and I reached over and put my sock on, and I felt a sting. So I pulled the sock back off and a spider run out of it. Well, I stomped it. I knew it was a brown recluse, pretty good size, so I scooped it up on a piece of paper to bring to the infirmary."

Leland shook his head at the memory and ran a bony hand over his short white hair. "But see, you can't just walk into the infirmary. You've got to fill out a whole deal called a Medical Service Request, and then they'll call you whenever they get to you. By the time I got up there, it was a couple hours later. The bite was swelled up to the size of a quarter. I showed it to the nurse, and she put a salve on it and sent me back. I mean, you could just look at it and see that it was going to get infected. It was swollen, throbbing, hurting like crazy. So a couple days later, I put in to go back, and she soaked my foot in a solution. It got to where she was doing that every three or four days. I would put up an MSR and she'd soak it and wrap it up again. I could tell it wasn't getting better, but I wasn't allowed to look at it or anything. I could get a conduct violation if I took the bandage off. Every time she unwrapped it, though, it looked worse. It was a big black welt on top of my foot, with a red hole in the middle. After a while, you could see my bone through the hole. It kept opening up more. At one point they had a doctor to lance it and drain out the pus. It looked like it might get better after that, but it didn't. It just swelled up more. Eventually, my whole foot got black. It was just a big black scab. That's when they started giving me antibiotics, but it was already too late. I couldn't even walk. Finally, the nurse took off the bandage one time and just run out of the room. She was really upset. I don't know what she told the doctor, but it wasn't a matter of a day before they was taking me to the hospital. The doctor said, "I'm gonna have to take it off." There was nothing I could say at that point. He told me, "If you refuse, it'll kill you." So I said, "Okay, take it off."

At fifty-eight, Leland couldn't have weighed more than 120 pounds, with knobby shoulders and elbows and a thick wisp of a neck. He rubbed his knees while he spoke, hunched over in his wheelchair, weak and almost emaciated. Toward the end of the interview, Karen, who had been struggling to remain silent, broke in to ask if he was okay. "You look like you're losing weight," she said.

He shrugged. "Well," he said. "You know, I can't get to the store by myself."

To someone on the outside, what happened to Leland's leg might sound, at the most fundamental, instinctive level, like a blatant case of malpractice. The notion of losing a leg to a spider bite has no place in the modern sensibility, and the suggestion that a person wait several weeks to receive antibiotics for an infection is almost unthinkable (though Leland's medical records confirm it). But like so many other things in prison, the term "malpractice" is inscrutable. On the outside, if a doctor does not conform to certain standards of care, then he is guilty of negligence, plain and simple, and finding a trial attorney to sue him is no challenge. By contrast, in prison, mere negligence is not necessarily enough for a lawsuit. Most prison malpractice cases are filed under the Eighth Amendment, which guarantees protection from cruel and unusual punishment. Unfortunately, in order to convict a prison doctor under these terms, the inmate must prove not only that the doctor provided substandard care but also that he did so intentionally. This rather elusive criterion is called "deliberate indifference," and under its protective banner a prison doctor is free to be as negligent and irresponsible and incompetent as he or she wants, just as long as he or she is not intentionally causing patients to suffer. Needless to say, this makes the practice of prison medicine significantly harder to regulate, and the care of patients harder to ensure. What could be more difficult to prove—or more secret—than a doctor's unstated intentions?

While I was visiting Karen and Leland in Kansas City, I placed a call to CMS headquarters in St. Louis, hoping to interview someone there. I did not have high expectations. I had already called several times from my home in New Mexico (another CMS state) trying to arrange interviews with hospital administrators and doctors and nurses, but I had mostly been ignored. On those occasions when my calls were returned, the CMS spokesperson had, in an exasperated tone, made it clear that virtually every member of his medical staff was far too busy to spend time with reporters, and that furthermore this would remain the case indefinitely, no matter how flexible my schedule was, no matter when I offered to visit. The timing, he explained, was simply awful, and it was not likely to get any better, ever.

Still, I held out some hope. Calling from within the state, I figured, would seem more real and immediate to them; and besides, I was no longer planning to ask for interviews with medical staff, or even company higher-ups, but to settle for a sit-down with the spokesperson, which seemed like a modest request, to say the least. I had even begun looking forward to that interview, wondering how the spokesperson might respond to the accusations I was hearing. I could imagine that some of his points might be reasonable. Certainly, prison med-

icine must be difficult to administer, and I assumed that the
spokesperson would be eager to point out just how difficult,
and to illuminate the challenges of working with convicts, of
sorting through faked illnesses and phony requests for medicine, ornery personalities, and violent outbursts.

But when Ken Fields, the spokesperson, called me back, and
I mentioned my desire to visit, he didn't sound nearly as eager
as I had hoped. "What do you want to talk about?" he asked.
"How were your interviews with inmates?"

I explained that most of them were angry at CMS, which
was why I wanted to get his point of view. "I think we're going
to have to handle this on the phone," he said. I suggested that
it would be preferable to meet in person, since I had met the
inmates in person and didn't want them to have an advantage,
but he replied, "We've had bad experiences with the media." I
assured him that I knew this, yet I felt that, as a member of the
company's communications team, he needed to communicate
the company's message, but he insisted, "I can't do it this week.
I'm too busy." I offered to return the following week, but he
repeated that he preferred to speak on the phone. So I repeated
my preference to meet in person, and he repeated that he was
too busy. Then I repeated my offer to return, and he repeated
his preference to speak on the phone. So it went, until finally,
perhaps just to stop the routine, he barked, "Well, I don't want
you to come back here. Why don't you just stop by tomor-
row?" I agreed and we hung up, but a couple of hours later, I
found a message on my voice mail from Fields, saying that he
had decided not to meet with me in person.

"It's a situation where we have been misquoted at times in the
past," he said, "and we're gonna respond to your questions in
writing. So I wanted to give you notice of that. Thanks, bye."

But even in response to written questions, Fields was hardly
forthcoming: of the fourteen questions posed, he offered only
eight complete answers. For example, he was willing to pro-

vide rudimentary statistics about the company, such as the total
number of patients under CMS care, but would not describe
any company protocols or reveal how much money the company actually spends on patients, except to insist that, of the
more than half a billion dollars that CMS receives in taxpayer
money each year, a "very, very significant portion goes to patient care." Although he was quick to claim that all CMS doctors and nurses are licensed in the states where they work, he
dodged the question of how many have been suspended or had
their licenses revoked in the past or in other states, insisting
that the company is "not obligated" to reveal those statistics.
Nor would he answer the question of whether or not the company has any plans to begin screening for hepatitis, claiming
that CMS leaves those decisions to state legislatures and individual doctors, a claim contradicted not only by the company's
detail-heavy and restrictive hepatitis pathway but also by the
internal communications of its regional medical director.

Since CMS officials were declining the chance to meet with
me, or to set up interviews, or even to talk on the phone anymore, I decided to contact some of their employees directly.
This turned out to be easier than I expected. Nurses tend to
know one another, and after speaking with a few nurses who
didn't work for CMS, I was able to reach a few nurses who had
once worked for CMS and, finally, nurses who still do. At the
very least, I hoped they would take the time to reassure me that
the gritty standard of "deliberate indifference" was not being
met; that nurses and doctors were not intentionally ignoring
their patients. But what I heard from CMS nurses was, in many
ways, more upsetting than what I had heard from inmates.
One conversation in particular stands out.

I had reached Christy through a series of referrals by other
nurses and their friends. At first, she was anything but eager to
speak with me. Her relationship with CMS was still good, and
she didn't want that to change. Although she was no longer

working in the jail in the northern United States where she had been a CMS supervisory nurse for half a decade (she had left to manage a hospital facility), she was considering a return to the company and didn't want to jeopardize her ability to do that. The money was good at CMS, she explained, and besides, she didn't need them as enemies. But after thinking about it and talking with her friends, Christy decided to speak with me anyway, mostly because, as she put it, she needed to tell somebody what she had seen and done, especially what she'd done.

I was immediately drawn to Christy's story, even before I had heard the details. As a supervisory nurse, she had been the highest-ranking member of the medical staff on duty, so she had been privy to many of the political and economic machinations behind company policy. I was also interested to hear about jailhouse medicine in general. People in prison, after all, have been convicted of a crime and have forfeited some of their rights (the right to vote, the right to own handguns, etc.), but most people in jail are still awaiting trial, and they haven't necessarily been convicted of anything. Not only have those awaiting trial not forfeited their rights; they are still officially innocent. Our legal system takes great pains to insist on this, so I was curious to know whether or not it made any difference to CMS.

The short answer, according to Christy, was no. "The way we treated inmates was a horror," she said. "Whenever a new inmate came in, they would have to see me, and I would assess their medical condition. If it looked like they were going to require any kind of serious treatment, I would go to the lieutenant and explain what I felt the cost of the treatment would be. I would say, 'We have this person here, and the treatment is going to be horrendously expensive. We need to get them out of here.' If they were a real serious criminal, like a murderer, the liability was high, so they would keep them under arrest and we would incur the cost of treatment. But if the lieutenant thought the person was not a serious risk to the community, he would proceed to get hold of judges and other people to try to release the inmate, or make arrangements to get the bail lowered. The lieutenants would often call judges late at night and on holidays to tell them the situation, then we would release the inmate, and take them to the hospital, so CMS wouldn't incur the cost of treatment. The lieutenants went along with it because they didn't want to incur the cost of a deputy to stay with the inmate in the hospital. So we would let them know, and they would make a call and release the inmate, then they would take them to the hospital. After the inmate got their medical treatment, we would immediately rearrest them.

"We did this frequently also with pregnant inmates. If they went into labor, we would release them or give them a signature bond, then rearrest them and the child was put into the custody of child services. I did that for years. You just ignore what you're doing. The whole atmosphere of the jail was, these criminals, these convicts, these scumbags, they get what they deserve.

"Appointments were made for weeks or months down the road, knowing that the inmate would not be there anymore. Or we would make appointments for days that we knew the inmate was going to be in court. They don't keep the trial dates in the medical file, but you just call the booking desk up front and ask them when the trial date is. Then you make their next appointment for that date. We were told to tell them, there was a canned phrase, 'Don't worry, you have an appointment. We just can't tell you when it is because of security reasons.' So you would be consoling someone, knowing full well that they weren't going to get to see anybody. You just put them right back at the bottom of the list again."*

---

* In response to these claims, CMS wrote, "Correctional health care staff make every effort to work with corrections agencies to coordinate such offsite trips in ways that do not create conflicts with scheduled court appearances."

"It was absolutely appalling, to the point that I can't even tell you. You knew that as long as you worked there, you did not challenge any of it. But your disgust builds as the horrible cases build. Even though a good majority of these people ended up being guilty. I just felt from a moral standpoint that it was wrong. They always play up, 'Well, look what they did to this other person,' so a lot of people say, 'Okay, justice is served.' But the way I feel is, we've all taken an oath and we have a license, and just because one person has died, that doesn't mean that a second person dying or being denied care . . . one doesn't justify the other. As far as I'm concerned, if you're sick and you get into one of these places, you might as well be signing your death certificate. Even if you don't have a death sentence."

The more I spoke with nurses like Christy, and looked at inmate medical files, and studied infectious-disease statistics, the clearer it became that, no matter where you looked or to whom you spoke, this was a medical system run amok, one that not only ignored sick patients but was actually skirting the limits of the law and, in the process, helping to unleash an epidemic on society. As one nurse put it bluntly, "We have no accountability. If I deny care, that's it. You have no recourse." Yet the clearer this reality became, the more baffling it seemed. Wasn't anyone keeping track? Where had the media been?

In the course of nearly a decade, only two newspapers had undertaken major investigations of CMS, and both were located in Missouri, which has become a kind of ground zero in the debate over prison medicine, largely because CMS is head-quartered there. Even more discouraging, the reporters who wrote those stories had, in the aftermath of their work, become just as tortured and frustrated as everyone else who confronts the company. Not long ago, one of them agreed to meet with me in the basement of his office, but within the first two minutes of our conversation he insisted that I keep his name out of my story. In the weeks after his articles appeared in the

Columbia Daily Tribune, he said, he had been under attack by CMS lawyers and publicists, who deluged his editors with denunciations, and he didn't want to be perceived as settling the score. He sat nervously with me, fidgeting, smiling, and trying to be as helpful as possible without getting further involved.

The other reporter I spoke with was less reserved, but only because he had less to lose. He had already lost it all. In 1998, Andrew Skolnick had been an editor at the *Journal of the American Medical Association* (*JAMA*), a recent recipient of the Harry Chapin Media Award, and an inaugural fellow of the Rosalynn Carter Fellowship in Mental Health Journalism, which is a $10,000 grant. Using these lofty connections, he had managed to get himself and two journalists from the *St. Louis Post-Dispatch* into CMS facilities, where they spoke with several inmates and doctors before publishing articles in both *JAMA* and the *Post-Dispatch*, revealing a national pattern of abuse and neglect by CMS. As the organizing force behind both projects, Andrew had helped expose several CMS doctors with checkered histories and had revealed more than a dozen cases of egregious mistreatment, some of which resulted in death. One story revealed a memo from the medical director of the New Mexico corrections department explaining that several prison doctors had quit because CMS administrative officials were "changing physicians' orders and adding orders without seeing the patient or consulting the physicians directly." Another story exposed a CMS doctor in Alabama who had been convicted of having sex with a sixteen-year-old "mentally defective" patient in Tennessee. Another described the chief of mental-health services for CMS in Alabama, whose license had been revoked in both Michigan and Oklahoma after he was found guilty of sleeping with patients, harassing female staff members, and defrauding insurance companies. The newspaper series had won awards from both Amnesty International

and the American Medical Writers Association in the late
1990s, but even still, looking back, Andrew said that he wasn't
always certain it had been a good idea to publish it. After the
articles appeared, he told me, CMS had sent a letter to *JAMA*
accusing him of hiding his involvement with the *Post-Dispatch*,
which they called "fraud," and threatening to sue the journal.
Within a week, *JAMA* had fired Andrew and, although CMS
later paid him to settle a defamation lawsuit,* his professional
life never quite recovered. Even today, the editors of *JAMA* refuse to comment on "the conditions surrounding his termination" or to defend his award-winning exposé, which has never
been refuted or retracted.

"I had an exploding career," Andrew told me, "and it
crashed. We may have won some awards, but the horrible fact
is we lost. CMS won. After the articles appeared, they went
to the state legislature in Missouri and protected themselves.
They got a law passed expunging the records of physicians who
are accused of malpractice in correctional facilities. So now,
anytime the medical board doesn't take action on an allegation
they disappear it. This means no pattern can emerge against a
doctor. That is our legacy. That's our achievement. We actually made it worse."

But Andrew's investigation had a resonance far beyond that.
It was his work that started CMS down the path of information
lockdown, building barricades to public scrutiny, hiding numbers and statistics and the names of employees, refusing even
to sit for a formal interview, and stifling the efforts of journalists to cover the field at all. Andrew's series had put pressure
on CMS, but that pressure had only deepened the company's

---

*According to CMS, "Company attorneys determined that a small settlement
of Mr. Skolnick's baseless claim was less expensive than the cost of ongoing
litigation."

aversion to publicity. CMS officials were happy to continue operating with public funds, but they were no longer willing to provide any serious accounting of them.

Like almost any wound, the weakness of an institution festers without proper attention, and as CMS has retreated into its shell, its facilities have only grown worse. Outside of anecdotal evidence, however, it is difficult to assess exactly how much worse—it is nearly impossible, for example, to know how many doctors and nurses it employs, or how adequate its facilities are, or even what pathways and protocols it adheres to. Few lawsuits have managed to expose details of the company's inner mechanisms, and aside from the Michigan hepatitis suit there is no major legal action pending against the company at the moment, only scattered individual lawsuits—the great majority of them, it is safe to say, doomed. In Massachusetts a small network of attorneys has been threatening to file a comprehensive class-action suit, but nothing has gained much traction so far. And although the U.S. Justice Department has reportedly kept an open file on CMS since the mid-1990s, collecting evidence and reviewing cases, no formal charges have been leveled against the company, and sources say it is not a high priority in the post-9/11 climate. Even activist Karen Russo has her doubts that CMS will change. "It's not going to happen," she says. "They don't want to be rehabilitated. They probably can't be rehabilitated. So the only solution is to get rid of them, and they're going to fight that in every state, at every step. They're going to use all their money and power, and they have a lot."

But if the battle over prison health care is beginning to seem lost, littered with the bodies of the wounded, the sick, and sickened alike, with inmates and nurses and journalists by the wayside, if the whole field seems deathly unwell and bordering on hopeless, it may, in the end, have more to do with the way we look at prisons in general than with anything CMS has done. This is not to obscure or to apologize for the company's failures and crimes. It is simply to suggest that the secrecy afforded to prisons would be easy enough to strip away. When we, as a culture, choose to see our prisoners as a part of our society (which they are, of course, and an ever-growing part), when we remove the wall of secrecy that surrounds the prison itself, when we are willing to face and bear witness to the punishments we disburse, there will be no more need to wonder what is being done on the inside, in our names.

Private Health Care in Jails
Can Be a Death Sentence
Paul von Zielbauer

February 2005

Brian Tetrault was forty-four when he was led into a dim county jail cell in upstate New York in 2001, charged with taking some skis and other items from his ex-wife's home. A former nuclear scientist who had struggled with Parkinson's disease, he began to die almost immediately, and state investigators would later discover why: The jail's medical director had cut off all but a few of the thirty-two pills he needed each day to quell his tremors.

Over the next ten days, Mr. Tetrault slid into a stupor, soaked in his own sweat and urine. But he never saw the jail doctor again, and the nurses dismissed him as a faker. After his heart finally stopped, investigators said, correction officers at the Schenectady jail doctored records to make it appear he had been released before he died.

Two months later, Victoria Williams Smith, the mother of a teenage boy, was booked into another upstate jail, in Dutchess County, charged with smuggling drugs to her husband in prison. She, too, had only ten days to live after she began complaining of chest pains. She phoned friends in desperation: the medical director would not prescribe anything more potent than Bengay or the arthritis medicine she had brought with her, investigators said. A nurse scorned her pleas to be hospitalized as a ploy to get drugs. When at last an ambulance was called, Ms. Smith was on the floor of her cell, shaking from a heart attack that would kill her within the hour. She was thirty-five.

In these two harrowing deaths, state investigators concluded, the culprit was a for-profit corporation, Prison Health Services, that had moved aggressively into New York State in the last decade, winning jail contracts worth hundreds of millions of dollars with an enticing sales pitch: Take the messy and expensive job of providing medical care from overmatched government officials, and give it to an experienced nationwide outfit that could recruit doctors, battle lawsuits, and keep costs down.

In the two deaths, and eight others across upstate New York, state investigators say they kept discovering the same failings: medical staffs trimmed to the bone, doctors underqualified or out of reach, nurses doing tasks beyond their training, prescription drugs withheld, patient records unread, and employee misconduct unpunished. The company has paid millions of dollars in fines and settlements.

Not surprisingly, Prison Health, which is based outside Nashville, is no longer working in most of those upstate New York jails. But it is hardly out of work. Despite a tarnished record, Prison Health has sold its promise of lower costs and better care, and become the biggest for-profit company providing medical care in jails and prisons. It has amassed eighty-six contracts in twenty-eight states, and now cares for 237,000 inmates, or about one in every ten people behind bars.

Prison Health Services says that any lapses that have occurred are far outnumbered by its successes, and that many cities and states have been pleased with its work. Company executives dispute the state's findings in the upstate deaths, saying their policy is never to deny necessary medical care. And they say that many complaints—from litigious inmates, disgruntled employees, and overzealous investigators—simply come with the hugely challenging work they have taken on. "What we do," said Michael Catalano, the company chairman, "is provide a public health service that many others are unable or unwilling to do."

As governments try to shed the burden of soaring medical costs—driven by the exploding problems of AIDS and mental illness among prison populations—the field has become a billion-dollar industry. It is an intensely competitive world populated by a handful of companies, each striving to find enough doctors and nurses for a demanding and sometimes dangerous job. The companies, overseen by local governments with limited choices and money, regularly move from jail to jail, and scandal to scandal—often disliked but always needed.

Perhaps the most striking example of Prison Health's ability to prosper amid its set of troubles unfolded in New York State. Despite disappointed customers and official investigations in Florida and Pennsylvania, the company still managed to win its largest contract ever in 2000, when New York City agreed to pay it $254 million over three years to provide care at the correctional labyrinth on Rikers Island.

The city, in fact, renewed that deal in January 2005 for another three years—despite the deaths upstate, and a chorus of criticism over Prison Health's work at Rikers, where employees and government monitors have complained of staff shortages and delays in drugs and treatments for HIV and mental illnesses. A rash of suicides in 2003 prompted a scramble by officials to fill serious gaps in care and oversight.

Along the way, though, Prison Health has acquired at least one tenacious adversary. The State Commission of Correction, appointed by the governor to investigate every death in jail, has moved over the last several years from polite recommendations to bitter denunciations, frustrated by what it says is the company's refusal to admit and address deadly mistakes. The commission has faulted company policies, or mistakes and misconduct by its employees, in twenty-three deaths of inmates in the city and six upstate counties. Fifteen times in the last four years, it has recommended that the state discipline Prison Health doctors and nurses. And since 2001, the commission, along with the State Education Department, which regulates the practice of medicine, has urged former Attorney General Eliot Spitzer (who in 2006 was elected governor of New York) to halt the company's operations in New York, saying that Prison Health lacks any legal authority to practice medicine because business executives are in charge. New York, like many other states, requires that for-profit corporations providing medical services be owned and controlled by doctors, to keep business calculations from driving medical decisions.

Prison Health says its work in New York is legal because it has set up two corporations headed by doctors to run medical care. But state investigators have called those corporations shams. Elsewhere, Prison Health did not go that far, until questioned by the *Times*. Now it says it is creating doctor–run corporations in eleven other states with similar laws, including New Jersey and California. "Had we realized this would be a question, we would have addressed it earlier," said Mr. Catalano, the company's chairman. "We have nothing to hide here."

But in one report after another, the state commission has exposed what it says is the dangerous way Prison Health has operated. One investigation found that the doctor overseeing care in several upstate jails in 2001, continually overruling the other doctors there, and refusing drugs and treatments, was not even licensed to practice in New York State. He did the job, the commission found, by telephone—from Washington.

The commission's gravest findings have involved deaths on the company's watch, mostly of people who had not been convicted of anything. Candy Brown, a forty-six-year-old Rochester woman jailed in 2000 on a parole violation, died when her withdrawal from heroin went untreated for two days as she lay in her own vomit and excrement in the Monroe County Jail, moaning and crying for help. But nurses did not call a doctor or even clean her off, investigators said. Her fellow inmates took pity and washed her face; some guards took it on themselves to ease her into a shower and a final change of clothes. Scott Mayo Jr. was only a few minutes old in 2001 when guards fished him out of a toilet in the maternity unit of Albany County Jail. It was the guards, investigators said, who found a faint pulse in the premature baby and worked fiercely to keep his heart beating as a nurse stood by, offering little help. "We're a jail," the nurse told state officials after the infant died. "There's no equipment for a fetus. Or a newborn."

In at least one death report, the commission took the opportunity to voice a broad indictment of the company. Frederick C. Lamy, chairman of the commission's medical review board, denounced Prison Health, or PHS as it is widely known, as "reckless and unprincipled in its corporate pursuits, irrespective of patient care."

"The lack of credentials, lack of training, shocking incompetence and outright misconduct" of the doctors and nurses in the case was "emblematic of PHS Inc.'s conduct as a business corporation, holding itself out as a medical care provider while seemingly bereft of any quality control." The examination shows that in many parts of the country, including counties in New Jersey and Florida, Prison Health has become a mainstay, satisfying officials by paring expenses and marshaling medical staffs without the rules and union issues that constrain government efforts. But elsewhere, it has hopscotched from place to place, largely unscathed by accusations that in cutting costs, it has cut corners.

Georgia, which hired Prison Health in 1995, replaced the company two years later, complaining that it had understaffed prison clinics. Similar complaints led Maine to end its contract in 2003. In Alabama, one prison has only two doctors for more than 2,200 prisoners; one AIDS specialist, before she left, called staffing "skeletal" and said she sometimes lacked even soap to wash her hands between treating patients.

In Philadelphia's jails, state and federal court monitors in the late 1990s told of potentially dangerous delays and gaps in treatment and medication for inmates under Prison Health, which nonetheless went on in 2000 to win a contract not far away in the Baltimore City Detention Center. There, two years later, the federal Department of Justice reported that better care might have prevented four inmate deaths. One guard, it said, complained that she had to fight nurses to get sick inmates examined.

Such stories can be heard around the country. In Las Vegas, after an HIV-positive inmate died in 2002, nurses and public defenders said the county jail's medical director had refused medications for AIDS and mental illness, calling inmates junkies. In Indiana, Barbara Logan, a former Prison Health administrator who filed a whistleblower suit last year, said in an interview that the pharmacy at her state prison was so poorly stocked that nurses often had to run out to a CVS pharmacy to refill routine prescriptions for diabetes and high blood pressure.

Before Prison Health even started in Georgia, there had been several inmate deaths in neighboring Florida that cost the company three county contracts, millions of dollars in settlements—and an apology for its part in the 1994 death of forty-six-year-old Diane Nelson. Jailed in Pinellas County on charges that she had slapped her teenage daughter, Ms. Nelson suffered a heart attack after nurses failed for two days to order the heart medication her private doctor had prescribed. As she collapsed, a nurse told her, "Stop the theatrics." The same nurse, in a deposition, also admitted that she had joked to the jail staff, "We save money because we skip the ambulance and bring them right to the morgue."

A Tough Business: Taking On Headaches, and Creating Some, Too

Few jobs are harder to get right than tending to the health of inmates, who are sicker and more dependent on alcohol and drugs than people outside. AIDS and hepatitis have torn through cellblocks, and mental illness is a mushrooming problem. In the last decade, state and local government spending for inmate health care has tripled nationwide, to roughly $5 billion a year.

Qualified doctors and nurses are difficult to find, as jails are hardly the most prestigious or best-paying places to work. The potential costs of failure, though, are high—because most inmates will eventually be let out, along with any disease or mental illness that went untreated. For decades the task fell to state and local governments that typically lacked resources or expertise, acting in sometimes conflicting roles as punisher and medical protector. Often, the results were tragic.

Three skeletons dug up at an Arkansas penal farm in 1968 led to the uncovering of a monstrous system in which a prison hospital served as torture chamber and a doctor as chief tormentor. The 1971 uprising at Attica state prison in upstate New York, which was sparked in part by complaints about health care, left forty-three inmates and guards dead. The debacle unleashed a flood of prisoner lawsuits that culminated in a 1976 United States Supreme Court decision declaring that governments must provide adequate medical care in jails and prisons.

But where governments saw a burden, others spotted an opportunity. Two years after the ruling, a Delaware nurse named Doyle Moore founded Prison Health, pioneering a for-profit medical care industry that offered local officials a grand solution: hand off the headache. About 40 percent of all inmate medical care in America is now contracted to for-profit companies, led by Prison Health, its closest rival, Correctional

Medical Services, and four or five others: though the remaining 60 percent of inmate care is still supplied by governments, most often by their Health Departments, that number has been shrinking as medical expenses soar.

A few big-city hospitals and other nonprofit enterprises have stepped into the fray and, while not perfect themselves, have performed the best by many accounts, bringing a sense of mission to the work. But that care usually costs more than governments want to spend, and most hospitals are neither equipped nor motivated to enter a jail or prison, where profit margins linger in the single digits.

In this world, where governments are limited in their choices, a half-dozen for-profit companies jockey to underbid each other and promise the biggest savings. "It's almost like a game of attrition, where the companies will take bids for amounts that you just can't do it," said Dr. Michael Puisis, a national expert and editor of *Clinical Practice in Correctional Medicine*, an anthology of articles by doctors. "They figure out how to make money after they get the contract."

Businesses with the most dubious track records can survive, and thrive. When cost trimming cuts into the quality of care, harming inmates and prompting lawsuits and investigations, governments often see no alternatives but to keep the company, or hire another, then another when that one fails—a revolving-door process that sometimes ends with governments rehiring the company they fired years earlier. Prison Health has mastered the game. When its mistakes have become public, the company has quietly settled lawsuits and nimbly brokered its exits by quickly resigning, thus preserving its marketable claim that it has never been let go for cause.

Even dissatisfied government clients can be reluctant to discuss their complaints openly, or share them with other counties or states. Some fear being exposed to lawsuits and criticism; others worry that the company dropped this year may return next year as the only bidder for the job. Or, as some former Prison Health customers discovered to their dismay, the new company they hire may be bought by the company they fired. "You've got the professionals dealing with amateurs," said Dr. Ronald Shansky, a former medical director for the Illinois prison system. He said most sheriffs and jailers were not sophisticated enough about medicine to know what to demand for their money until things go wrong. Local laws requiring that contracts be regularly put out for bid—and go to the lowest bidder—can force officials to switch providers constantly, disrupting care and demoralizing staffs.

Prison Health has prevailed on this playing field by thinking big, buying up competitors, and creating a nationwide pharmacy to supply its operations. Its revenues have risen in the last decade to an estimated $690 million last year from $110 million in 1994, and its stock has leapt to $27.46 a share—its closing price as of February 2005—from a split-adjusted price of $3.33. But day by day, Prison Health—like all of its competitors—faces the most basic challenge: finding people to do the job. For openings in Philadelphia last year, it advertised on a Web page called the Job Resource. "Psychiatrists—Feel shackled to an unsatisfying job? Discover correctional medicine!" said one ad. A Las Vegas posting urged, "Come do some time with us!"

Those whom Prison Health hires wind up responsible for the legion of people locked up every day. When the doors shut behind them, the care those prisoners get is shuttered from public view. Deaths behind bars provoke scant outcry.

Cutting a Lifeline: For Parkinson's Patient, a Countdown to Death

Four days into his stay at the Schenectady County Jail, it all began to come apart for Brian Richard Tetrault. He could no longer walk the four steps from his bunk to the door of Cell 22, in A-block, where a nurse was waiting with his small ration of pills. Since his arrest, the state commission later reported, he had been denied most of the medication he had used for a decade to control his Parkinson's disease and psychological problems. The medical staff knew about his ailments from the day he arrived, soft-spoken and clutching a plastic pill organizer; they even phoned his doctor for his charts.

But the jail's medical director took him off all but two of his seven medications, and nurses concluded that the new inmate was more uncooperative than ill, state investigators said. Mr. Tetrault, a former nuclear scientist at the nearby Knolls Atomic Power Laboratory, had only seven days left before an agonizing death that investigators would label "physician induced."

Mr. Tetrault was medically mistreated immediately upon arriving at the jail, according to the state commission. Without seeing Mr. Tetrault, the jail's medical director, Dr. W.J. Duke Dufresne, prescribed Sinemet and an antiulcer drug, but none of the other five medications for his Parkinson's, pain, and psychiatric troubles.

On his second day in jail, Mr. Tetrault saw Dr. Dufresne, the only physician for the jail's 300 or so inmates. In a brief visit, the commission said, the doctor reduced even his antiulcer drug Sinemet. As for the mental-health drugs, Dr. Dufresne later told investigators that only a psychiatrist should prescribe them. But no one ever arranged for Mr. Tetrault to see the jail psychiatrist, the commission said. And never again did he see Dr. Dufresne, who told investigators he had believed that Mr. Tetrault was merely feeling the typical ups and downs of Parkinson's; he had planned to check on him in three months.

Mr. Tetrault had only days. On his fourth day in jail, medical records show he exhibited clear symptoms as his body withdrew from the medications that had sustained him for years.

On the sixth day, he lay in his bunk, steeped in his own urine and unable to move. "Continues to be manipulative," a nurse wrote.

On the seventh day, the commission said, nurses continued to look in on him, and chronicled his deterioration and failed to do much about it. "Inmate remains very stiff," one wrote. "Head arched back, sweating profusely," another noted. A third nurse forced him to walk to the jail clinic, though he could barely move.

On the eighth day, alerted by a nurse's phone call, Dr. Dufresne ordered Mr. Tetrault hospitalized. At Ellis Hospital in Schenectady, emergency-room doctors diagnosed the ravages of his untreated Parkinson's. "I suspect, in the prison setting, he was not getting his full dose of medication as needed," wrote Dr. Richard B. Brooks. There was not much the hospital could do. On the tenth day, Mr. Tetrault went into septic shock. On the eleventh, he died.

The state commission ultimately referred Dr. Dufresne to the State Board for Professional Medical Conduct for what it alleged was "grossly inadequate" care, urged Prison Health to fire him, and asked the county to fire Prison Health.

The commission found that Dr. Dufresne had never given Mr. Tetrault a physical examination, and nurses had transcribed the doctor's orders incorrectly, reducing even the Sinemet.

The medical conduct board has taken no action against Dr. Dufresne. The company, in its lawyer's response to the commission, disputed virtually all of the commission's findings, saying that Mr. Tetrault sometimes resisted taking his medication, and that he was well able to move when he wanted. The company's internal one-page review of Mr. Tetrault's care passed no judgment on the doctor or the nurses. But it did recommend six minor changes, such as keeping medical records in chronological order. Dr. Dufresne, who is now the company's regional medical director for upstate jails, did not return calls seeking comment.

Richard D. Wright, the president and chief executive of Prison Health, would not discuss details of the case, citing a lawsuit by Mr. Tetrault's son Zachary. He said that overall, Schenectady County "was extremely pleased with the work of the company."

But the county moved to fire Prison Health the day after the commission's report was made public in June 2004. "We were going to terminate them for cause," said Chris Gardner, the county attorney. "But they approached us and we mutually agreed to terminate the relationship."

The humiliation of Mr. Tetrault did not end with his passing, or with Prison Health, the commission said. On the day he died, November 20, 2001, sheriff's officials altered records to change the time of his release from custody, in the early evening, to 2:45 P.M.—ten minutes before he was pronounced dead, the commission said. The Sheriff's Department denied the charge, and said it had done nothing untoward in trying to formally release Mr. Tetrault.

But the commission said the time change allowed the department to avoid an investigation, at least for a while. Commissioners learned of Mr. Tetrault's death by reading a newspaper article about Zachary's lawsuit, twenty months later.

The Revolving Door: After Trouble in Florida, Moving On, and Up

If Schenectady County was learning hard lessons about Prison Health, it was old news in South Florida, where several counties had tangled, and re-tangled, with the company years earlier. By the time Pinellas County hired Prison Health in 1992, the company was hitting its stride. Fourteen years after its founding, it had established a wide beachhead in the state and had just begun a nationwide push that by the end of the decade would put it in the three biggest cities of the Northeast and the prison systems of entire states. A year earlier, the company began selling stock under the name of a holding company, America Service Group.

But for Pinellas, halfway down Florida's Gulf Coast, things were headed downhill. Everett S. Rice, who was sheriff then, said that Prison Health understaffed the county jail in Clearwater. The company seemed reluctant, he said, to send seriously ill inmates to hospitals, which could cost it thousands of dollars a day. Inmates were regularly showing up in court incompetent to stand trial, said Bob Dillinger, the county public defender, because they were not getting their psychiatric medicines.

The sheriff's office learned that even the most basic care had to be spelled out in the contract. When one inmate died after a delay in calling for help, Mr. Rice said, the agreement was rewritten to require that Prison Health call 911 at a specific time after the start of a medical emergency.

Then, in March 1994, came the death of Diane Nelson, who collapsed of a heart attack in front of the nurse whose words would echo in news reports: "We save money because we skip the ambulance."

Saving money was the reason the county had hired Prison Health. Pinellas was actually on its second round with the company, having first enlisted it in 1986 because of worries about the ballooning costs of the county's own jail health care. When the contract went back out for bid three years later, Pinellas switched to a cheaper competitor; three years after that, Prison Health bid the lowest and retook the job. But Mr. Rice said the bidding process never turned up a whisper of criticism about Prison Health, or any of its competitors. "Every time we'd be up for renewal, we'd talk to the other counties and institutions, and surprisingly, most of them had glowing reports," he said.

In the end, the deal with Prison Health "probably saved a little money," Mr. Rice said, but the human and political costs were too high. "I thought if I'm going to get the blame for this, I'm going to bring it back inside," he said. The county did that in April 1995, going back into the business of jail medical care. Three months later, an hour's drive to the east, rural Polk County—which had hired Prison Health the same year as Pinellas—broke off with the company after three inmate deaths that cost Polk taxpayers thousands of dollars in settlements. "There were instances where we would actually send somebody to the hospital by ambulance because PHS wouldn't do so," said David Bergdoll, counsel to the Polk County Sheriff's office.

Since 1992, at least fifteen inmates have died in eleven Florida jails in cases where Prison Health appears to have provided inadequate care, according to documents and interviews with state and county officials. As it grew, Prison Health proved adept at ingratiating itself with local politicians, hiring lobbyists, and contributing to campaigns for sheriff. Under a promise of immunity from prosecution, the nurse who founded the company, Mr. Moore, testified at a 1993 Florida corruption trial that he had paid the Broward County Republican chairman $5,000 a month—"basically extortion," he said—to keep the contract there and in neighboring Palm Beach County.

There have been other costs. Last year, the company dismissed a nurse and reprimanded two others after an inmate's baby died; the mother, Kimberly Grey, said in a federal lawsuit that although she had been leaking amniotic fluid for five days, nurses refused to examine her until she gave birth over a cell toilet. But Colonel Parrish said that mistakes, and second-guessing, were part of the job, no matter who does it. "Anybody who is in the health care business for inmates is going to get blasted because inmates have nothing better to do than complain and sue and find somebody who is going to make a big stink about nothing," he said.

Certainly, a litany of complaints followed as Prison Health expanded across the nation. In Philadelphia, a 1999 federal court monitor's report warned that the company's failure to segregate inmates who were suffering from tuberculosis posed "a public health emergency." Pregnant inmates, it said, were not routinely tested or counseled for HIV, endangering their babies. Dr. Robert Cohen, a state court monitor, said in an interview that Philadelphia doctors "actually encouraged women to refuse pelvic examinations."

Prison Health still works in Philadelphia, where officials have persistently prodded it to improve care. Like many governments, the city has moved from a fixed-cost contract in which the company's profit comes out of whatever it does not spend, to one that covers most medical costs and pays Prison Health a management fee. When other governments have shown less patience, Prison Health has survived, and even grown, by buying rivals like Correctional Health Services, of Verona, New Jersey. In 1999, its biggest purchase, EMSA Government Services, brought with it contracts with dozens of prisons and jails.

Back in Florida, the purchase brought some unwelcome déjà vu to Polk County, which thought it was through with Prison Health when it hired EMSA. When Prison Health bought EMSA, Polk officials soon replaced it yet again. "PHS was the lowest bidder, but we didn't accept their bid," said Mr. Bergdoll, the sheriff's counsel. "That should tell you something." Since then, he said, the number of lawsuits has fallen so sharply that the county's insurer lowered its premiums.

The EMSA purchase also brought Prison Health back to Broward County, Florida, which had dropped it years earlier because it had been unhappy with the medical care. Two years after its return, three state judges noticed the phenomenon that had played out in Pinellas—a parade of inmates showing up in court incoherent—and ordered the company to stop withholding psychiatric drugs. "My impression was that it was money," Judge Susan Lebow said in an interview. "The doctors were under corporate direction to not continue the medications." Prison Health denies it gave any such order. The Broward sheriff would not comment on the company, which the county replaced again in 2001. But the revolving door of for-profit health care spins on. Last December, Broward hired Armor Correctional Health Services, a company formed just a few weeks earlier by a familiar figure: Doyle Moore, the nurse who founded Prison Health.

A Jailhouse Birth: Chaos on a Cell Floor as a Baby Is Discovered

It could not have been much worse. A newborn baby lay in a pool of blood on the floor of the Albany County Jail. At least four adults were there: the mother, a registered nurse and two correction officers who struggled to save the tiny boy. But the nurse looked on passively, tending to the dazed mother, convinced that little could be done, state records show. The baby, who was named Scott Mayo Jr., died two days later.

The mistreatment and missed chances to help the young mother, Aja Venny, began soon after her arrival eleven days earlier, investigators said. A twenty-two-year-old secretary and community-college student from the Bronx, she knew she had done something stupid: taken a ride with a drug dealer she knew from her neighborhood. When a state trooper pulled them over, she stuffed his small bags of drugs into her bra. She was booked into jail on August 30, 2001, nearly six months pregnant.

The medical staff made an appointment with an obstetrician

it paid to visit every two weeks, but Ms. Venny never saw him, state investigators said; nurses ordered her files from a Bronx women's clinic, but never received them. The one concession to her condition, it seems, was her assignment to the maternity unit, a six-bunk cell with a toilet cordoned off by a white curtain.

On September 9, Ms. Venny awoke before dawn with excruciating cramps. Another inmate told the guard that Ms. Venny was about to give birth. After two calls to the nursing supervisor, Donna Hunt, a jail sergeant sent an officer to fetch her immediately. When she arrived at 7:15 A.M., Ms. Hunt found Ms. Venny sitting on the toilet crying and "blood everywhere," she told investigators. She cleaned off and consoled the inmate, and told the officers to call an ambulance. She said later that she assumed that Ms. Venny had miscarried and saw no reason to check the toilet. But ambulance technicians, on the phone with the sergeant, asked if there was a baby. Guards looked in the toilet and discovered the infant, still in his placental sac. Guard Dave Verrelli scooped him out using a red biohazard waste bag and laid him on a towel on the cell floor as Nurse Hunt watched. "I knew that there was probably nothing we could do for this fetus," she told investigators.

Guard Verrelli detected a slight pulse. "What should I do now?" he frantically asked the nurse, who told him to cut open the sac. Verrelli cut it, removed the baby and uncoiled the umbilical cord from its neck. Ms. Hunt confirmed that there was a faint heartbeat, investigators said, but did nothing to get the baby breathing in the quarter-hour before ambulance workers arrived and administered oxygen. At the hospital, the boy was placed on a ventilator, his heart pumping but his temperature too low to be measured. On his third day of life, he died.

The State Board of Regents found that three Prison Health nurses, including Ms. Hunt, had failed to care properly for Ms. Venny or her baby. Each nurse was placed on a year's probation and fined $500. The State Commission of Correction did not say whether anyone might have saved the child, but it emphasized that Ms. Hunt did not take basic steps to help. She did not return calls seeking comment.

The commission also found more deep-seated failures: a disorganized staff and prenatal training for nurses that consisted of e-mail messages with instructions copied from a university Web site. Prison Health's lawyers defended Nurse Hunt—saying she found the child in the toilet, but was pushed aside by guards—and accused the commission of ignoring "inconvenient facts."

Ms. Venny, who completed a six-month boot-camp prison program after her son's death, now lives in the Bronx with her husband, Scott, and their twenty-month-old daughter, Skye. The ashes of Scott junior are kept in a golden urn in the bedroom. "I know what I was doing was wrong," she said. But still, "I can't find a reason why a baby had to die."

Connecting the Deaths: A Pattern Emerges, and a Battle Begins

It was late 2000 when state investigators began to notice something strange. Reviewing deaths that had occurred in jails in upstate New York, they were not struck by the number or even the grim details of the cases, which they routinely examined as employees of the State Commission of Correction. Something else was wrong.

Working out of a cluttered office in Albany, the three commissioners and a six-member medical review board noticed that low-level employees were doing work normally done by better-credentialed people. Nurses without the proper qualifications, they said, were making medical decisions and pronouncing patients dead.

In Rochester, where Candy Brown had died that September, pleading for help as she withdrew from heroin, investigators found that one of the nurses responsible for her had been suspended by the state three times for negligent care.

In that case and others, commission members said, the people offering the most help and compassion were guards and inmates. And the company, it turned out, was always the same: Prison Health. "Our sense was that what we were dealing with was not clinical problems but business practices," said James E. Lawrence, the commission's director of operations.

It was the start of a long fight to get the company to change its ways, and when that failed, to get other officials in Albany to step in. Four years later, the commission has been stymied on both fronts.

Mr. Lawrence said Prison Health seemed unfamiliar with New York's tradition of regulated health care, "and dismissive of it." When the agency sought out those in charge, it would often be routed to lawyers or executives at the company's headquarters in Brentwood, Tennessee, who bristled at the suggestion that they were answerable to New York State regulators. "The rules were not of any consequence," Mr. Lawrence said.

Prison Health entered New York in 1985 as medical provider for the Dutchess County Jail. Orange and Broome Counties hired the company for a few years, but ended those contracts in the 1990s. By late 2000, when the company began to attract the state commission's notice, it had signed contracts with Schenectady, Ulster, Monroe, and Albany Counties. The Albany jail superintendent at the time called the company "a godsend." The commission called it a disaster. "Grossly and flagrantly inadequate," for instance, was its verdict on the care given Candy Brown. Prison Health, in turn, challenged the commission's authority, and even sued over its report on one inmate's treatment, saying the panel had acted maliciously. The suit was dismissed on its merits.

The commission in 2001 moved beyond the specific criticisms in its reports to sound a general alarm. Asking state education officials to investigate, it said Prison Health was allowing "dangerously substandard medicine" by hiring doctors and nurses with questionable credentials. A month later, spurred by the commission, the Department of Education alerted the state attorney general that the company was operating illegally in New York by not having doctors in charge of medical care. "Nobody really noticed that they weren't licensed," one commission doctor said of Prison Health's presence in New York.

In the three years since, nothing has come of either complaint. The only agency with the power to enforce the state law—the attorney general's office—finally replied in October of 2004, telling the commission to resolve the matter on its own. In a heated exchange of letters, an assistant attorney general, Ronda C. Lustman, scolded the commission for refusing to meet with executives.

The company says that it is acting legally because it has set up local corporations with doctors in charge. But there is abundant evidence, state investigators say, that those corporations are shams. For example, Dr. Trevor Parks is listed as the sole shareholder of PHS Medical Services PC, which the company says provides all medical care at Rikers Island, free of any influence from Prison Health executives. But investigators say that when they interviewed him, he had little idea of his role, or his corporation's. Moreover, records show that Dr. Parks' corporation went out of business in July, for nonpayment of taxes and fees. After the *Times* pointed that out to company executives in December, Prison Health paid the money. Dr. Parks did not respond to phone calls and e-mail messages.

If frustration mounted at the commission, a sense of impending trouble was growing at the jail in Albany County, where the commission said doctors' decisions on inmate treatment were being overruled by a regional medical director in

Washington who was not licensed to practice in New York. The doctor, Akin Ayeni, said in an interview that he never overruled any doctor there. But a former medical director at the jail said she quit in April 2001 because she felt the company's policies, and Dr. Ayeni's decisions, were dangerous. "I told my staff, 'I know it's only a matter of time before they kill someone,'" she said, asking that her name not be used because she feared retribution. "I knew there was going to be a death. I could feel it." In the six months after she left, two people died and a third was seriously injured after poor treatment by Prison Health, the state commission found; the dead included Aja Venny's newborn son. The county and the company parted ways six months later, said Thomas J. Wigger, the jail superintendent, because he was unsatisfied with the quality of care.

One by one, other counties have followed suit. Ulster County, for example, caught Prison Health overbilling it for thousands of dollars of nurse hours and switched to another company in 2001. The company, for its part, said it lost most of the upstate contracts to competitors who had underbid them. Strangely, it said it had no record of working in Orange County, even though the state commission faulted the company in two inmate deaths, in 1989 and 1990.

Last October, Schenectady County dropped Prison Health after the death of Mr. Tetrault, the inmate with Parkinson's disease. The jail director, Major Robert Elwell, said in an interview that the medical director, Dr. Dufresne, had discouraged treatment for anything but the most urgent problems. "When you're dealing with a for-profit corporation, those are the types of decisions that get made," Major Elwell said.

The company's only remaining outpost in upstate New York is Dutchess County. "I believe they are a good company," said David W. Rugar, the county jail administrator. "It's just an intense thing to do, when you provide medical services." Indeed, just days before it renewed its deal with Prison Health in 2002, the jail had an intense experience that would cost the company's medical director there his job.

Cries from the Heart: Despite Days of Agony, "Nobody Will Help Me"

When they cleaned out Cell 6 in Unit 10 on Feb. 16, 2002, workers at the Dutchess County Jail found a letter that Victoria Williams Smith had written to her husband. "My chest is tight & burns, my arms are numb," it said. "I been to the nurse about five times & nobody will help me. I need to get out of this jail. It feels like I'm having a stroke, no bull." Actually, it was a heart attack, and it had killed Ms. Smith a few hours earlier at the age of thirty-five. The letter was just one in a skein of increasingly panicked pleas for help during her last ten days in jail.

Ms. Smith was born in Brooklyn, but settled in North Carolina with her second husband, Justin Smith. They married in 1997, shortly after he was sent to a prison in Dutchess County for attempted robbery. She shipped him canned food that he could sell for cash, and in January 2002 drove to the prison for what friends said was a visit allowed to married couples. The reunion was called off by state troopers, who were waiting at the prison to search her. They found about seven ounces of heroin clearly intended for her husband to use or sell, state records show.

Thirteen days passed, state investigators said, before Ms. Smith was examined by a doctor: Vidyadhara A. Kagali, the part-time medical director at the jail in Poughkeepsie, who worked only on Wednesday and Friday evenings even though he was responsible for about three hundred inmates. Dr. Kagali, who was board certified only as a pathologist, had never treated patients in a hospital and had "limited knowledge of his responsibilities as jail medical director," according to commission records.

On February 6, when she began to complain of chest pains and numbness, Dr. Kagali told her she was suffering from inflamed cartilage in her chest, and had her continue taking the Vioxx arthritis medication that friends in North Carolina mailed to her. The next day, after Ms. Smith was found crying in pain in her cell, an electrocardiogram revealed abnormalities in her heart. But Dr. Kagali, notified by a nurse, did not see her, according to the state commission. On her third day in jail, records show, a second EKG showed the same heart problem, but the doctor still did not see her.

On the seventh day, a nurse turned to the jail's part-time psychiatrist for help in easing Ms. Smith's chest pain and labored breathing. Without seeing her, he prescribed a drug for intestinal problems. On the eighth day, Dr. Kagali saw Ms. Smith; he ordered a spinal X-ray and recommended Bengay. Two days later, in tears, she phoned her North Carolina friends, Chris and Marjorie Bowers, three times. "She said these people would not help her at all," Ms. Bowers said.

In the early morning of February 16, Ms. Smith's untreated heart ailment became an emergency, according to jail records and sworn statements from nurses and guards. Around 4:30 a.m., a guard found her rocking on her bunk, clutching her chest, and called Barbara Light, the registered nurse on duty. Ms. Light concluded that Ms. Smith was having an anxiety attack—even though, the commission said, the nurse had never seen the inmate's medical record.

A half hour later, Ms. Smith, weeping, told the guard she wanted to go to a hospital—a plea Nurse Light dismissed as an attempt to get drugs. Minutes after that, the guard placed a frantic third call to the nurse, who arrived to find the inmate on the floor, shaking. An ambulance rushed Ms. Smith to Vassar Brothers Medical Center, where she died in less than an hour. The state commission, in its report, urged that Dr. Kagali be fired for "gross incompetence," and referred Ms. Light to state regulators for discipline. State health authorities eventually suspended the doctor's license for six months, but have not taken action against Ms. Light. Neither she nor Dr. Kagali would comment. The company's confidential review of Ms. Smith's death found no fault with her treatment, but recommended that its staff offer grief counseling to colleagues and inmates after future jail deaths.

In a letter to the commission, Prison Health defended Ms. Light and Dr. Kagali. It said that over Ms. Smith's five weeks in jail the doctor had seen her numerous times and provided medications, knee braces, and even an extra mattress for her arthritis. Ms. Smith had no known history of heart disease, the company said, and any suggestion that her death could have been prevented was "20-20 hindsight." The letter was signed by Dr. Dufresne, whom the commission would later blame for Brian Tetrault's death.

Joseph Plambeck contributed reporting for this article.

The Riot Academy:
Guards Stage Mock Prison Riots
to Test the Latest High-Tech Gear
Jennifer Gonnerman

May 30, 2000

Moundsville, West Virginia—The prison guards climbed into their costumes—faded gray cotton jumpsuits held shut by a strip of Velcro. Pretending to be prisoners, they tossed a football around the South Yard of the West Virginia Penitentiary. Last week, this defunct, Civil War–era prison was transformed into a classroom as prison officials from around the country came here to learn new tactics for subduing prisoners. They packed the bleachers inside the penitentiary's yard on this afternoon, and some pulled out video cameras to record the inmate football game.

A disagreement over a call soon escalated into a fight. The mock prisoners targeted one inmate, who had ratted them out to the guards. "Snitch motherfucker!" they shouted at him. "Did you talk shit on us?" As the prisoners pummeled the traitor, thirty masked men marched into the prison yard in lockstep. These men were guards assigned to Pennsylvania's Corrections Emergency Response Team (CERT). In this skit, they played themselves, and each resembled a walking arsenal. Pump-action shotguns jutted from under their arms, revolvers bulged in their holsters, and grenade launchers hung across their chests. "Get on the ground!" the guards hollered.

The prisoners refused to surrender. Instead, they reveled in their roles. Five prisoners stared down the approaching guards, gestured to their groins, and together shouted, "Suck this!" Laughter rippled through the bleachers.

This football-game-turned-mini-revolt was among the twenty scenarios staged during an event dubbed the Mock Prison Riot, held here May 14 to 17, 2000. This annual event is part training session and part trade show. Inventors and vendors set up booths to show off the newest law enforcement technology, everything from laser shields to guns that shoot pellets of pepper powder. To try out the equipment and hone their riot-quelling skills, tactical teams of prison guards staged uprisings inside the penitentiary's cell blocks and recreation yards.

The Office of Law Enforcement Technology Commercialization (OLETC) began organizing the Mock Prison Riot in 1997. OLETC is part of the National Institute of Justice, which is the research arm of the U.S. Department of Justice. Attendance at the Mock Prison Riot has skyrocketed since the first year, when 107 people showed up. This year's event drew 1,315 participants from twenty-five states and included eleven members of the Emergency Services Unit on Rikers Island.

The popularity of the Mock Prison Riot is a sign of the times. The nation's prison population has quadrupled over the last two decades, climbing to two million. At the same time, the law enforcement technology industry has also exploded. Its annual sales now exceed $1 billion, according to OLETC. (This figure includes stab-proof vests, helmets, shields, batons, and chemical agents.) All this new equipment for suppressing inmate revolts can create the impression that prison riots are on the rise. They are not. Rather, the hunger of companies for new customers in this post–Cold War era and the availability of government dollars have fueled a military-style buildup inside many of the nation's prisons.

"Gimme food!" "Gimme food!" The prisoners pounded the mess hall floor with their chairs. Unhappy about the day's lunch menu, they flung their paper plates across the room. "Gimme food, damn it!" they shouted. In this scenario, criminal justice students from a nearby college played the prisoners. Only the foam plugs in their ears and the few inches of denim sticking out beneath their inmate jumpsuits made this scene slightly unreal.

An officer cracked open the cafeteria door and threw in a "flash-bang," a grenade that stuns by momentarily blinding its target while delivering an ear-piercing boom. The prisoners clapped their hands over their ears as a team of officers stormed in. These men belonged to the "disturbance control team" at the Federal Correctional Institute in Manchester, Kentucky. They played themselves in this scenario and wore their usual uniform: padded gloves, plastic shin guards, Kevlar helmets, and flak vests.

Two guards wielded PepperBall guns, a new weapon they were trying out for the first time. The pellets in this gun envelop their target in a cloud of pepper spray, as they did when Seattle police fired them at World Trade Organization protesters in November 1999. But the student-prisoners were spared a gassing; the officers had loaded their guns with inert pellets. Within a minute or two, all the prisoners obeyed the guards' commands and sprawled on the cement floor, their cheeks mashed against the beans, peas, and carrots they had earlier refused to eat. Officers bound each inmate's wrists with a pair of plastic cuffs before leading them out.

The officers gathered afterward on a grassy patch outside the mess hall and passed around the PepperBall rifle. "I really like this gun," said one officer as he stroked the thirty-three-inch launcher. The team's leader, Jon Pell, a senior lieutenant, added, "We're really hoping to get some of these." Several steps away, the student-inmates checked their wrists for scratches and bruises. Not surprisingly, they were less excited about the PepperBall gun. "One of the balls hit me right in the toe," said a student-prisoner. "Boy, did that hurt. It felt like a baseball hitting you."

At times, the Mock Prison Riot seemed to be as much about boosting morale as it was about practicing high-tech responses to inmate rebellions. "For a long time in corrections, we were the stepchild of law enforcement—and the emphasis had been on street officers," says Captain John Kingston, the coordinator of Pennsylvania's Western Region CERT. Now, he says, correction officers are receiving the attention they deserve with a conference—and a booming industry—specially tailored for them. "They like to come here and see what's hot," Kingston says of the seventy guards he brought here. "Tactical officers are just like soldiers—they love new toys."

For this event, organizers transformed the Prison Industries Building into an exhibit hall. Where prisoners once made license plates, prison officials now strolled around carrying plastic bags stuffed with glossy brochures advertising the latest high-tech gear. Here, vendors sprinkled their sales pitches with the vocabulary of this burgeoning industry: "pursuit management" equipment to track escapees, "compliance technology" to subdue unruly prisoners, and—the industry's favorite catchphrase, used by every other salesman—"less than lethal."

Ironically, the most popular piece of equipment at the Mock Prison Riot was neither new nor for sale. Parked in front of the exhibit hall sat an armored personnel carrier bearing the logo of the New York City Department of Correction. A captain had bought the forty-year-old carrier at a military surplus sale a couple of years ago, and it made the twelve-hour journey from Rikers Island to West Virginia aboard a tractor-trailer.

This 26,000-pound machine became a magnet for prison guards with cameras, eager for memorable snapshots to bring home. Some officers even climbed inside so they could pose for a photo with their heads poking out the hole in the top. "We'd like New York to let us use it for a month," joked Darcy Regala, the director of operations at Cambria County Prison in Pennsylvania. Regala admitted he did not need an armed personnel carrier to handle his facility's 430 prisoners, but he said he would love to park it in front of his jail. "Just to let people know corrections is high-tech now," he said. "When you see equipment like this, you know corrections is not playing anymore."

Some participants at the Mock Prison Riot sounded like veterans swapping war stories as they traded their own tales of quashing inmate protests. The crowd included guards who had worked at the West Virginia Penitentiary in 1986, when prisoners seized control for fifty-three hours. They held seventeen employees hostage and killed three fellow prisoners who they believed were snitches.

Today, this penitentiary is a tourist attraction and this bloody revolt has become one of the many stories tourist guides tell as they lead visitors around inside the prison's thirty-foot sandstone walls. The West Virginia Penitentiary shut down a few years ago after the state supreme court ruled that imprisonment here qualified as "cruel and unusual punishment." By today's standards, the cells are tiny—just five feet by seven feet—and each cell held two or three prisoners.

The West Virginia Penitentiary will soon add a new chapter to the nation's penal history, as OLETC plans to transform it into a year-round training center for correction officers. Already, Congress has allocated $1.4 million. And the Mock Prison Riot, co-sponsored by the Moundsville Economic Development Corporation and the West Virginia Department of Corrections, has already proven to be a moneymaker. This year's participants injected about $625,000 into the local economy, eating at restaurants, renting cars, and filling nearby hotels.

One attendee at this year's Mock Prison Riot hopes that the event's focus will shift as it continues to grow. "I think it's a terrific event, but I think we need to move to the next step," says Bert Useem, a sociology professor at the University of New Mexico and the coauthor of *States of Siege: U. S. Prison Riots 1971–1986.* "This is mainly about how these tactical units operate, but we need to know how to manage and control and best deploy them. Whether inmate assault is advisable is a difficult tactical, moral, and strategic question."

That question was barely on the agenda at this year's Mock Prison Riot. Useem tackled it during a workshop titled "What Causes Prison Riots?" which drew several dozen prison guards and managers. But almost all of the other events at the Mock Prison Riot concerned how best to employ force.

Looming over any conference about prison riots is the memory of the 1971 uprising at New York's Attica prison, which left forty-three people dead. That riot was part of a wave of inmate revolts that swept through the nation's prisons in the late 1960s and early 1970s. Another wave of riots occurred in the late 1980s and early 1990s. Since then, the nation's prisons have been relatively quiet, with about a dozen riots each year, according to Useem. Still, the Mock Prison Riot continues to grow, and so do sales of weapons such as the PepperBall gun, all fueled by rhetoric about avoiding another Attica. During each scenario enacted at the Mock Prison Riot—and throughout the exhibit hall set up for the event—the goal was the same: to perfect the art of breaking a prisoner's will without taking his life.

In the prison's South Yard, no one following the football-match-turned-brawl was surprised that the gun-wielding officers quickly seized control. Before the carefully choreographed scenario concluded, though, one inmate torched a station wagon parked nearby. An army helicopter landed inside the prison's walls to pick up an injured inmate. And the tactical officers escorted the prisoners from the yard by jamming the barrels of their guns between the prisoners' backs and cuffed wrists.

Six prisoners in this scenario were actually guards from Colorado, and afterward they sat on the sidelines comparing notes. Everyone said they liked Pennsylvania's strategy for escorting prisoners, which they dubbed the "chicken-wing technique," and they discussed using it on their own prisoners. "It's effective, and you're not going to cause injury to the individual," said Jim Romanski, commander of the Special Operations Response Team for the Colorado Department of Corrections.

As a team of local firefighters doused the flaming car at the far end of the football field, the crowd began to pack up. A full day of wrestling prisoners, capturing escapees, and rescuing hostages seemed to have tired everyone. The Mock Prison Riot was winding down, and soon the crowd would depart— their spirits lifted as they headed home armed with business cards, brochures, and plans to ask their bosses for the latest "less than lethal" weapons.

Mapping the Prison Telephone Industry
Steven J. Jackson

March 2007

Elaine is one of millions of people in the United States with family members in the criminal justice system.[1] Since the late 1990s her son has been serving time in Oklahoma, with no likelihood of parole before 2008. In recent months, Elaine has contracted what appears likely to be a terminal illness, leaving her unable to work and, no less important, unable to leave her home in Texas to visit her son (who, like a sizeable portion of the incarcerated population of the United States, is functionally illiterate). Under these circumstances, Elaine faces some hard choices. She can foot the cost of long-distance phone calls billed at 89 cents per minute plus a hefty connection fee—no small sum on her current disability allowance of $573 per month. Or she can do what most other people in her situation have in fact done: severely restrict and/or give up contact altogether with family members—parents, spouses, children, siblings, and other relatives—in prison. Elaine and her son have worked out what they believe to be the best possible compromise under the circumstances: once a month, she will receive a collect call from the Oklahoma prison where her son is housed, and they will talk for no more than 15 minutes—a call that will show up on her next phone bill at $20 or more. If he calls again in the month, she will have to refuse the charges.

As this brief vignette will suggest, pricing and other abuses in the prison telephone system further exacerbate the deep and deepening divide between the insides and outsides of American penology. By further restricting an already limited range of options for connecting prisoners to family members and communities on the outside, exploitative phone rates contribute directly to patterns of isolation and lost or severely limited contact with direct and destructive consequences for prisoners, family members, and their broader communities. This chapter surveys the dynamics driving the escalation of prison phone rates through the 1990s and early 2000s, exploring in particular how prison collect calling, through the vagaries of restructuring in the telecommunication industry along with the national correctional explosion of the 1980s and 1990s, has become a significant and controversial revenue generator within the wider prison industrial complex. At the heart of these developments lies a series of questionable contracts entered into by local, state, federal, and private prison operators with telephone service providers that have in many instances driven the costs of prison calling significantly *up*—over precisely the same period that the costs of intra- and interstate long-distance calling have plummeted within the domestic telecommunications market at large. The net result of this activity is a long-term trend toward excommunication—a move with deeply disturbing implications along penal policy, social, and ethical lines.

Background and Origins

The roots of the current prison telephone industry can be traced to the early 1970s, when prison calling was first introduced as a now-routine feature of correctional life. Departing from the highly limited phone policies widespread before this time, in 1973 the federal Bureau of Prisons introduced an expanded telephone access program that would "permit constructive, wholesome community contact" while addressing security concerns through rudimentary call monitoring capabilities. Citing contemporary recidivism studies showing a strong correlation between weakened family and community bonds and the likelihood of reoffense, federal prison officials argued that a more liberal regime of telephone access could help to maintain prisoner-community connections valuable to the rehabilitation process. State correctional departments throughout the country (and later, private facilities) generally followed suit over the course of the 1970s. By the early 1980s, inmate calling via widespread (though by no means universal) commercial pay phone service had become a common practice within the American correctional landscape.

Throughout this period, like most other segments of the American telecommunications industry, the fledgling prisoner telephone market remained under the purview of AT&T. Within the relatively staid and stable world of the regulated AT&T monopoly, rates for operator-assisted collect calling from prisons (the only form of service available to prisoners) largely tracked price trends in the outside world. Under such circumstances, apart from the distinctive security requirements operative in the correctional setting, there was little to distinguish the basic dynamics of the prison telephone market from the broader dynamics governing the provision and pricing of telephone service in the American telecommunications market at large. Prison collect calling was relatively expensive, but then so was the consumer long-distance market in general (at least by the standards of 2006). Beyond absorbing the costs of the required security systems, there were no additional incentives to "game" the system, in the form of windfall profits to be produced and distributed in the interests of securing ongoing service contracts.

This structural dynamic changed in 1984, when AT&T entered into a consent decree with the Department of Justice under which the telecommunications giant agreed to divest itself into a long-distance company retaining the AT&T name and a series of seven separate Regional Bell Operating Companies (or "Baby Bells") that took over the local service functions of the former AT&T. This move, and the subsequent Telecommunications Act of 1996, reflected a regulatory sea change by which competition and market innovation became enshrined as the guiding principles of American information policy. The move to a pro-competitive framework introduced far-reaching changes into almost every corner of the American telecommunications world, throwing long-standing practices and arrangements up for grabs, and substantially rewriting the rules of the telecommunications game.

The prison telephone market was no exception to this rule. Market restructurings and interim steps away from the AT&T monopoly were enacted throughout the middle and latter part of the 1980s, and by the end of the decade AT&T and the Baby Bells were facing their first real competition for prison telephone contracts, in the form of dedicated and aggressive correctional service divisions at rivals MCI, Sprint, and GTE. These established players were soon joined by other niche firms catering exclusively to the correctional market.[2] As these markets grew and competitors flooded in, however, the unique competitive dynamics pertaining in the prison telephone industry quickly became apparent. Simply put, in stark contrast to most other major sectors of the post-monopoly telecommunications world, far from causing end-user rates to fall (a common experience across most of the American telecommunications landscape through this period) competition in the prison telephone industry has *driven prices up*. Armed with a uniquely effective monopoly sourcing power, county, state, federal, and private prison officials have entered into what amount to profit-sharing agreements with telephone service providers, awarding exclusive service rights in exchange for cash or percentage payments, back into correctional authority and/or state general funds.[3] Under such conditions, the incentives of price competition—instrumental in driving down long-distance rates by more than 80 percent in the residential consumer market between 1984 and 2005—have proven fundamentally perverse, as companies compete to secure contracts by effectively offering the *highest* prices and passing along a portion of the windfall revenues in the form of "commissions" paid to the contracting agencies (i.e., public or private correctional facilities). The net result of post-divestiture "competition" across vast stretches of the prison phone industry, then, has been a significant *rise* in prices—even as consumer rates available elsewhere in the American telecommunications landscape have plummeted.

By the mid-1990s, this perverse competitive dynamic had driven prison phone commissions to unprecedented heights. According to an American Corrections Association survey published in 1995, nearly 90 percent of correctional systems nationwide received a percentage of the profits derived from inmate-placed collect calls, ranging from 10 to 55 percent of gross revenues.[4] For states struggling to keep up with the costs of the unprecedented national explosion in incarceration of the past twenty years, phone revenues represented a welcome and multimillion-dollar source of income; under such circumstances, expected commission revenue became a principal determinant in the awarding of prison phone contracts in the 1990s.[5] According to the results of the 1995 ACA survey, based on state self-reporting, Ohio was making $21 million annually in prison phone commissions, while New York brought in $15 million, California $9 million, Florida $8.2 million, and Michigan $7.5 million. Nationwide, the thirty-two state departments of correction and twenty-four city and county jails surveyed—a far from complete count of the national total—reported phone commission revenues in 1994 exceeding $100 million. By 2000, commissions on prisoner calling had reached new levels, with California at 44 percent, Georgia 46 percent, South Carolina 48 percent, Illinois, Ohio, and Pennsylvania 50 percent, Indiana 53 percent, Florida 57 percent, and New York a national high of 60 percent. At least ten states were taking in $10 million or more from prisoner calling, with California, New York, and the Federal Bureau of Prisons leading the pack with more than $20 million in prison phone revenues each. Such patterns were broadly if unevenly replicated at the local level, with city and county jails— home to more than 700,000 prisoners, or about 35 percent of individuals incarcerated nationwide—entering into similar commission-based phone contracts.[6]

Such windfall profits for the states (along with the undisclosed profits of the telephone companies themselves) have been accompanied and enabled by a significant rise in the price of prison collect calling—an increase made all the more dramatic when set against the momentous rate drops experienced across the general long-distance market over precisely the same period. As of 1994, respondents to the ACA survey reported initial connection fees running between $1 and $3, followed by per-minute charges ranging as high as 90 cents for local calls and $2.25 for long distance. Fifteen-minute phone calls billed at $20 or more were routine, while monthly phone bills for family members receiving prisoner collect calls climbed into the several-hundred-dollar range (and sometimes higher). Some twelve years later, such extortionate rates remain largely in place.[7] Recent data show charges for fifteen-minute out-of-state calls ranging from $3.75 in Nebraska (one of the few states to charge no commission) to $17.77 in Washington, with a significant percentage of states falling in the $13–17 range.[8] The cost of in-state long-distance calling has been similarly steep, ranging from $2.25 (Nebraska) to $11.57 (Kansas) for a fifteen-minute call.[9]

As the work of a growing chorus of prison advocates and family members reveals, the social costs of this pricing regime have been enormous. By 2000, low-income families with monthly phone bills running to several hundred dollars, and in some cases thousands, faced a series of hard financial decisions. Family members contacted in the course of this research have reported forgoing medical operations or prescription drugs in order to meet payments on their MCI, AT&T, or other phone bills. For some, telephone service surpassed rent as the largest household monthly bill. Many more had had their numbers blocked, suspended, or permanently disconnected over unpaid prison bills, thus losing telephone service altogether. Some had seen their credit ratings permanently ruined.[10]

More disturbingly still, in the face of the financial pressures noted above, several had been forced to severely restrict, and in some cases cut off, contact with incarcerated relatives—an outcome with deep personal, and ultimately social, costs. As these accounts suggest, the ultimate effect of profit-sharing and what amount to price-gouging arrangements in the prison phone sector has been a long-term trend toward excommunication, making contact between prisoners and family members on the outside more costly and therefore more difficult to maintain. But this goes directly against the findings of several decades of recidivism and community impact studies, some of which were used to justify the introduction of prison calling in the first place. Such studies have found that a powerful predictor for reoffense is the failure to maintain family and community contact while under incarceration. As this work suggests, a reliable way of increasing the likelihood that prisoners *will* reoffend is to break all ties with the outside world and then place them back on the street years later, with little reentry support, in a community to which they have become a stranger. This is compounded by a pronounced geographic shift in American penal policy that has seen the vast bulk of recent prisons built in remote rural areas, far from the urban areas from which most prisoners originate. Under such circumstances, telephones are frequently the only viable means of sustained family contact. Beyond such individual-level outcomes, numerous scholars have pointed to the wider social costs associated with the disruption of family and community contact, in the form of weakened parent-child relations and more general damage to community social networks and authority structures.[11] For families with one or both parents in prison, telephone calls represent an important and sometimes the sole means of maintaining parental contact with children, particularly where constraints of distance, financial constraint, and/or illiteracy rule out the possibility of visitation or written correspondence. These costs are borne immediately and disproportionately by low-income communities and those of color—but in the long run by society as a whole, through downstream costs in policing, educational decline, and future costs passed through the juvenile and adult correctional systems. To support a policy and pricing regime that encourages precisely this outcome amounts to a staggeringly shortsighted piece of public policy.

Protest, Alternatives, and the Limits of Regulatory Action

Since the late 1990s, pricing and other abuses in the prison telephone sector have attracted a growing chorus of critics and opponents. Sporadic actions against rate hikes (usually following new contracts) occurred in relative isolation throughout the 1990s, in the form of locally organized telephone boycotts of varying scales and duration. In January 2000, Citizens United for the Rehabilitation of Errants (CURE) launched its national Campaign to Promote Equitable Telephone Charges, with the goal of eliminating excessive rates and improving access by calling the issue to legislative, administrative, and public attention. Promoting alternatives such as debit calling and advocating legislative reform along with the reduction or outright elimination of state and county commissions, the CURE campaign has targeted lawmakers, correctional authorities, and media outlets in states where correctional phone contracts are up for renewal. Community groups such as Brooklyn's Fifth Avenue Project and the Los Angeles Metropolitan Churches have pursued prison telephone reform efforts at the local and state levels. In 2005, the New York–based Center for Constitutional Rights (a key litigator of several of the prison telephone suits described below) along with advocates from the Fifth Avenue Project and Prison Families of New York launched the New York Campaign for Telephone Justice, which seeks to "end the kickback contract between Verizon/MCI and the New York State Department of Correctional Services, reform the exorbitant rates, and deliver choice, affordability and equitable service to the families and friends of those incarcerated in New York State."[12]

Despite these efforts—and the real and destructive consequences of prison phone price gouging—opponents of the practice have met with general indifference in the regulatory and legal arenas to date. As early as 1996, the Federal Communication Commission, in a series of rule makings sorting out the terms of pay phone service provision in the wake of the 1996 TCA, acknowledged the potential for "locational rents" to produce exorbitant rates in situations where no effective calling alternatives existed. Under such circumstances,

The location provider can contract exclusively with one PSP [pay phone service provider] to establish that PSP as the monopoly provider of payphone service. Absent any regulation, this could allow the PSP to charge supracompetitive prices. The location provider would share in the resulting "locational rents" through commissions paid by the PSPs. To the extent that market forces cannot ensure competitive prices at such locations, continued regulation may be necessary.[13]

A related concern was voiced in FCC rule makings around the contentious issue of "billed party preference," or the question of whether recipients of collect calls from pay phones should be able to select from a competitive range of service providers, or whether that right could be effectively contracted (or "sold") by location owners to a single monopoly provider. Under such circumstances, noted the FCC, the much-celebrated price benefits of competition once again cut the other way. In a statement attached to the ruling (which found *against* billed party preference, on the grounds that the "buyer beware" remedy of prior rate disclosure sufficiently served the public interest by allowing customers to seek out alternative locations from which to place the call) Commissioner Gloria Tristani acknowledged:

> Unfortunately, operator services from payphones are a rare example of competition leading to higher prices for consumers. When more OSPs [Operator Service Providers] compete for the right to serve a particular location, they must pay higher commissions to the location's owner. OSPs often recover those higher commissions from consumers in the form of higher calling charges.[14]

In these and subsequent proceedings, the FCC has consistently recognized and criticized the basic economic principles driving the prison phone escalation, while refusing to grant effective regulatory relief. In charting this course (and in contrast to its vaunted pro-competitive position on most other issues before it) the FCC has bent to the predictable but ultimately disingenuous arguments advanced by MCI, AT&T, Sprint, and a variety of other industry players: namely, that expense, security, and penological concerns unique to the correctional setting overbalance the potential benefits to be derived from either real competition in the sector or an effective cap on rates or commissions.[15]

The record of action at the state level has been only marginally better. Here the principal regulatory actors have been the state-level public utility or interstate commerce commissions, who retain nominal (but weak) oversight of consumer telecommunication tariffs. In theory, this oversight is achieved through the system of filed rates, under which telecommunication carriers agree not to exceed a set of maximum rates posted and nominally reviewed by state utility regulators. In some instances, this has served as a partial if still weak check on the prison price escalation. Carriers in some states (e.g., Louisiana, Florida) have been forced to cap rates and/or issue refunds following regulatory proceedings in which prison phone providers were found to be charging rates in excess of posted tariffs and therefore in violation of state law. In other cases (e.g., Colorado, South Carolina) regulatory actions at the commission level have been effectively overturned by state legislatures, which have passed measures exempting inmate calling from the traditional mechanisms of regulatory review. Even where enforced, however, the filed rate doctrine serves as only a nominal check on pricing abuses, primarily because filed rates track only the most expensive (and in the outside world, rarely used) calling options, and therefore fail entirely to reflect the real options and prices available to consumers twenty-plus years into the competitive telecommunications landscape.

The track record among formal legal challenges to the prison calling system has been similarly discouraging to date. In a series of class action suits, the Center for Constitutional Rights has attacked such arrangements on constitutional grounds, arguing that the present system constitutes a case of unlawful taxation, and moreover that the high prices resulting from monopoly service provision in state, county, and private prison facilities violates First and Fourteenth Amendment rights to free speech, association, and equal protection of both inmates and family members.[16] Other suits have sought to restrict commissions on competition grounds, arguing that the contractual monopolies between corrections authorities and phone service providers violate the provisions of American antitrust law. Still other suits have challenged prison phone commissions under a variety of state law claims. These challenges have so far met with limited success. Courts at the district and circuit level have remanded some cases to relevant state regulators and the Federal Communication Commission under the filed-rate and primary-jurisdiction doctrines, declining to rule on constitutional issues until the rate questions have undergone appropriate administrative review. Other cases have been dismissed on grounds long familiar to plaintiffs of prison-related suits: the requirement for prior exhaustion of lengthy, obscure, and frequently futile internal appeal procedures under the Prison Litigation Reform Act of 1995; the court's traditional deference to the discretion of prison administrators, and the concomitant low levels of judicial scrutiny applied to security-inspired abrogations of the constitutional rights of prisoners; and the perennial imbalance in resources available to legal aid and public interest lawyers versus those of corporate and government legal departments.[17]

Arguably the most successful advocacy efforts to date have come in the associated spheres of public opinion and legislative pressure. CURE campaign organizers point to more than 150 articles and a dozen sympathetic editorials in the mainstream press, and report overwhelmingly favorable responses to targeted and more general public lobbying campaigns. In some cases, this has been translated into significant, if still partial, victories. In April 2001, legislation was passed in Vermont that would see all prison phone commissions phased out by the end of 2006. In 2002, California once again entered into exclusive no-bid contracts with MCI and Verizon, but agreed to a reduction in state commissions that would reduce the cost of inmate calling by as much as 25 percent.[18] During summer 2003, in apparent response to pressures emanating from the legislature and state Public Utility Commission, MCI and the New York Department of Corrections announced that state correctional facilities would move to a flat-rate pricing system, with all in-state calls, local or long distance, priced at 16 cents a minute with a $3 connection fee—an increase over local fees under the previous system, but delivering substantial long-distance savings. In June 2005, the New York State Assembly passed its Family Connections Bill, which would emphasize fair-market pricing and make it illegal for the state to profit from prison telephone contracts.[19] Under the terms of HB 1765, effective as of July 1, 2006, Virginia prisons saw debit calling options added, with commissions capped at 10 percent. Legislatures in Missouri, Kentucky, and several other states have instructed state purchasing and correctional officials to prioritize price over commission revenue in the awarding of new correctional phone contracts (though the track record in following these guidelines, as evidenced in subsequent contracts, would appear to be mixed). Additional resolutions that would cap rates and commissions and mandate debit calling have been introduced in several more states, only to die on the floor after encountering stiff opposition from correctional authorities and/or telephone providers.[20] At the federal level, in December 2005 Illinois congressman Bobby Rush introduced House Resolution 4466, the Family Telephone Connection Protection Act of 2005. The proposed act would have instructed the Federal Communications Commission to establish and enforce maximum per-minute rates and connection fees, mandate debit calling options, require competition, and prohibit commission payments on all prisoner-originated calls.[21] The proposed legislation went no further, however, and was not ultimately enacted. In an early and significant development frequently cited by price reform advocates, the Federal Bureau of Prisons (BOP) in 1995 began adding debit calling options to its previous collect-only phone system. The BOP's debit calling system remains subject to monopoly provision and all the usual security features, but appears in most cases to have resulted in substantial savings over previous collect rates.

Conclusion

At the time of writing, in mid-2006, the political and economic future of the prison telephone industry remains fundamentally up for grabs. The efforts of a growing movement of family members and advocates to raise the issue to legal, legislative, and public attention have created new political pressures and occasional openings to curb the worst abuses of the commissioned monopoly system. In some cases, such efforts have produced breakthroughs and concessions that have led to partial rollbacks of the rising prices and commissions experienced in the 1990s. This has occurred in tandem with what seems to be a renewed interest in questions of reentry and recidivism, if the recent statements of prison officials are to be taken at face value. But despite these developments, both real and professed, prison telephone monopolies remain firmly in place and ineffectively regulated throughout large parts of the country. Many of the principal legal challenges to pricing abuses in the prison phone industry have foundered on the rocks of the filed-rate doctrine and primary jurisdiction and/or continue to languish before state and federal courts and regulatory agencies. In light of the manifest reluctance of legal and regulatory authorities to act on this matter, the best long-term hope for reform may lie in efforts to build public support and pressure against current practices, which may then be translated into legislative action. But that strategy will rest in turn on public perceptions around the unprecedented social experiment in incarceration that has dominated American criminal and corrections policy over the past twenty-five-plus years. Like many of the other prison industries reviewed in this book, justice and sound policy in the prison telephone sector remain at heart questions of deep public ethics—and will be fought for, achieved, or denied at that level.

Shocked and Stunned:
The Growing Use of Tasers
Anne-Marie Cusac

June 2005

High-powered tasers are the new fad in law enforcement. They are becoming ever more prevalent even as their safety is increasingly in question. The proliferation of tasers in police departments across the country has led to unconventional uses. Among those hit by tasers are elderly people, children as young as one year old, people apparently suffering diabetic shock and epileptic seizures, people already bound in restraints, and hospital mental patients. Police used tasers against protesters in Miami in 2003 at the Free Trade Area of the Americas demonstration and against rowdy fans at the 2005 Fiesta Bowl. School systems are employing the weapons, with some officers carrying tasers even in elementary schools.

But doctors, reporters, and human rights groups have raised questions about the safety of the devices, which shoot two barbs designed to pierce the skin. The barbs are at the end of electrical wires carrying 50,000 volts. The *New York Times* reported on July 18, 2004, that at least 50 people had died within a short time after being hit with tasers. By April 1, 2005, when Amnesty International released its own report, that number had risen to more than 101. An earlier Amnesty report released in November 2004 listed 70 taser-related deaths.

In February 2005, Chicago police used the device against a fourteen-year-old boy, who went into cardiac arrest but survived, and a fifty-four-year-old man, who died. The Chicago Police Department, which had recently purchased a hundred of the devices, decided not to distribute them until it had investigated the incidents.

The Department of Justice is conducting its own investigation into the safety of the devices. It has selected researchers at Wake Forest University and the University of Wisconsin to run independent taser studies.

Taser International, the biggest manufacturer of the weapon, denies that its product caused any deaths. The company insists that its products are safe. "The ADVANCED TASER has a lower injury rate than other non-lethal weapons and has had no reported long-term, adverse after-effects," says the company Web site.

Early tasers, those used from the 1970s until the early 1990s, were lower-wattage devices. "The original taser operated on only five watts and was followed by Air Taser on seven watts," says the November Amnesty International report.

William Bozeman, a medical doctor at the Wake Forest University department of emergency medicine, is investigating the safety of tasers for the Justice Department. "They've increased the amount of wattage that's delivered," he says. Above fourteen watts, he says, you get "electro-muscular disruption."

According to Taser International, that's the point. The "uncontrollable contraction of the muscle tissue" allows the taser "to physically debilitate a target regardless of pain tolerance or mental focus," says the company Web site. The tasers "directly tell the muscles what to do: contract until the target is in the fetal position on the ground."

Taser International introduced its "Air Taser" in 1994. Then, in 1998, "the company began Project Stealth: the development of the higher-power weapons to stop extremely combative, violent individuals who were impervious to non-lethal weapons." Project Stealth led to the M26, a taser with twenty-six watts of power.

In 2003, Taser International started selling an additional version of the twenty-six-watt taser, called the X26, which is light enough for police officers to carry at all times.

Police like tasers, sometimes for good reason. Greg Pashley, officer and spokesperson for the Portland Police Department, says the taser "is a tool that is effective in ending what could otherwise be a violent conflict without injuries. We're finding that time and again."

Many other officers add praise of their own. "It's increasingly a less lethal weapon of choice," says Scott Folsom, police chief at the University of Utah. "It doesn't have residual effects. It's proven to be a relatively safe and effective tool."

The Department of Justice is not the only governmental authority inquiring into tasers. On January 7, 2005, Taser International issued a press release that said the U. S. Securities and Exchange Commission was investigating what Taser International described as "company statements regarding the safety" of the company's products. Arizona's Attorney General, Terry Goddard, is also investigating their safety.

Taser International did not respond to repeated requests for an interview, or answer written questions posed to them. The company did, however, send several press releases by e-mail. One of those press releases concerned stories by Associated Press and CBS about a study they said linked the taser to heart damage in pigs. The company disputed the news reports, saying, "TASER International is deeply concerned that CBS News and the Associated Press would publicize erroneous links between the TASER and heart damage conflicting with the study author's own assertions and relying solely on statistically insignificant readings."

In Portland, Oregon, police used a taser to shock a seventy-one-year-old blind woman four times on her back and once on the right breast. They also pepper-sprayed her and beat her.

On June 9, 2003, Eunice Crowder was home when a city

official came to clean up her messy yard. When Crowder objected, he called the police. The Portland *Oregonian* reported that Crowder, who claimed to be hard of hearing, ignored police commands and tried to climb into a city truck to retrieve her possessions. The police claimed that when they tried to stop Crowder, she kicked at them. That's when they pepper-sprayed her and used the taser. Then they handcuffed Crowder's arms and yelled at her to stand up. "And she says, 'I bet you wouldn't yell at your mom like that,'" her lawyer, Ernest Warren Jr., told a radio station. One of the officers responded, "My mom is seventy-four." She said, "Well, I'm seventy-one."

In 2004, Crowder agreed to a $145,000 settlement from the city of Portland. The police department admitted no wrongdoing.

"We don't have age restrictions" for use of tasers, says Pashley of the Portland Police Department. But he says that policy is currently "under review."

Crowder wasn't the oldest person hit by a taser. The oldest one on record was seventy-five-year-old Margaret Kimbrell of Rock Hill, South Carolina, who describes the electricity from the taser as traveling "all over your chest like a big snake or something worming to try to get out." Kimbrell says, "I prayed, 'Lord, Jesus, make it quicker.' I was waiting to die so the pain would go away." Police used the taser on Kimbrell when she refused to leave a nursing home and, the police claimed, tried to hit an officer.

Some of Taser International's own materials suggest that shocking senior citizens may pose a danger. In its November report, Amnesty International cites a "certified lesson plan" from the company that warns it is "not advisable" to use its high-power devices on someone who is pregnant or elderly.

A study of available medical literature commissioned by Taser International and available on the company's Web site says that older people may have particular vulnerabilities. "Elderly subjects and those with preexisting heart disease are perhaps at an increased risk of cardiac complications and death following exposure to large quantities of electrical energy," wrote Anthony Bleetman of the University of Birmingham. "Since the elderly and heart patients don't often require to be subdued or controlled with a high level of force, then this is unlikely to pose a common problem."

Scientists and medical doctors have several theories, some of them conflicting, about how tasers affect bodies. Electricity near the heart can be dangerous, explains John Webster, professor emeritus in biomedical engineering at the University of Wisconsin, "because it might cause ventricular fibrillation." Webster and a team of University of Wisconsin researchers are investigating the taser's effect on the heart for the U.S. Department of Justice. While suggesting that the taser may be relatively safe for the heart, they speculate that an excess of potassium, produced when muscles contract violently but also produced by cocaine use, may be a key ingredient in the deaths associated with the device.

The Department of Justice study appears to have serious conflicts of interest. It turns out that Webster had hired four paid advisers for the DOJ-sponsored taser study, including Robert Stratbucker, a Nebraska physician who is also Taser International's medical consultant. Within days of Stratbucker's participation being made public in *USA Today* in May 2005, Webster removed him from the study.

Others suggest that some deaths may be attributable to a combination of restricted breathing—due to being extremely excited, held forcibly on the ground, or strapped down—possibly in combination with the stress of enduring a taser shock. A 2001 article in the medical journal *The Lancet* notes that in one study, cardiac arrests following incidents of taser use "occurred 5–25 min[utes] after the tasers were fired." This long after the shock, wrote the *Lancet* authors, "taser-induced muscle contractions would no longer be present, and one would expect the individuals to be relaxing and able to breathe in a way that would compensate" for the rise of acid levels in the blood. "Such may not be the case if the individuals remained agitated or were prevented from breathing freely."

Werner Spitz, a consultant forensic pathologist and the former Medical Examiner for Wayne and Macomb Counties in Michigan, says some deaths that occurred after suspects suffered both physical restraint and shocks with the taser may be due to the restricted breathing, also called positional asphyxia, rather than to the electrical shock. "Positional asphyxia is certainly much more common than many people want you to believe," says Spitz. However, he also believes that tasers can be dangerous and notes that there are "documented taser cases," in which coroners said the weapon contributed to the deaths. "The taser is not as innocuous as the taser company suggests," says Spitz.

Many police departments say that use of tasers has reduced injuries and fatalities. The city of Phoenix saw a 54 percent drop in police shootings the year it began to use tasers. In 2003, Seattle, which also uses tasers, had no shootings that involved officers for the first time in fifteen years. This type of correlation has made tasers popular.

"As of October 2004, over 6,000 police departments in the United States and abroad had purchased TASER products," says the company Web site. "Over 200 police departments—including Phoenix, San Diego, Sacramento, Albuquerque, and Reno—have purchased TASER products for every patrol officer."

But Amnesty International says the tasers are making it too easy for the police to use excessive force. "Claims that tasers have led to a fall in police shootings need to be put into perspective, given that shootings constitute only a small percentage of all police use of force," says the November report. "In contrast, taser usage has increased dramatically, becoming the most prevalent force option in some departments. While police shootings in Phoenix fell from twenty-eight to thirteen in 2003, tasers were used that year in 354 use-of-force incidents, far more than would be needed to avoid a resort to lethal force."

A number of the stories in the Amnesty report involve police use of tasers on people who were already restrained, including two who were strapped to gurneys and on their way to, or already inside, hospitals. In one such case in Pueblo, Colorado, "a police officer applied a taser to the man while he was restrained on a hospital bed, screaming for his wife," said Amnesty. This example supports claims that tasers are being used primarily for torture and abuse rather than as a substitute for lethal force.

"That was a case where a rookie officer did not understand appropriate use of a taser," says Pueblo Police Chief Jim Billings. Although the incident involved a misunderstanding of policy, rather than maliciousness, he says, the officer received "a pretty heavy suspension."

Amnesty International wants the devices temporarily banned "pending a rigorous, independent, and impartial inquiry into their use and effects." The investigation should "be carried out by acknowledged medical, scientific, legal, and law enforcement experts who are independent of commercial and political interests in promoting such equipment," says the human rights organization.

In response to the Amnesty report, Taser International issued a press release accusing the human rights organization of being "out of step with law enforcement worldwide."

Tasers in Prisons and Jails

Tasers started as a police tools, and police are still the chief users of the electroshock weapons. But in addition to their spread into schools and hospitals, tasers are emerging in jails and prisons. In its November report, Amnesty cites information from Taser International indicating that "at least 1,000 U.S. jails and prisons have adopted the new generation M26 or X26 Tasers."

Prisons and jails lag behind police departments in taser purchases. Taser International says that won't be the situation for long. "Give us enough time, you'll have that attitude changed 180 degrees," Taser International spokesman Steve Tuttle told the Associated Press.

But some prisons aren't buying, in part because they feel the confrontational relationship that comes with a taser is more useful for police than for prison guards, who must build communication and relationships over time with the inmates. Sam Sublett, security operations administrator for the Arizona Department of Corrections, in Taser International's home state, told the Associated Press that he was concerned tasers could pose a danger in a prison, saying, "We have a big concern about a taser being taken away from someone and then used against them."

But because they can be shot from a distance, tasers may be useful in prison and jail situations, particularly dangerous ones like riots. In Monterey County, California, where prisoners took over their housing units in March 2004, SWAT teams carrying tasers helped guards reclaim the jail.

Amnesty International has expressed concern about "reports that tasers have been used to gain compliance in the case of emotionally disturbed, intoxicated or uncooperative individuals in the booking section of jails." In one case, noted Amnesty, a prisoner who refused to open his hand for fingerprinting received a shock, as did another who would not "provide a blood sample." Deputies allegedly shocked a woman who "failed to remove an eyebrow ring."

The overuse of tasers doesn't stop after booking. In Clear

Creek County, Colorado, says Amnesty, citing an incident report, a prisoner got a jolt when he threw a food tray to the
floor of his cell and would not pick it up. At the jail in Greene
County, Missouri, a group of prisoners filed a lawsuit in 2004
alleging numerous uses of, or threats to use, the taser "for failing
to comply with orders." Both counties say that, because of the
pending lawsuits, they cannot comment on the allegations.

In December 2004, the *Los Angeles Times* reported that deputies shocked a man awaiting trial at the Orange County jail
when he "draped a bed sheet around his neck," in what his
lawyer told reporters was a bid for the guards' attention. Jon
Fleischman, spokesman for the Orange County Jail, confirms
that deputies did use a taser on the prisoner and that the action was "within proper regulations in the department." The
Orange County jail, says Fleischman, is mostly concrete. "In
general, if you've got a choice between taking an inmate" to
the cell floor and using a taser that, Fleischman says, "has a
zero chance of causing permanent damage," a taser is preferable to "the laying on of hands." Tasers, he says, "apply a very
minimal charge for a short time. My question is, what's the
alternative?"

But the easy availability of the devices may lead to misuse.
In March 2005, a police officer resigned after he used a taser
on an Escambia County, Florida, jail prisoner. "He pulled the
taser out when the individual wouldn't get out of the chair,"
says Escambia County assistant Chief Chip Simmons. The
officer moved out of range of the video cameras during the
shock, but the sound of the taser firing was noticeable on an
audiotape. Simmons says that the county conducted an internal
affairs investigation on the incident and determined that the
officer tased the prisoner unnecessarily. Pensacola police chief
John Mathis "was going to recommend that he be terminated,"
says Simmons. "He resigned prior to that."

In response to the incident, Simmons conducted a review

of taser use in the police force and made recommendations, which have since been incorporated into department policy. Among other stipulations, the changes would prohibit use of tasers in corrections facilities, require that the weapons be used only for active (rather than passive) resistance, and limit use of the devices on children, elderly people, and people with serious medical conditions.

In February 2005, James Telb, Sheriff of Lucas, County, Ohio, announced that his department would no longer use tasers. The department was responding to the death of Jeffrey Turner, who was shocked nine times, four of those from guards at the county jail. An early autopsy on Turner's death was inconclusive. Telb did not respond to requests for comment.

But autopsies of some deaths following taser shocks delivered at jails did conclude that the taser was partly at fault. Local news reports on one such incident say that in mid-August 2004, William Malcolm Teasley, a prisoner at the detention center in Anderson County, South Carolina, rushed up to guards and attempted to use a pen as a weapon. "The subject, who was acting violently, began to assault the officers and was restrained with a taser," says Robert Daly, Director of the Anderson County Detention Center. Teasly collapsed during the shock and died at a hospital. "The cause of death was cardiac arrhythmia," says Daly. "The subject had serious cardiac and vascular disease that placed him at risk for arrhythmia." The county's Deputy Coroner told a reporter from the *Greenville News* that the shock, together with Teasly's heart disease, helped cause his death.

And at the Monroe County, Indiana, jail in November 2003, a guard shocked a handcuffed prisoner named James Borden. Borden died while still in the jail's booking room. "A pathologist determined Borden's death resulted from an enlarged heart, pharmacological intoxication and electric shock," reported the Associated Press. "An autopsy indicated that he had received six electric shocks." Monroe County sheriff Stephen E. Sharp declined to comment, saying, "We've got pending litigation on this case."

Amnesty International has also noted numerous reports of people receiving shocks while restrained or during transport to and from prisons and jails. In some cases, notes the human rights organization in its November report, "individuals have been shot with taser darts, then threatened or stunned with repeated jolts of electricity while the darts remain in place during transportation or custody."

Tasers have made an appearance not only in our domestic prisons and jails but at military detention facilities in Iraq. In December 2004, the Pentagon announced that the U.S. military was disciplining four Special Operations personnel because they had physically mistreated detainees at an interrogation camp in Baghdad. "Based on the results of this specific investigation, four individuals received administration punishments for excessive use of force," said Pentagon spokesman Lawrence Di Rita, according to a *New York Times* report. "In particular, I'm advised that it was the unauthorized use of Taser."

The abuse became public after the release of a letter by Vice Admiral Lowell J. Jacoby of the Defense Intelligence Agency. In that letter, Jacoby wrote, among other allegations of abuse, that officials with his agency had seen prisoners who had burn marks along their backs.

Tasering Children

On December 10, 2004, police in Pembroke Pines, Florida, used a taser on a twelve-year-old boy who tried to stab another child with a pencil and then became combative with police. Commander Ken Hall, public information officer for the Pembroke Pines police, says the case "was looked at very closely, obviously because of the controversial nature," and found to be "within the parameters of our policy."

In November 2004, a Miami–Dade officer shocked a twelve-year-old Florida girl who was playing hooky. At the moment he shocked her, she was running from him. Although Miami–Dade police did at the time consider tasers to be an appropriate weapon for use on children, the director of the Miami–Dade Police Department has raised questions about the event. "It was his opinion that that incident may not have been within our guidelines" because the girl was not posing a threat to herself or others, says Detective Juan DelCastillo, who handles media relations for the Miami–Dade police. The director is reviewing the incident.

Back in May 2004, a nine-year-old runaway girl in Tucson who was already handcuffed by police and sitting in a police vehicle was shocked with a taser when she began to kick at the car and bang her head. The Pima County attorney general's office conducted an investigation of the incident and decided not to bring criminal charges against the officer who used the taser. "In all likelihood, the use of the taser prevented" the girl "from injuring herself any further," wrote David L. Berkman, the chief criminal deputy, in explaining his decision.

Even one-year-olds have been shocked, according to records Taser International supplied to the Associated Press. The company also told the *San Jose Mercury News* that its taser can be used safely on toddlers.

In October 2004, in a widely reported incident, police in Miami shocked a six-year-old. The officers were dispatched to an elementary school where they encountered "a mentally disturbed student bleeding and holding a piece of glass," says the police report. "Upon their arrival, the officers were confronted by a highly agitated and disturbed male bleeding and smearing blood on his face while clutching a piece of glass in his left hand." The officers tried to talk the boy into giving up the glass and tossing it into a wastebasket. The boy refused and "attempted to cut his leg with the shard of glass." The report says that officers then shocked the boy to keep him from hurting himself more extensively. The boy "dropped the glass and was subdued without further incident."

The officers shot the boy with the taser "for his own safety and to stop him from hurting himself," says DelCastillo of the Miami-Dade police. As for the appropriateness of shocking a six-year-old, DelCastillo says, "Our understanding is that there has been research" and that the taser causes "no after-effects." He says there is "no reason that would cause harm to someone younger than an adult."

But the research is not nearly so clear-cut.

A scientist who tested some of the early tasers for the Canadian government recommended that the government ban the devices. Andrew Podgorski says his tests showed the devices could cause death. He says that children could be especially vulnerable.

The use of a taser on the six-year-old disturbed Rudolph Crew, superintendent of Miami-Dade schools. In a November 16, 2004, letter to the police department, Crew wrote, "While I acknowledge the need of law enforcement officers on occasion to subdue and to restrain members of the public, I believe that certain tactics should never be used in dealing with young children—particularly within a school." Crew recognized that the student "was agitated and injured." But, he said, "police officers have dealt with other children in this condition without resorting to a taser." Crew requested that the police department "refrain from deploying or discharging tasers against elementary school students in Miami-Dade County public schools" and that officers use the taser only as a "last resort" on older students.

Tony Hill, the Democratic whip in the Florida State Senate, was so concerned that he sponsored a bill that would prohibit schools from using tasers on schoolchildren. "Every day here in Florida," says Hill, there are reports of "use of a taser on someone." But, he says, it was a group of tasings at schools near Palatka, Florida, that first made him wonder about the appropriateness of the weapon. "They all were African American kids," he says. "That raised a red flag."

In early January 2004, the Miami-Dade police revised their guidelines. The new policy "requires officers to consider factors such as age, size, and weight," in addition to other considerations, reported the Associated Press.

Crew and Hill are bucking a trend: the increasingly common use of tasers against students. Taser International says that 32 percent of the police departments it interviewed include tasers in local school systems, reported the *Birmingham News*.

In Birmingham, Alabama, officers armed with tasers will soon patrol the hallways of many schools. Superintendent Wayman Shiver says he's okay with that. "You have got to have something that the children fear," says Shiver, who has heard about people who were injured or who died after being hit with a taser. "We have to be in a position to control these schools by whatever means possible."

For Virginia Volker, a Birmingham school board member, "whatever means possible" is too much. "It's easier for systems to say, 'Zap them, throw them out,' something technical, when there's not a technical fix," she says. "It's a human problem."

Like Shiver, Volker also talks about problems with fighting in the schools, but she opposes the taser. "It's treating the children as criminals," she says. "It doesn't address why the children are acting out."

In the South, electronic shocking devices have a disturbing precedent, says Volker. Back in the time of the civil rights marches, sometimes the police department would use cattle prods on protesters. "When I think of the taser," she says, "I think of that."

Dexter Massey is president of the PTA at Parker High School in Birmingham. He says he took a taser instruction course from the police academy, but he still has doubts about the device when it comes to kids. The trainers, he said, told him that the average shock from the taser is three seconds. "Who's to say how many seconds it takes to die?" he asks. "Got my drift?"

Mass Market for Tasers

Taser International, which features the slogan "Saving Lives Every Day" on its Web site, is also hawking tasers directly to consumers.

"Choose your citizen taser device," says the company. Calling them "home self-defense systems," the company says tasers are a "safe and effective defense" that is "easy to use" and has "no aftereffects or contamination." The company offers three different consumer models, including one with a fifteen-foot range. The police version, the M-26, has up to a twenty-one-foot range. So, presumably, in a taser duel between a police officer and a consumer, the officer would win.

On January 26, 2005, Jim Weiers, House Speaker in the Arizona legislature, announced that he would propose a bill that would give police officers—and citizens—the upper hand against consumers who buy the tasers. It would allow the state's "police officers and ordinary citizens the use of lethal force in confronting people who threaten them with remote stun guns such as tasers," reported the Associated Press.

The consumer models sell for $399.95, $599.95, or $999.00.

For-Profit Transportation Companies: Taking Prisoners and the Public for a Ride

Alex Friedmann

July 2006

With approximately 2.2 million people currently incarcerated in prisons and jails nationwide,[1] the need to transport many of those prisoners has created a thriving new industry. Prisoners are moved both within and between states on a regular basis for a variety of reasons, including court appearances, medical visits, detainer extraditions, and interstate compact transfers.[2]

While there are no firm statistics for the total number of prisoners transferred and extradited annually, the U.S. Marshals Service, which is responsible for the transportation of prisoners and immigration detainees in federal custody, moves an average of nearly 300,000 prisoners each year.[3]

On the state and local level, individual jurisdictions are responsible for their own prisoner transportation needs. Although almost all sheriff's offices and state departments of correction maintain their own prisoner transport services, they also rely on privately operated companies, especially for interstate extraditions, due to cost and convenience. Staff shortages occur when county or state guards are used to transport prisoners, expenses such as gas and meals are incurred, and overtime pay may result. It is often logistically simpler and less expensive to pay a private company to provide such services.[4]

However, private companies by their nature are primarily concerned with making a profit. To this extent, problems within the prisoner transportation industry mirror those that exist in other areas where correctional services have been privatized: the inherent profit motivation of private transport services, with a corresponding need to lower costs and increase revenue, has resulted in escapes, deaths, injuries, and mistreatment of prisoners.

Private Prisoner Transportation as Big Business

Private prisoner transport companies operate pursuant to the Extradition Clause of the U. S. Constitution[5] and the Extradition Act,[6] which give them the same authority as public agencies that move prisoners. Private transportation guards—called "agents" in the industry[7]—can take custody of and move and house prisoners while en route to their destination; they are allowed to carry weapons and use deadly force but are not sworn law enforcement officers.

While there are numerous private transport services, most are relatively small operations. At the top of the industry are multi-million-dollar companies such as TransCor America, LLC, the undisputed market leader.

TransCor is a wholly owned subsidiary of Corrections Corporation of America (CCA). TransCor, based in Nashville, Tennessee, was founded in 1990 and acquired by CCA in 1994; it has approximately 300 employees and 80 vehicles, and moved more than 25,000 prisoners in 2005. The company states it can save public agencies between 30 and 40 percent on interstate transportation costs.[8]

TransCor's finances are consolidated with those of CCA, its parent company, so precise financial data are difficult to obtain. However, according to documents filed with the SEC, the company has been steadily losing money for years: TransCor took in gross revenue of $14.6 million in 2005, $19.1 million in 2004, and $18.9 million in 2003.[9] In 2005, TransCor's expenses were a whopping $21 million, with a net loss of $6.5 million. Nevertheless, the company manages to control an estimated 85 percent of the private transport market.[10]

Besides TransCor, other major prisoner transportation companies include PTS of America, LLC, located in Nashville and founded in 2001 by a former TransCor employee;[11] Con-Link Transportation Corp., which began business in 2001 and is based in Memphis, Tennessee;[12] U.S. Extraditions, Inc., located in Palm Bay, Florida, and started in 2004;[13] Security Transport Services, headquartered in Topeka, Kansas, and formed in 1995;[14] and Court Services, Inc., founded in January 2002 and based in Riverside, California.[15]

Prisoner transportation fees range from approximately 80 cents to $1.50 per mile, with $1.00 per mile being the industry average.[16] Additional costs may apply for transporting juveniles or prisoners with medical needs, and some companies impose a fuel surcharge.[17] These fees add up. Following a TransCor study of Montana's prisoner transport system in 1993, the company concluded that it could save the state about $350,000 from its present transportation expenditure of approximately $1 million per year.[18] From 2000 to 2006, State Extraditions billed Orange County, Florida, around $1 million for transportation services.[19] And according to separate fixed-cost contracts between the state of Nevada, TransCor, and PTS, the companies will receive payments of up to $2 million each over a two-year period ending February 2007.[20]

The History of Privatized Transport Services

Prisoner transportation companies expanded in number and scope during the 1990s as the U.S. prison and jail population almost doubled over a ten-year period, largely due to tough-on-crime laws that resulted in a surge of convictions and longer sentences.[21] The greater number of prisoners meant a greater need for prisoner transfers and extraditions, and an industry was born.

Initially, most transport services were mom-and-pop operations, sometimes literally two-person businesses.[22] At first there was little regulation of privatized prisoner transportation companies. While there were federal regulations for moving livestock and safety requirements for commercial truck drivers, few if any guidelines were in place for transporting prisoners.[23] As Florida's U.S. representative Bill McCollum (R) put it, "Anyone with a vehicle and a driver's license can engage in this business and with very little accountability when things go wrong."[24]

The greatest expenses for private transportation companies are those related to its employees—wages, benefits, staffing levels, and training. In the 1990s private transport services had fairly low training requirements; prior to 1999, for example, TransCor required only forty hours of in-house training for its transport guards[25] (in comparison, U.S. Marshals Service officers receive a comprehensive sixteen-week training course).[26] Employee background checks weren't always performed, and drivers were held to demanding travel schedules to ensure the company maximized its profit on each trip.

As a result, prisoners who were extradited by private transportation services raised repeated complaints, such as transport guards speeding, driving recklessly, and staying behind the wheel for lengthy periods of time—even to the point of falling asleep while on the road.[27] Prisoners were sometimes held in full restraints with no stops for food, water, or restroom breaks for over twelve hours at a time. Some prisoners claimed they received just one or two meals a day, typically from fast-food restaurants.[28] "There is virtually no government regulation of the conditions prisoners live in while they are shackled all day long without sanitary facilities in these cramped transport vans," said Mark Silverstein, legal director of the Colorado ACLU, in 1999.[29]

Private transport services have also been criticized for taking their imprisoned passengers on unnecessarily meandering routes across the country and overpacking their vans with prisoners to boost their profits.[30] Such "diesel therapy," in which prisoners may be on the road for a week or more, can be physically and mentally debilitating, as well as dangerous. The longer prisoners are in transit, the greater the possibility of an accident; also, the more times that a transport vehicle stops for food or fuel, the greater the risk of an escape.

William Minnix was extradited from Ohio to Colorado on a parole violation in July 1997. He was transported by Trans-Cor on a twenty-day trip that took him through more than seven states as other prisoners were picked up and dropped off along the way.[31] Nor have things changed much since then. On February 14, 2004, Rick Hollon, a veteran charged with failure to pay child support, was extradited by TransCor to Nevada from Kansas. Along the way he passed through Missouri, Oklahoma, Texas, and New Mexico over a seventeen-day period.[32]

Private transportation companies that are more concerned with their profit margins than the public good also tend to avoid costly security precautions. For example, public agencies often use "chase cars" that follow a transportation vehicle to provide an added level of security.[33] Private transport services, however, typically eschew this practice due to the additional expenses.

Many private transportation companies also use larger fifteen-passenger vans that have significantly lower safety ratings in order to transport more prisoners at a time and thus make extradition trips more profitable. Although the National Highway Traffic Safety Administration (NHTSA) has repeatedly issued warnings regarding the larger-capacity vans,[34] Court Services, Con-Link, U.S. Extraditions, and PTS continue to use such vehicles.[35]

Due to the initial lack of regulation of private transport companies and the resulting negative impact on safety and security, prisoner transportation services experienced a plethora of accidents and escapes, and their employees extradited prisoners under dangerous, inhumane, and abusive conditions with frightening frequency.

Problems in the Past: Reflections in the Rear-View Mirror

Smaller transportation companies, which are typically understaffed, run the risk of having their transport guards overpowered by their charges. On August 28, 1996, Rick Carter and Sue Smith, a husband-and-wife team who ran R&S Prisoner Transport, were overpowered by six convicts when they stopped at a Texas rest area. The unarmed couple was held hostage during an escape attempt that ended in a high-speed police chase.[36]

Larger prisoner transport services, including the top names in the business, don't necessarily fare much better. On July 30, 1997, Dennis Glick, a convicted rapist, took a gun from a Federal Extradition Agency (FEA) guard who had fallen asleep in the transport van when they stopped in Colorado. Despite its official-sounding name, the FEA is a private company founded by former bounty hunter Clyde Gunter. Glick took seven prisoners, a guard, and a local rancher hostage, and stole two more vehicles and a horse during his escape.[37] On October 23, 1997, four prisoners absconded from a Federal Extradition Agency van near Swanton, Ohio, taking a shotgun with them. The transport guards had left the vehicle unattended with the engine running.[38] And two Federal Extradition Agency guards were arrested in Dalton, Georgia, on December 27, 1997, after drinking and fighting with each other while they were transporting nine prisoners.[39]

TransCor had a bad year in 1997, too. Three of eleven extradited prisoners escaped en route on December 4, 1997: they removed their restraints, threw a rookie guard out of the van, and drove away while another guard was inside a Burger King in Owatonna, Minnesota.[40] This was the second time in only four days that that particular TransCor van was used in an attempted escape. On November 30, 1997, prisoner Whatley Roylene had removed his handcuffs and taken a shotgun from a sleeping TransCor guard when the same van had stopped at a gas station in Sterling, Colorado.[41]

A succession of accidents and escapes occurred over the following years. When an Extraditions International van stopped for a restroom break in Canyon Country, California on January 23, 2000, two of the nine prisoners they were transporting jumped into the front seat and drove off.[42] After two Nevada prisoners, James Prestridge and John Doran, escaped from an Extraditions International vehicle in California on March 25, 2000, Nevada officials decided to discontinue using the company.[43] And Evelio Escalante, an alleged gang leader, fled from TranCor guards in Waterbury, Connecticut, on October 27, 2000.[44]

On May 24, 2000, a van operated by Extraditions International was involved in a fatal accident in Great Barrington, Massachusetts. One guard, Scott Lee Bellon, was killed and a second guard and a prisoner were injured.[45] On November 20, 2000, thirty-nine Wisconsin prisoners filed a federal lawsuit against TransCor. They claimed that during a thirty-hour bus ride from a state prison to a CCA-operated facility in Sayre, Oklahoma, on January 25, 2000, the TransCor vehicle had no heat, no working toilet, and an inoperable muffler that let exhaust fumes inside the vehicle. They said they were denied meals and medication; wearing only jumpsuits in subzero weather, some reportedly arrived in Sayre with frostbite and hypothermia. The case was settled in November 2002.[46]

But the above incidents, while illustrative of the shortcomings of private transportation services, pale in comparison to the most devastating incident to befall the industry to date. On April 3, 1997, six prisoners were burned alive when the van owned by FEA extraditing them caught fire near Dickson, Tennessee.[47]

A female prisoner who had been dropped off just before the accident said the van had been making "knocking noises." Court records indicate that when the transport guards stopped in Memphis they informed the company's main office about the problem but were told to continue. The van's drive shaft apparently came loose, bounced off the road, and punctured the gas tank; the 1995 Ford E150 had logged more than 240,000 miles in two years. The prisoners who died in the blaze were Richard King, Monty Crain, John Cannon, Steven Hicks, James Catalano, and David Speakman.[48]

On February 28, 2001, a federal jury in Nashville awarded $10.5 million to the ten-year-old daughter of James Catalano on civil rights and negligence claims.[49] A second jury awarded $20 million in compensatory and punitive damages to the estate of John Cannon, another prisoner who died in the accident, on December 20, 2001.[50] James R. Omer Sr., an attorney with the law firm that litigated both of the lawsuits, said the company's insurance carrier paid the damage awards up to the limit of its policy. The remaining amount could not be collected because Federal Extradition Agency had gone out of business.[51]

Beyond accidents and escapes, some of the most troubling reports are of rapes and sexual abuse of female prisoners during transportation by male guards. TransCor guard Jack ter Linden was accused of fondling and sexually assaulting two female prisoners, Beverly Hirsch and Joann Gwynn, in separate incidents during extraditions to Colorado in 1993. Gwynn related that during a six-day trip through seven states she was repeatedly raped by ter Linden, and another guard failed to report the sexual abuse. A TransCor official stated at the time that male guards transporting female prisoners "had no impact on prisoner safety." Gwynn and Hirsch both sued the company and reached undisclosed settlements in March 1999.[52]

Cheryl Nichols and other prisoners were being extradited by two TransCor guards on October 25, 1997. Nichols accused one of the guards, Angel Rivera, of raping her in a gas station bathroom in Louisiana. TransCor fired him, and on August 6, 1998, Nichols filed a lawsuit in state court in Tennessee. TransCor settled the case for a confidential amount.[53]

In October 1999, Cheryl Schoenfeld was sexually assaulted by two TransCor employees while being transported through Texas. TransCor guards Michael Jerome Edwards and David Jackson forced her to expose her breasts and perform oral sex, then penetrated her vaginally with a flashlight and a gun barrel.[54]

Both Edwards and Jackson were charged with sexual assault. Jackson pled guilty, while Edwards was convicted and sentenced to ten years plus a $5,000 fine.[55] Schoenfeld and Annette Jones, another prisoner who said she had been mistreated by Edwards, filed suit against TransCor on February 24, 2000. The company agreed to settle the case in April 2002 for $5 million, of which $4 million was paid by its insurance carrier.[56]

In another sexual assault case involving TransCor, forty-three-year-old Catherine Jamison was repeatedly raped over a five-day period in March 1998 while being transported by TransCor guards in Colorado. On March 1, 1999 the ACLU, representing Jamison, filed a federal lawsuit against the company. "It is time for TransCor to take full responsibility for the safety and treatment of prisoners that the government entrusts to its care," said Colorado's ACLU Legal Director Mark Silverstein. The suit was settled on April 24, 2002, for an undisclosed though "substantial" amount.[57]

But it was neither the repeated rapes of female prisoners nor the six convicts who died while locked inside a blazing van in rural Tennessee that ultimately resulted in much-needed regulatory reform; it was yet another escape.

On October 13, 1999, Kyle Bell was aboard a TransCor bus that stopped to refuel in New Mexico. Bell was serving a life sentence for molesting and killing eleven-year-old Jeanna North. While two TransCor guards were asleep and two others were occupied outside the vehicle, Bell removed his restraints, crawled through a ceiling ventilation hatch, and slipped to the ground as the bus pulled away. The guards didn't notice he was missing until nine hours later, and delayed notifying law enforcement authorities. Bell was eventually captured in Texas in January 2000.[58]

Kyle Bell's escape resulted in far more than bad press and sharp criticism of TransCor; it accomplished what more than a decade of deaths, accidents, sexual assaults, and numerous other escapes had not—comprehensive federal regulation of the private prisoner transportation industry.

Federal Intervention Results in Regulatory Reforms

In 1999, U.S. Senator Byron Dorgan of North Dakota introduced a bill containing a broad range of regulatory measures for prisoner transport services. Entitled the Interstate Transportation of Dangerous Criminals Act, it was more commonly referred to as "Jeanna's Law" after Jeanna North, the child whom Bell had murdered.[59] Senator Dorgan's proposed legislation included the following provisions:

- Minimum standards for the length and type of training that employees must receive before they are allowed to transport prisoners
- Limitations on the number of hours that employees can be on duty during a specific period

• Minimum standards for the number of employees necessary to supervise violent prisoners
• Standards requiring certain violent prisoners to wear brightly colored clothes that identify them as prisoners
• A requirement that when transporting violent prisoners, private transport companies must notify local law enforcement officials twenty-four hours before scheduled stops in their jurisdiction
• A requirement that in the event of an escape by a violent prisoner, private transportation services must immediately notify law enforcement officials[60]

Dorgan's bill was passed by Congress and signed into law on December 21, 2000.[61] However, the U.S. Department of Justice (DOJ) failed to formulate regulations to enforce the bill's provisions until more than a year after the 180-day deadline for doing so. The regulations, codified at 28 C.F.R. §97, were not approved until December 2002.[62] "Tragically, incidents Jeanna's Law was designed to prevent have occurred since the regulations were supposed to be in place," stated Dorgan.[63]

Those incidents included the escape of David R. Puckett, seventeen, who fled from a TransCor guard at a Wisconsin airport on June 19, 2001. The guard escorting the teenager had failed to handcuff him.[64] Another escape occurred on September 28, 2001, when Christopher Paul Savage hijacked a TransCor van at a gas station in Clarksburg, West Virginia. Savage pretended he was sick and convinced the guards to stop; after his handcuffs were removed he overpowered both guards and stole the van, which contained a shotgun and ammunition.[65]

Further, Extraditions International lost a van transporting a dozen prisoners on September 11, 2001, when the vehicle stopped at a McDonald's in Mentor, Ohio. One of the prisoners, Lawrence Tutt, overpowered a female guard and drove away while a second guard was ordering food.[66]

Other incidents of sexual abuse occurred, too. During a four-day van trip beginning May 13, 2001, two male guards employed by Extraditions International transported Robin Darbyshire, forty-one, a pretrial detainee, from Nevada to Colorado. One of the guards, Richard Almendarez, made crude sexual comments to Darbyshire; he then threatened to take her out into the desert, shoot her, and claim she had tried to escape. When they reached a rest area he escorted Darbyshire into a bathroom, where he removed her restraints, ordered her to lie down, and forced her to expose herself. Almendarez, who weighed over 300 pounds, pinned her to the floor by standing on her hand while he masturbated and ejaculated on her.[67]

After the van stopped at Extraditions International's headquarters in Commerce City, Colorado, Darbyshire's complaints were ignored and she was placed back in the same van with Almendarez to continue the trip. Her subsequent testimony resulted in investigations in Colorado and New Mexico, and prompted a lawsuit filed by the Colorado ACLU in April 2002.[68] During the course of the litigation it was learned that Extraditions International knew Almendarez previously had been fired from the Texas prison system for abusing a prisoner.[69]

On March 14, 2003, the ACLU announced that Extraditions International had agreed to settle Darbyshire's suit for an undisclosed sum. "This case provides an excellent example of why contracting with private for-profit companies to conduct correctional functions can be dangerous to prisoners and the public," said the ACLU's National Prison Project staff attorney David Fathi.[70]

The DOJ regulations that were eventually implemented for Jeanna's Law contained specific standards intended to remedy the escapes, abuses, and related problems among private prisoner transport services. A minimum of a hundred hours of training was required before private guards could transport violent prisoners. The maximum driving time for transport guards was made the same as for commercial motor vehicle operators under Department of Transportation rules. Although the one-to-six guard-to-prisoner ratio was preserved, public agencies that contract with private transport companies can require lower ratios. Law enforcement agencies must now be notified within fifteen minutes of escapes.[71]

Standards to ensure the safety of prisoners, though less precise, were also set forth, such as a vague provision that transport vehicles be "safe and well-maintained." Also included was a requirement that companies establish policies to prohibit mistreatment of prisoners, including sexual misconduct and the use of excessive force. Further, juvenile prisoners are required to be separated from adults and female prisoners separated from males "where practicable." Female guards are to be available when female violent prisoners are transported, also "where practicable." Another regulation states that private transport companies are responsible for ensuring the well-being of prisoners, including "necessary stops for restroom use and meals, proper heating and ventilation of the transport vehicle." No minimum schedule for rest stops or meals was specified, however. The regulations also included civil penalties of up to $10,000 for each regulatory violation, liability for the cost of prosecution, and payments to public agencies for expenses incurred due to escapes.[72]

Notably absent from the DOJ regulations were requirements related to seatbelts or other safety restraints for imprisoned passengers. TransCor, for example, doesn't provide seatbelts for prisoners.[73] This is despite a 2003 Pennsylvania court verdict against the company in a case in which a female prisoner was thrown into a metal screen separating the passenger area from the driver's compartment when the TransCor van she was riding in came to a sudden stop. She suffered back and knee injuries, and received a $166,323 judgment against the company.[74]

Also missing from Jeanna's Law were heightened liability insurance requirements for prisoner transport companies. Most private transportation services are subject to minimum amounts of insurance mandated by the Federal Motor Carrier Safety Administration (FMCSA), which requires at least $1.5 million in public liability coverage for commercial vehicles in interstate transit.[75] Such minimal coverage may be insufficient; consider that lawsuits following the Federal Extradition Agency van fire resulted in jury awards over $24 million.[76]

Despite these shortcomings, Senator Dorgan said his legislation was a "common sense law that will do much to protect the safety of the American people if and when state and local governments use private companies to transport violent criminals."[77] Unfortunately, it appears he was overly optimistic.

Effective Regulation Inherently at Odds with Industry?

Notwithstanding the regulatory provisions of Jeanna's Law and its civil penalties, accidents, escapes, and abuses continue to occur among prisoner transport companies—often resulting from the same security lapses and deficiencies that predated the new federal regulations. This may be because although the rules have changed, the profit motivation of these private companies has not. So long as prisoner transportation services are primarily concerned with making money, not ensuring public safety, such incidents will persist.[78]

TransCor, for example, continued to experience a fairly high number of escapes and other incidents. Prisoner Floyd W. Stolin Jr. escaped from a TransCor van in Brighton, Colorado, on August 4, 2004, fleeing from the vehicle when it made a traffic stop.[79] Several months later, on October 24, 2004, David Randal

Moser, who was being extradited by TransCor, fled from the company's transport van in Oxford, Mississippi.[80]

In yet another high-profile sexual assault case involving the company, Denna Ann Jensen was being transported from California to Nevada on September 2, 2003, when TransCor guard Jason Parker pulled behind a remote, abandoned truck stop. Parker removed Jensen's restraints and forced her to perform oral sex. He then raped her. After being dropped off at a jail in Goldfield, Nevada, Jensen told one of the jail staff about the sexual assault.[81]

Parker was arrested and eventually convicted of four felony charges. On September 29, 2003, Jensen sued TransCor in federal court. Asked why Jensen had been transported alone by a male guard in violation of company policy, an attorney representing TransCor said, "That's the big question, isn't it?" Jensen's lawsuit was settled in January 2004 under undisclosed terms.[82]

Further, on September 2, 2004, four maximum-security Montana prisoners removed their wrist, leg, and waist restraints, pried a screen from the back window of a TransCor van, and escaped while the vehicle was stopped at a Burger King in Helena. A trainee guard had stayed with the van while a more experienced guard went inside to get food—which, according to a TransCor official, did not violate the company's safety policies.[83]

Other private transportation companies have also experienced recent escapes and security-related problems. On November 18, 2003, Robert L. South, a Tennessee prisoner being transported by Con-Link, absconded during a stop at a Subway restuarant in Lewisburg, West Virginia.[84] And Dominic Reddick, charged with attempted murder of a police officer, escaped from State Extraditions after the company's transport van broke down in Florida on December 5, 2005. Reddick reportedly complained that his leg shackles were hurting him, and one of the guards obliged by taking them off. He slipped away while the transport guards were occupied with other prisoners.[85]

Most recently, in La Crosse, Wisconsin, three prisoners escaped from a transport van operated by PTS on June 6, 2006. One of the company's guards initially claimed that a prisoner had used his eyeglasses to pick the locks on his handcuffs and shackles and to open the van door. However, an investigation by PTS revealed that a prisoner had stolen the guard's key ring.[86]

Public Transport Services Imperfect

Publicly operated prisoner transportation services are not immune to escapes, accidents, and other problems, of course. For example, in a bizarre incident in November 2005, a Florida state prison van crashed through a parking garage wall at a medical center in North Miami Beach and plummeted four stories. The driver and a prisoner inside the vehicle survived the fall.[87] That same month Carlos Kidd, a Texas state prisoner, escaped from a prison transport van by slipping out of his wrist and ankle restraints, leaving them locked on the floor behind him, and squeezing through a small rear window unseen by the two guards in the front seat.[88]

And on April 11, 2006, in downtown Hilo, Hawaii, a jail guard shot and killed a prisoner who was attempting to escape. Thane K. Leialoha had removed his handcuffs, fled from a jail transport van, and scuffled with the guard before running across a busy street. He was shot in the back of the head.[89]

However, compared with their privatized counterparts, government-run prisoner transport services don't appear to suffer from a similar number of incidents. This may be because public law enforcement agencies aren't intent on making a profit and thus are willing to invest in more costly security and safety measures such as chase cars and additional guards. They also tend to employ more experienced, more professional, and better-trained staff.

It should be noted that while comprehensive information can be obtained from government agencies, similar data is not readily available from private transport companies, which makes accurate comparisons difficult. But this illustrates another problematic aspect of the prisoner transportation industry: the lack of transparency and public accountability. While documents can be requested from federal, state, and local agencies through public records laws or Freedom of Information Act requests, such is not the case with private companies which are, in general, under no duty to disclose such documentation.[90] As Thor Catalogne, founder of PTS, stated, his company doesn't usually "give anyone any information."[91]

But some hard data, particularly concerning escapes, which are usually reported, can be compared. According to an exposé on private transport services published in *Mother Jones* magazine, from 1994 to 2000 TransCor experienced twenty-five escapes, while other transportation companies had twelve escapes. Over the same period of time the U.S. Marshals Service, which moves an estimated twice as many prisoners each year as the entire private prisoner transport industry combined, had zero escapes.[92]

A Road Map for the Future: Where to Go From Here

Although federal regulation is beneficial, it apparently isn't sufficient in its present form to cure the ongoing problems that seem endemic to private prisoner transport companies. What, then, is an effective solution?

While Jeanna's Law provides numerous rules and standards, it doesn't go far enough. Congress should impose further re-

straints on the private transportation industry, including regulations that address (1) higher minimum insurance requirements, (2) the types of vehicles permissible for transporting
prisoners, (3) specific rules for the maintenance and inspection
of prisoner transport vehicles, (4) mandatory seatbelt or other
safety restraint requirements for prisoners being transported,
and (5) increased civil penalties for regulatory violations based
on a company's annual revenue. Further, federal law should
require that all escapes, accidents, and other incidents that en-
danger public safety be reported to a government agency and
made available to the public.

Even absent further regulation on the federal level, state and
local authorities can impose their own rules and regulations on
prisoner transportation services, as the provisions of Jeanna's
Law "do not pre-empt any applicable federal, state, or local
law that may impose additional obligations on private prisoner
transport companies or otherwise regulate the transportation
of violent prisoners."[93] Supplemental state and local regulations
can address such issues as licensing for prisoner transportation
companies, employee training (including firearms training and
certification), and standards for licensing and inspection of
transport vehicles.

On a more basic level, law enforcement agencies that uti-
lize private transportation services should insist on contractual
provisions that enhance public safety. Contracts can specify
that chase cars be used during particular prisoner transports,
that private transportation companies maintain a lower guard-
to-prisoner ratio, that their transport vehicles not stop at nonsecure locations for meal or refueling breaks, and so on.

Public law enforcement agencies should further conduct
comprehensive background checks before using private transportation companies. During the ACLU's litigation against
Extraditions International in the Darbyshire case discussed
above, it was discovered that the company had operated il-

legally, without proper licenses and insurance.[94] And when Evelio Escalante escaped from TransCor guards in Connecticut in October 2000, it was revealed that the company wasn't even licensed to do business in the state.[95]

Private transport services that do not, or cannot, meet more stringent governmental regulations or contractual requirements should not be used. Terminating or suspending business with prisoner transportation companies has proven necessary in the past. In November 2000, then Connecticut Governor John G. Rowland[96] ordered state officials to stop using TransCor after Escalante's escape. The Nevada Department of Correction ceased using Extraditions International in 2000 following two separate escapes.[97] And Montana prison officials plan to resume control over prisoner transportation services after the state's contract with TransCor expires on June 30, 2006, partly due to the September 2004 escape of four maximum-security prisoners.[98]

When a company begins to lose customers it is motivated to make changes to ensure its continued profitability, even at greater cost to its bottom line. Only those prisoner transport services that provide safe and effective services in compliance with government regulations will survive. One that didn't, State Extraditions, apparently went out of business earlier this year following a high-profile escape and concerns over security violations.[99]

Increased litigation has been another powerful motivator to force private transport services to change their operating policies, or to force them out of business by way of large damage awards and settlements.

Federal Extradition Agency shut down in 1998 following the van fire in which six prisoners died.[100] Extraditions International folded in January 2002 following an undisclosed settlement in a suit filed by the ACLU on behalf of Robin Darbyshire, who was sexually assaulted by one of the company's employees.[101] And lawsuits against TransCor by female prisoners who were raped by the company's guards have resulted in a number of settlements—one for $5 million—that serve as an incentive for the company to adopt safer policies and practices.[102]

It will only be through additional state and local regulations, stricter contractual requirements, and continued litigation, in conjunction with vigorous enforcement and expansion of Jeanna's Law, that the private transport industry will be held accountable for the mistakes and misdeeds that have historically resulted from its inherent need to generate profit. Government agencies must also be willing to pay higher fees for safer prisoner transportation services; alternatively, they may prefer to invest such funds in their own prisoner transport services and avoid contracting with for-profit companies altogether.[103]

Author's Note

This book is the third in a series about the workings of the mass incarceration experiment. Previous books include *Prison Nation: The Warehousing of America's Poor*, also edited by Tara Herivel and Paul Wright (Routledge, 2002), and *The Celling of America: An Inside Look at the U.S. Prison Industry*, edited by Daniel Burton-Rose, Dan Pens, and Paul Wright (Common Courage Press, 1998).

Acknowledgments

We would like to thank all the authors whose excellent work appears in this book, and our editor, Diane Wachtell. Special acknowledgement to Alex Friedmann for his research assistance on the fly. The editors also wish to acknowledge the writings of Bill Quigley, which has greatly influenced our work, as well as the following folks, to whom we are deeply grateful for all their efforts and patience: David Fathi, Margot Schlanger, Paul Street, David Ladipo, Lonnie Burton, Leah Caldwell, and Matt Clarke. We also wish to mark the passing this year of James Quigley, Harmon Wray, and Thomas Sellman—advocates for the rights of prisoners.

Contributors

Anne-Marie Cusac, Assistant Professor in the Department of Communication at Roosevelt University, is a George Polk Award–winning journalist. For ten years, she was an editor and investigative reporter for *The Progressive* magazine. Cusac is also the author of two books of poetry, *The Mean Days* (Tia Chucha, 2001) and *Silkie* (Many Mountains Moving Press, 2007).

Alex Friedmann served ten years in Tennessee prisons and jails and was released in November 1999. While incarcerated he wrote for *Prison Legal News* (*PLN*), served as the resources editor for *Prison Life* magazine, and self-published the *Private Corrections Industry News Bulletin*. Presently employed as *PLN*'s associate editor, he has also worked for several law firms, as the advocacy coordinator for a nonprofit group for prisoners' families, and as a volunteer mediator at juvenile court. His area of specialty is prison privatization.

Jennifer Gonnerman is a staff writer for the *Village Voice*, where she has reported on the criminal justice system since 1997. Her work has also appeared in the *New York Times Magazine*, *Vibe*, *The Nation*, *The Source*, *Newsday*, and many other publications. Her stories have won numerous prizes, including the Gold Typewriter Award for Outstanding Public Service from the New York Press Club. Awards include the Meyer

Berger Award from the Columbia University School of Journalism as well as the Livingston Award for Young Journalists.

Judith Greene is a criminal justice policy analyst whose essays
and articles on criminal sentencing issues, police practices, and
correctional policy have been published in numerous books,
as well as in national and international policy journals. She
has received a Soros Senior Justice Fellowship from the Open
Society Institute, served as a research associate for the RAND
Corporation, as a senior research fellow at the University of
Minnesota Law School, and as director of the State-Centered
Program for the Edna McConnell Clark Foundation. From
1985 to 1993 she was Director of Court Programs at the Vera
Institute of Justice.

Tara Herivel is a public defense attorney in Portland, Oregon. She is the co-editor of this book and of *Prison Nation: The
Warehousing of America's Poor* (Routledge, 2002), also with Paul
Wright, which was a recipient of the Gustavus Myers Award
for Advancing Human Rights. She is also the author of numerous articles in the alternative press.

Gregory Hooks is professor and chair of the Department of
Sociology at Washington State University. He pursues a multi-
faceted examination of regional economic growth and the social costs that are associated with growth. Hooks has worked
with several collaborators to explore the widely held, though
inaccurate, belief that prisons bring economic growth and employment to hard-pressed rural communities. Hooks has served
as a Soros Senior Justice Fellow, and he is continuing research
into the local impacts of prison construction.

Gary Hunter is a Texas state prisoner who has been writing for
magazines such as *Prison Legal News* for six years. He managed

to parlay his first nine years in Texas prisons into three college degrees, including a BS in sociology and an MA in humanities. Gary is awaiting release on a twenty-five-year sentence, with his eye on a PhD in English and a desire to use his inside experience to draft legislation for progressive prison reform.

Wil S. Hylton is a writer at large for *GQ* magazine. He covers politics, science, and the law, and has contributed to *Esquire, Rolling Stone,* and *Harper's.*

Steven J. Jackson is an Assistant Professor at the University of Michigan School of Information, coordinator of the School's Information Policy Specialization, and a core member of the UM Science, Technology, and Society Program. His areas of research range from information and communication policy to the social study of science and technology and to information infrastructure, community, and international development.

Comments and suggestions regarding his article are welcome at: Dr. Steven Jackson, School of Information, University of Michigan, 1085 South University Avenue, Ann Arbor, MI USA 48109-1107, e-mail sjackso@umich.edu.

Kirsten D. Levingston directs Public Initiatives and the Living Constitution Project at the Brennan Center for Justice at New York University School of Law. For over a decade she has pressed for fair and effective administration of criminal justice and promoted social reintegration for those who come into conflict with the law. Her work in this area includes addressing debilitating criminal debt imposed against people in the system, strengthening public defender offices, and racial disparities in the system.

Clayton Mosher joined the faculty in the Department of Sociology at Washington State University in 1995, having previously served as a Senior Research Associate in the Department of Anthropology and Sociology at the University of British Columbia. Dr. Mosher transferred to the Vancouver campus of Washington State University in the spring of 1999 and was granted tenure and promotion to associate professor in the spring of 2001. He also serves as research faculty in Washington State University's Alcohol and Drug Abuse Program and is a faculty associate in the Social and Economic Sciences Research Center. Dr. Mosher's general research focus is on issues of social inequality, with specific areas of specialization in criminal sentencing policies; race, crime, and criminal justice; racial profiling; drug legislation; drug treatment, and the relationship between substance abuse and crime. He is also an expert in research methodology (including evaluation research) and statistics, and has received grants and contracts from federal, state, and local agencies to support his research.

Kevin Pranis is a policy analyst with Justice Strategies, a nonprofit organization that provides research to advocates and policymakers in the fields of criminal justice and immigrant detention. Mr. Pranis has produced educational materials, training manuals, and reports and white papers on topics that include corporate accountability, municipal bond finance, prison privatization, and sentencing policy. Recent reports authored or co-authored by Mr. Pranis include "Cost-Saving or Cost-Shifting: The Fiscal Impact of Prison Privatization in Arizona" (Private Corrections Institute, 2005); "Alabama Prison Crisis" (Justice Strategies, 2005); "Treatment Instead of Prisons: A Roadmap for Sentencing and Correctional Policy Reform in Wisconsin" (Justice Strategies, 2006); "Disparity by Design: How Drug-Free Zone Laws Impact Racial Disparity—and Fail to Protect Youth" (Justice Policy Institute, 2006); and "Hard Hit: The Growth in the Imprisonment of Women, 1977–2004" (Women's Prison Association, 2006).

David M. Reutter is a Florida state prisoner originally from Michigan, serving a twenty-five-year sentence for murder. He has been imprisoned since 1988 and while imprisoned obtained a paralegal certificate, which he has used to both assist other prisoners with their legal needs and successfully assert his civil rights. Since 2000 David has been a contributing writer to *Prison Legal News*.

Samantha M. Shapiro is a journalist and writer whose work has appeared in the *New York Times*, *Mother Jones*, *The Forward*, and other publications.

Silja J. A. Talvi is a freelance investigative journalist who emphasizes gender, ethnicity, and prison/criminal justice issues. Talvi is also a senior editor for *In These Times* magazine, and her work appears in numerous book anthologies, including *Prison Nation* (Routledge, 2003) and *Body Outlaws* (3rd edition, Seal Press, 2004). In 2006, Talvi was awarded the top award in immigrant rights reporting as a part of the New America Media awards. She has also been honored with two national PASS awards for magazine journalism from the National Council on Crime and Delinquency, and twelve SPJ Western Washington Journalism awards for her work on gender, ethnicity, and prison/criminal justice issues. She is currently based in Seattle, where she is working on a book about women in prison for Seal Press/Avalon.

Ian Urbina is a reporter for the national desk of the *New York Times*. Before joining the *Times* he wrote freelance and his work has been published in *Harper's*, *The Nation*, the *Los Angeles Times*, and elsewhere. He is based in Washington, D.C.

Paul von Zielbauer has been a reporter for the *New York Times* since 1990. From 2003 through 2005, he covered prisons for the newspaper and published a Pulitzer-nominated four-part series in 2005 that examined the world of correctional health care and, in particular, the work of Prison Health Services, Inc., the largest nonpublic health care provider to American jail and prison inmates. That article is included in this book. He earned a bachelor's degree in English from Iowa State University and a master's degree with honors from Columbia University's Graduate School of Journalism. He lives in Brooklyn, New York.

Peter Wagner is an attorney and the executive director of the Prison Policy Initiative who teaches, lectures, and writes about the negative impact of mass incarceration in the United States. His current focus is on working to demonstrate—through graphics, legal research, and state-by-state analyses—the distortion of the democratic process that results from the U.S. Census Bureau's practice of counting the nation's mostly urban prisoners as residents of the often remote communities in which they are incarcerated. The *New York Times* editorial board has written nine editorials supporting his efforts to change the way prisoners are counted, and the *Boston Globe* identified him as the "leading public critic" of the prisoner miscount. He has presented his research at national and international conferences and meetings, including a Census Bureau Symposium, a meeting of the National Academies, and keynote addresses at Harvard and Brown Universities.

Peter B. Wood (Ph.D., Vanderbilt University) is professor of sociology, director of the Program in Criminal Justice and Corrections, and a research fellow in the Social Science Research Center at Mississippi State University. Dr. Wood also served as President of the Southern Criminal Justice Association in 2005–06. His research includes the study of factors that motivate and maintain habitual offending, and issues associated with correctional policy and practice. His work has appeared in *Criminology, Justice Quarterly, Journal of Research in Crime and Delinquency, Punishment and Society, Prison Journal, Crime and Delinquency, Journal of Offender Rehabilitation, Journal of Criminal Justice*, and *Deviant Behavior*.

Paul Wright is a former Washington state prisoner, jailhouse lawyer, political activist, and journalist. Paul is the co-founder and editor of *Prison Legal News*, a monthly magazine published since 1990 that is primarily prisoner-written and edited. He also co-edited *Prison Nation: The Warehousing of America's Poor* (Routledge, 2002), with Tara Herivel, and *The Celling of America: An Inside Look at the US Prison Industry* (Common Courage, 1998), with Daniel Burton-Rose.

About Prison Legal News

Prison Legal News (*PLN*) is an independent, monthly magazine founded and edited by *Prison Profiteers* co-editor Paul Wright. Published since 1990, *PLN* is the longest-running independent, prisoner-produced magazine in U.S. history. With a national circulation of more than 7,000 subscribers, *PLN* focuses on reporting news and legal developments involving prisons, jails, and the criminal justice system. Each issue is packed with news, analysis, book reviews, and legal information. *PLN*'s content is uncensored.

PLN is a 501(c)(3) nonprofit and is almost entirely reader-supported. If you believe in the concept of an independent media that reports on prison and jail issues from a perspective other than that of the government, the private prison industry, or the "lock 'em up" crowd, subscribe to *PLN* today.

For more information about *PLN*, our back issues, and other related information, please go to *PLN*'s Web site: www.prison legalnews.org. The staff of *Prison Legal News* thank you for reading this book. We hope your interest in this important topic does not end here. To continue receiving regular updates and articles about the U.S. prison system, prisoner struggle, human rights in American detention facilities, organizing, and legal and political developments found nowhere else, subscribe to *Prison Legal News* today.

Prison Legal News
2400 NW 80th St., PMB 148
Seattle, WA 98117
(206) 781-6524
PLN@prisonlegalnews.org
www.prisonlegalnews.org

Notes

"Banking on the Prison Boom" by Judith Greene

1. Corrections Corporation of America, Form 10K for the fiscal year ended December 31, 2005, filed with the U.S. Securities and Exchange Commission, Washington, D.C.
2. Roy Walmsley, *World Prison Population List*, 6th ed. (London: King's College International Centre for Prison Studies, 2006).
3. Paige M. Harrison and Allen J. Beck, *Prisoners in 2004* (Washington, DC: Bureau of Justice Statistics, 2005).
4. Institute on Money in State Politics. *Policy Lockdown: Prison Interests Court Political Players*, April 2006. This figure includes contributions from private prison firms, investment and construction companies, food service providers, health care management, and counseling services that do business with them.
5. Elliott Sclar, *You Don't Always Get What You Pay For: The Economics of Privatization* (Ithaca, NY: Cornell University Press, 2000).
6. Scott D. Camp and Gerald G. Gaes, *Growth and Quality of U.S. Private Prisons: Evidence from a National Survey* (Washington, DC: Federal Bureau of Prisons/Office of Research and Evaluation, October 2001).
7. John DiIulio, "The Duty to Govern," in Douglas C. McDonald, ed., *Private Prisons and the Public Interest* (New Brunswick, NJ: Rutgers University Press, 1990).
8. American Friends Service Committee, "Minute on Prison Privatization," at http://www.afsc.org/az/prispriv.htm.
9. Catholic Bishops of the South, "Wardens from Wall Street: Prison Privatization," at http://www.catholiclabor.org/church-doc/CBS-2.htm.

Notes

. Julianne Nelson, "Appendix 1: Comparing Public and Private Prison Costs," in Douglas McDonald, Elizabeth Fournier, Malcolm Russell-Einhorn, and Stephen Crawford, *Private Prisons in the US: Assessment of Current Practice* (Cambridge, MA: Abt Associates, 1998).

11. James Austin and Garry Coventry, *Emerging Issues on Privatized Prisons* (Washington, DC: Bureau of Justice Assistance, 2001).

12. Judith Greene, "Bailing Out Private Jails," *American Prospect*, September 10, 2000.

13. Barbara Stolz, "Privatizing Corrections: Changing the Corrections Policy-Making Subgovernment," *Prison Journal*, 77, 1 (1997).

14. Richard Locker, "Personal, Political, Business Ties Bind CCA, State," *Commercial Appeal* (Memphis), May 25, 1997.

15. Cary Spivak and Dan Bice, "Tennessee Prison Exec Opens Wallet for Wisconsin Campaigns," *Milwaukee Journal-Sentinel*, February 18, 1999.

16. Erin Sullivan, "Jail Sell," *Metroland*, May 11, 2000.

17. Ziva Branstetter and Barbara Hoberock, "Private Prisons Benefit Politicians," *Tulsa World*, December 19, 1999.

18. Judith Greene, "Massachusetts, Missouri, and Oklahoma Establish Sentencing Commissions," in Michael Tonry and Kathleen Hatlestad, eds., *Sentencing Reform in Overcrowded Times* (New York: Oxford University Press, 1997).

19. Anthony Thornton, "Resignation Underscores Prison Crisis," *Daily Oklahoman*, August 25, 1996.

20. "Senator Formally Challenges Governor's Recommendation," *Catoosa Times-Herald*, September 4, 1996.

21. Barbara Hoberock, "Five Private Prisons Seek More Funding," *Tulsa World*, December 8, 1996.

22. Anthony Thornton, "Private Prisons Risky, Senator Warns Town," *Daily Oklahoman*, November 4, 1997.

23. Barbara Hoberock, "Board OKs Jump in Private Prison Beds," *Tulsa World*, April 23, 1998.

24. Paul English, "Keating Foe Attacks Private Prison Links." *Daily Oklahoman*, September 30, 1998.

25. "Candidates Keating, Boyd Share Little Common Ground," *Daily Oklahoman*, October 28, 1998.

26. Brian Ford, "Prison Bill Will Get Another Go," *Tulsa World*, October 1, 1998.

27. John Greiner and Mick Hinton, "Lawmakers Rewrite Truth in Sentencing," *Daily Oklahoman*, July 1, 1999.

28. Barbara Hoberock, "Packed Prisons Posing Problem," *Tulsa World*, July 21, 1999.
29. Brian Ford, "Lawmaker to Repeal State 'Cap Law,'" *Tulsa World*, July 30, 1999.
30. Ziva Branstetter and Barbara Hoberock, "Private Prisons Benefit Politicians," *Tulsa World*, December 19, 1999.
31. Mark Oswald, "Cost Savings of Private Prisons Inconclusive," *Santa Fe New Mexican*, August 26, 1996.
32. Mike Gallagher, "History of N. M. Prisons Written in Blood," *Albuquerque Journal*, September 19, 1999.
33. Angela Shah, "New Mexico Officials Pledge to Advance Private Prisons," *Bond Buyer*, July 15, 1996.
34. Carla Crowder, "Lawsuit Puts Brakes on New Prisons," *Albuquerque Journal*, November 21, 1996.
35. Mark Oswald, "Aragon, Coll Bring Fight out into the Open," *Santa Fe New Mexican*, November 21, 1998.
36. "Lea County Won't Buy New Prison," *Albuquerque Journal*, May 7, 1998.
37. Wackenhut/GEO would remain the owner of its prison in Santa Rosa but would transfer ownership of the Hobbs prison to Correctional Properties Trust, a real estate investment trust that acquired eight Wackenhut prison facilites in 1998.
38. Tim Archuleta, "Aragon Gets Private-Prison Job," *Albuquerque Tribune*, June 4, 1998.
39. Technically these county lock-ups are operated as public facilities, but enterprising local officials, including sheriffs, seek contracts to house state prisoners for the extra revenue they add to the county budgets, competing directly with private corporations in the "market" created by prison privatization.
40. Judith Greene, "Mississippi Churning," *American Prospect*. September 10, 2001.
41. Bryan Gruley, "Prison Building Spree Creates Glut of Lockups," *Wall Street Journal*, September 6, 2001.
42. Bob Libal, "Prisons for Fun and Profit," *ZNet*, June 17, 2006, http://www.zmag.org/content/showarticle.cfm?ItemID=10441.

"Doing Borrowed Time" by Kevin Pranis

The author would like to acknowledge Judy Greene, May Va Lor, Mafruza Kahn, and Phillip Mattera for their contributions to the growing body of prison finance knowledge.

1. A bond is a security that guarantees its owner payment of interest and principal—the "face" amount of the bond—on a fixed schedule. Bonds can be bought and sold in the marketplace like stocks but are generally considered a safer investment because the bondholder's eventual return is largely predetermined.
2. Cooperative endeavor agreements are legal structures that allow the state of Louisiana to engage in partnerships with private parties to fund activities which are supposed to benefit state residents.
3. The Tallulah story is discussed more fully in a later chapter in this book by Tara Herivel.
4. According to PublicBonds.org, in 1996 capital expenditures accounted for $1.3 billion of $22 billion in total corrections spending.

"Making the 'Bad Guy' Pay" by Kirsten D. Levingston

The author wishes to thank Nora Christenson, a Brennan Center summer intern, and Bran Noonan, a volunteer lawyer, for their essential research and drafting for this article, as well as Brennan Center colleagues Lynn Lu, for her tireless work on all aspects of this chapter, and Chris Muller, for his always helpful review and insights. Finally, the author thanks Rene Kathawala, Mick Peters, and their firm, Orrick, Harrington, and Sutcliffe, LLP, for their expert cite-checking.

1. *James v. Strange*, 407 U.S. 128, 141–142 (1972).
2. Michigan State Senator Alan Cropsey, chair of the Judiciary Committee and member of the Appropriations Committee, Karen Imas & Rachel McLean, The Council of State Governments Eastern Regional Conference, Issue Brief, "Policymakers Discuss Practical Solutions to Financial Obligations of People Released from Prisons and Jails," 1, May 2006.
3. The Honorable Judge John Andrew West of the Court of Common Pleas in Ohio, Karen Imas & Rachel McLean, The Council of State Governments Eastern Regional Conference, Issue Brief, "Policymakers Discuss Practical Solutions to Financial Obligations of People Released from Prisons and Jails," 2, May 2006.
4. NAACP Legal Defense and Educational Fund, Inc., Web site, http://www.naacpldf.org/content.aspx?article=524.
5. Appeals Court Decision and Opinion Vacating Order to Pay Costs, *State v. Rideau*, No. 2005-1470, 2006 WL 3091892 at *3, *1 (La. Ct. App. November 2, 2006). The first reversal, handed down by the

U.S. Supreme Court, called Rideau's trial a "kangaroo court," and the events leading up to it a "spectacle."

6. Motion to Vacate March 15, 2005 Order, *State v. Rideau*, No. 15321-01, 1 (May 2, 2005), *available at* http://www.naacpldf.org/content/pdf/rideau/Louisiana_v._Rideau_Motion_to_Vacate_3-15-2005.pdf.

7. *See* Appeals Court Decision and Opinion Vacating Order to Pay Costs, *State v. Rideau*, No. 2005-1470, 2006 WL 3091892 at *1 (La. Ct. App. Nov. 2, 2006), *see also* Adam Liptak, *Debt to Society is Least of Costs of Ex-Convicts, New York Times*, February 23, 2006.

8. See Appeals Court Decision and Opinion Vacating Order to Pay Costs, State v. Rideau, No. 2005-1470, 2006 WL 3091892 at *9 (La. Ct. App. November 2, 2006).

9. Appeals Court Decision and Opinion Vacating Order to Pay Costs, State v. Rideau, No. 2005-1470, 2006 WL 3091892 at *16 (La. Ct. App. November 2, 2006).

10. Appeals Court Decision and Opinion Vacating Order to Pay Costs, State v. Rideau, No. 2005-1470, 2006 WL 3091892 at *9 (La. Ct. App. November 2, 2006).

11. See Original Application for a Supervisory Writ of Review Filed on Behalf of the Applicant, State of Louisiana, *State v. Rideau*, No. KA-05-1470 (La. Ct. App. November 29, 2006).

12. Jon Wool and Don Stemen, Vera Institute of Justice, "Changing Fortunes or Changing Attitudes? Sentencing and Corrections Reforms in 2003," (2004), 4.

13. See Brief in Support of Plaintiffs' Motion for Summary Judgment, *Williams v. Clinch County*, No. 7:04-CV-124-HL at 1 (M.D. Ga. October 11, 2005).

14. Carlos Campos, "Jail Inmates No Longer Charged Rent: Pretrial Detainees in Clinch Had Paid Room and Board," *Atlanta Journal-Constitution*, April 18, 2006.

15. Ibid.

16. Ibid.

17. *Dean v. Lehman*, 18 P.3d 523, 533 (Wash. 2001). For further discussion of the fee issues in this case, see infra at 25–26.

18. Carlos Campos, "Poverty Keeps Woman Jailed, Lawsuit Says," *Atlanta Journal-Constitution*, September 19, 2006.

19. "To many taxpayers, it seems unfair to be burdened with providing food, clothing, shelter, medical, and other expenses for persons convicted of criminal wrongdoing." Donald J. Amboyer, Jail Administrator, Macomb Sheriff Department, Mt. Clemens, Michigan,

U. S. Department of Justice, National Institute of Corrections, *Large Jail Network Bulletin* 2, summer 1992.

20. "[L]egislators are reluctant to introduce new taxes to fund the operations of the judiciary." Imas and McLean, "Policymakers Discuss Practical Solutions to Financial Obligations of People Released from Prisons and Jails," 2 (quoting Assemblywoman Shelia Leslie, a member of the Nevada State Assembly and Specialty Courts Coordinator in Reno).

21. "'Inmates are being held financially accountable for their crimes and the pain and suffering that they have caused victims and their families,' said [New York State Department of Corrections] Commissioner [Glenn] Goord." "Inmates Pay $4M Annually in Fines, Fees to Taxpayers, Crime Victims," New York State Department of Corrections Services, *DOCS Today* (Apr. 2004), 4. Commissioner Goord retired from the DOC's post in July 2006.

22. Fahy G. Mullaney, U. S. Department of Justice, National Institute of Corrections, *Economic Sanctions in Community Corrections* (1988) 1–2; emphases appear in original. (Hereinafter referred to as "Economic Sanctions Report") available at http://www.nicic.org/pubs/pre/006907.pdf.

23. Former New York Corrections Commissioner Goord explains fees "teach inmates: [they] are either imposed to deter misconduct that often-times endangers staff or other inmates, or to teach inmates that there is a cost associated with the privileges that they seek." "Inmates pay $4M annually in fines, fees to taxpayers, crime victims," 4.

24. *See* Federal Bureau of Prisons Program Statement, Inmate Financial Responsibility Program, Section 545.10, 1 ("staff will assist the inmate in developing a financial plan for meeting [legitimate financial] obligations and . . . shall consider the inmate's efforts to fulfill those obligations as indicative of that individual's acceptance and demonstrated level of responsibility").

25. Imas and McLean, "Policymakers Discuss Practical Solutions to Financial Obligations of People Released from Prisons and Jails," 2.

26. Ibid. (quoting the Honorable Judge John Andrew West of the Court of Common Pleas in Ohio).

27. Marc Mauer, *Race to Incarcerate* (New York: New Press, 2006), 178.

28. New York State Bar Association, *Re-entry and Reintegration: The Road to Public Safety, Report and Recommendations of the Special Committee on Collateral Consequences of Criminal Proceedings* (2006), 200 (citation omitted).

29. Mark H. Bergstrom & R. Barry Ruback, *Economic Sanctions in Criminal Justice: Purposes, Effects and Implications*, 33 Crim. Justice & Behav. 242, 264 (2006) (citations omitted).

30. Paige M. Harrison & Allen J. Beck, U.S. Dep't of Justice, Bureau of Justice Statistics, *Prisoners in 2005*, 8 (2006), *available at* http://www.ojp.usdoj.gov/bjs/pub/pdf/p05.pdf.

31. Ibid.

32. Carmen DeNavas-Walt, Bernadette D. Proctor & Cheryl Hill Lee, U.S. Census Bureau, *Income, Poverty, and Health Insurance Coverage in the United States: 2005*, 5 (2006), available at http://www.census.gov/prod/2006pubs/p60-231.pdf.

33. Ibid.

34. The Census Bureau uses a set of money income thresholds that vary by family size and composition to determine who is in poverty. For example, for a family of four that includes two related children under 18 the threshold amount is $19,806. Income above this amount means the family is not in poverty, while income below the sum means the family is in poverty. For a list of the poverty thresholds in 2005, *see* Carmen DeNavas-Walt, Bernadette D. Proctor & Cheryl Hill Lee, U.S. Census Bureau, *Income, Poverty, and Health Insurance Coverage in the United States: 2005*, 45 (2006), *available at* http://www.census.gov/prod/2006pubs/p60-231.pdf.

35. Ibid., 13–15.

36. Ibid., 13–14.

37. Office for Victims of Crime Legal Series Bulletin, *State Legislative Approaches to Funding for Victims' Services* 1 (2003).

38. As early as 1988, the National Institute of Corrections observed that economic sanctions against people involved in the criminal justice system were expanding. Economic Sanctions Report at 1. The number of states charging a probation fee, for example, grew from 9 in 1980 to 24 in 1986. Ibid.

39. 730 Ill. Comp. Stat. 5/5-5-10.

40. Kan. Stat. Ann. § 22-4529.

41. Minn. Stat. Ann. § 611.27.

42. Jon Wool & Don Stemen, Vera Institute of Justice, *Changing Fortunes or Changing Attitudes? Sentencing and Corrections Reforms in 2003*, 4 (2004).

43. Karen Imas & Rachel McLean, The Council of State Governments Eastern Regional Conference, Issue Brief, "Policymakers Discuss Practical Solutions to Financial Obligations of People Released from Prisons and Jails," 2–3, May 2006. NIC expressed this

sentiment twenty years earlier in the Economic Sanctions Report: "Concurrent with these leaps has been an incremental growth resulting from the piecemeal adoption of fees, program by program, agency by agency." Economic Sanctions Report at 1.

44. Lauren E. Glaze & Thomas P. Bonczar, U.S. Dep't of Justice, Bureau of Justice Statistics, *Probation and Parole in the United States, 2005*, 1 (2006), *available at* http://www.ojp.usdoj.gov/bjs/pub/pdf/ppus05.pdf.

45. Economic Sanctions Report at iv.

46. Economic Sanctions Report at iv.

47. "In New York, and all across the country, state legislatures are increasing existing fees, fines, and surcharges and creating new ones. Parole and probation supervision fees, surcharges for convictions of violations, misdemeanors, and felonies, incarceration fees, and DNA databank fees are all examples of financial penalties." Center for Community Alternatives, "Sentencing for Dollars: Policy Considerations," *available at* http://www.communityalternatives.org/articles/policy_consider.html.

48. Gabriel Jack Chin & Margaret Colgate Love, *Introduction to Symposium on the Collateral Sanctions in Theory and Practice*, 36 U. Tol. L. R. ix (2005) *available at* http://law.utoledo.edu/students/law review/volumes/v36n3/index.htm. The American Bar Association recently recommended that state "legislature[s] should collect, set out or reference all collateral sanctions in a single chapter or section of the jurisdiction's criminal code" in order to "provide the means by which information concerning the collateral sanctions that are applicable to a particular offense is readily available." Am. Bar. Ass'n, Standards for Criminal Justice Section Standards, Collateral Sanctions and Discretionary Disqualification of Convicted Persons, Standards §§ 19-2.1, 19-1.2(a)(iii) (2006), *available at* http://abanet.org/crimjust/standards/collateral_blk.html.

49. N.Y. State Bar Ass'n, *Re-entry and Reintegration: The Road to Public Safety, Report and Recommendations of the Special Committee on Collateral Consequences of Criminal Proceedings* 163 (2006).

50. Gabriel Jack Chin & Margaret Colgate Love.

51. Economic Sanctions Report at vii–viii.

52. Mark H. Bergstrom & R. Barry Ruback, *Economic Sanctions in Criminal Justice: Purposes, Effects and Implications*, 33 Crim. Justice & Behav. 242, 260 (2006).

53. For example in Washington "'cost of incarceration' means the cost of providing an inmate with shelter, food, clothing, transportation,

supervision, and other services and supplies as may be necessary for
the maintenance and support of the inmate while in custody of the
department. . . ." Dean v. Lehman, 18 P.3d 523, 533 (Wash. 2001).
54. Mark H. Bergstrom & R. Barry Ruback, *Economic Sanctions in Crim-*
inal Justice: Purposes, Effects and Implications, 33 Crim. Justice & Behav. 242, 249 (2006).
55. Ibid., 250.
56. According to the U.S. Department of Justice Office for Victims of
Crime, "nearly every state has some form of general offender assessment, penalty, or surcharge that all convicted defendants must pay"
that goes to funds set aside for victim services or compensation.
U.S. Dep't of Justice, Office for Victims of Crime, "State Legislative Approaches to Funding for Victims' Services," Legal Series
Bulletin #9, 1 (2003), *available at* http://www.ojp.usdoj.gov/ovc/
publications/bulletins/legalseries/bulletin9/ncj199477.pdf.
57. Lauren E. Glaze & Thomas P. Bonczar, U.S. Dep't of Justice, Bureau of Justice Statistics, *Probation and Parole in the United States*,
2005, 1 (2006), *available at* http://www.ojp.usdoj.gov/bjs/pub/pdf/
ppus05.pdf.
58. Paige M. Harrison & Allen J. Beck, U.S. Dep't of Justice, Bureau of
Justice Statistics, *Prisoners in 2005*, 1 (2006), *available at* http://www
.ojp.usdoj.gov/bjs/pub/pdf/p05.pdf.
59. Ibid.
60. *See* note 66.
61. Ibid.
62. Ibid., 6, tbl. 2.
63. Ibid., 9, tbl. 6.
64. Ibid.
65. Barbara Krauth & Karin Stayton, U.S. Dep't of Justice, Nat'l Inst.
of Corr., *Fees Paid by Jail Inmates: Fee Categories, Revenues, and Man-*
agement Perspectives in a Sample of U.S. Jails, 1 (Connie Clem, ed.,
2005) (hereinafter referred to as "NIC Jail Fees Report"), *available*
at http://nicic.org/Downloads/PDF/Library/021153.pdf.
66. Ibid., 4. "Responses were received from jurisdictions in 28 states
and the District of Columbia. . . ."
67. NIC Jail Fees Report at 6.
68. NIC Jail Fees Report at 15.
69. Ibid., 15–16.
70. NIC Jail Fees Report at 2. Ibid.
71. U.S. Dep't of Justice, Nat'l Inst. of Corr., *Fees Paid by Jail In-*
mates: Findings From the Nation's Largest Jails, Special Issues in Cor-

rections, 2 (February 1997), *available at* http://www.nicic.org/
pubs/1997/013599.pdf.

72. Kentucky law requires prisoners to reimburse "costs of confinement." See Ky. Rev. Stat. Ann. § 441.265 ("a prisoner in a county jail shall be required by the sentencing court to reimburse the county for expenses incurred by reason of the prisoner's confinement as set out in this section, except for good cause shown." Ibid. § 441.265(1). In Campbell County, jailors confiscate an initial $20 from an arrestee's possessions and subsequently deduct 25 percent daily from inmate accounts as reimbursement for costs of confinement, up to $50 per day, and a mandatory $30 "booking fee." In neighboring Kenton County, jailors deduct 50 percent from a prisoner's account until charges are paid in full. *See Sickles v. Campbell Cty*, 439 F. Supp. 2d 751, 752 (E.D. Ky. 2006); *see also* Plaintiff's Class Action Complaint and Jury Demand, *Sickles v. Campbell Cty.*, 2005 WL 1530654 at ¶ 13 (May 17, 2005).

73. Paul A. Long, *Judge OKs seizing inmates' money*, Kentucky Post, July 25, 2006. The federal Bureau of Prisons requires prisoners in its facilities to pay their "cost of incarceration," and runs the "Inmate Financial Responsibility Program" (IFRP), which ostensibly "encourages each sentenced inmate to meet his or her legitimate financial obligations [by assisting] the inmate in developing a financial plan for meeting those obligations." *Program Statement: Financial Responsibility Program, Inmate*, U.S. Dep't of Justice, Federal Bureau of Prisons, § 545.10-1 (Aug, 15, 2005). The IFRP requirements do not apply to pre-trial or detainee inmates. Ibid. § 545.10-6.

74. 18 P.3d 523, 526 (Wash. 2001). Specifically, it permitted deduction of 35 percent of such funds, rerouted as follows: (i) 5 percent to the public safety and education account for the purpose of crime victims' compensation; (ii) 10 percent to a department personal inmate savings account; and (iii) 20 percent to the department to contribute to the cost of incarceration.

75. Ibid., 527.

76. Ibid., 533 (citation omitted). The appellate court upheld the finding that the statute unlawfully diverted interest earned on the inmate savings accounts to cover costs of incarceration since "it belonged to the inmates." Ibid., 536.

77. *See Slade v. Hampton Roads Reg'l Jail*, 407 F.3d 243, 247 (4th Cir. 2005) (finding this policy is not a violation of due process because the charge does not amount to a punishment).

78. "A governing unit may require that each person who is booked at a

city, county, or regional jail pay a fee based on the jail's actual booking costs or one hundred dollars, whichever is less, to the sheriff's department of the county or police chief of the city in which the jail is located. The fee is payable immediately from any money then possessed by the person being booked, or any money deposited with the sheriff's department or city jail administration on the person's behalf." Wash. Rev. Code Ann. §70.48.390 (2002).

79. Order Granting Plaintiff's Motion for Partial Summary Judgment, *Huss v. Spokane*, No. CV-05-180-FVS at 15 (E.D Wa. Aug. 29, 2006).
80. In *Matthews v. Eldridge*, 424 U.S. 319, 333 (1976), the U.S. Supreme Court set forth three factors courts must consider in deciding whether the government provided the individual being deprived of her private interest "the opportunity to be heard at a meaningful time and in a meaningful manner."
81. Order Granting Plaintiff's Motion for Partial Summary Judgment.
82. Ibid., 12.
83. Ibid., 13.
84. Order Granting Plaintiff's Motion for Partial Summary Judgment, *Huss v. Spokane*, No. CV-05-180-FVS at 13-14 (E.D. Wa. Aug. 29, 2006).
85. *See Allen v. Leis*, 213 F.Supp.2d 819, 830 (S.D. Ohio 2002) (finding Hamilton County's "Pay for Stay" program offered no procedural protections and therefore violated due process even though it was possible to obtain a refund).
86. *Dean v. Lehman*, 18 P.3d 523, 539-40 (Wash. 2001). For a full discussion of incarceration's impact on the family, *see* Donald Braman, *Doing Time on the Outside: Incarceration and Family Life in Urban America* (2004).
87. Jon Wool & Don Stemen, Vera Institute of Justice, *Changing Fortunes or Changing Attitudes? Sentencing and Corrections Reforms in 2003*, 4 (2004), available at http://www.vera.org/publication_pdf/226_431.pdf. *See* Kirsten D. Levingston, op-ed, *The Cost of Staying out of Jail*, N.Y. Times, April 2, 2006, § 14, at 11 (describing a 2006 proposal by New York Governor George Pataki to permit counties to institute monthly probation supervision fees).
88. *See* S. Christopher Baird, Douglas A. Holien & Audrey J. Bakke, U.S. Dep't of Justice, Nat'l Inst. of Corr., *Fees for Probation Services* 14 tbl. 3.1, 15 (1986), *available at* http://www.nicic.org/pubs/pre/004274.pdf.

89. Am. Probation and Parole Ass'n., "Supervision Fees," available at http://www.appa-net.org/about%20appa/supervis.htm.

90. S. Christopher Baird, Douglas A. Holien & Audrey J. Bakke, U.S. Dep't of Justice, Nat'l Inst. of Corr., *Fees for Probation Services* 1 (1986), *available at* http://www.nicic.org/pubs/pre/004274.pdf.

91. Mark H. Bergstrom & R. Barry Ruback, *Economic Sanctions in Criminal Justice: Purposes, Effects and Implications*, 33 Crim. Justice & Behav. 242, 255 (2006); *see also* S. Christopher Baird et al., Nat'l Council on Crime and Delinquency, *Projecting Probation Fee Revenues* 9, 10 tbl. 2 (1986) (draft), *available at* http://www.nicic.org/pubs/pre/004915.pdf (finding that 49 percent of agencies sampled in a study of probation fees "consciously g[a]ve less priority to [collection of probation] fees" and that 64.2 percent of the agencies used "Late Payment Notices" as collection methods versus only 12.5 percent who garnished probationers' wages).

92. Mark H. Bergstrom & R. Barry Ruback, *Economic Sanctions in Criminal Justice: Purposes, Effects and Implications*, 33 Crim. Justice & Behav. 242, 255 (2006) (stating that collection rates were higher when a factor in job performance evaluations).

93. La. Code Crim. Proc. Ann. art. 895.1(B).

94. Ibid., arts. 899, 900.

95. Ohio Rev. Code Ann. § 2951.021.

96. Ohio Rev. Code § 2951.021.

97. Ariz. Rev. Stat. Ann. § 13-902(C).

98. For example, Florida allows the clerk of the court to assess a collections fee of up to 40 percent of the debt for defendants who default on payments. Fla. Stat. Ann. § 28.246. Similarly, in Ohio, once a financial sanction is imposed, it is subject to enforcement through civil remedies, and collections are conducted by the clerk of the court. See Ohio Rev. Code Ann. § 2929.18(A)(5)(a), (D), (F) (governing the imposition and collection of fees for community control sanctions); ibid., § 2929.15 (enumerating community control sanctions, including probation).

99. Gerald R. Wheeler et al., *Economic Sanctions in Perspective: Do Probationers' Characteristics Affect Fee Assessment, Payment and Outcome?* at 12 (1989) (manuscript), *available at* http://www.nicic.org/pubs/pre/007810.pdf.

100. Ibid., 9–10 (miscellaneous fees and fines were assessed on "52.1% of those with unstable employment histories . . . whereas 41.9% of those with stable employment histories" were assigned such fees and fines).

101. Mark H. Bergstrom & R. Barry Ruback, *Economic Sanctions in Criminal Justice: Purposes, Effects and Implications*, 33 Crim. Justice & Behav. 242, 255–56 (2006).
102. Ariz. Code of Judic. Admin. pt. 4, ch. 3, § 4-301(e)(7), *available at* http://www.supreme.state.az.us/orders/admcode/pdfcurrentcode/4-301%20section.pdf.
103. Ibid.
104. Am. Probation and Parole Ass'n., "Supervision Fees," available at http://www.appa-net.org/about%20appa/supervis.htm (emphasis omitted). The APPA also notes "[t]he ability to impose strong sanctions (e.g. jail, work release) is moderately associated with increased collections." Ibid.
105. Carlos Campos, *Probation Fees Unfairly Punish Poor, Critics Say*, Atlanta Journal-Constitution, Sept. 24, 2003, at C1.
106. S. Christopher Baird, Douglas A. Holien & Audrey J. Bakke, U.S. Dep't of Justice, Nat'l Inst. of Corr., *Fees for Probation Services* viii (1986), *available at* http://www.nicic.org/pubs/pre/004274.pdf.
107. *See Bearden v. Georgia*, 461 U.S. 660, 661–62 (1983). Even those individuals who escape the most draconian sanction of incarceration stemming in part from nonpayment may nevertheless be subjected to other restraints on liberty, such as driver's license suspension or forced community service. See, e.g., Fl. Stat. Ann. § 948.01, Wash. Rev. Code Ann. § 9.94A.634. In some states, nonpayment of criminal justice debt may preclude the restoration of civil rights, including the right to vote. See, e.g., Wash. Rev. Code Ann. § 9.94A.637.
108. N.Y. Penal Law § 420.40; N.Y. Penal Law §420.10(6).
109. *See* Wash. Rev. Code Ann. § 9.94A.760(3), (9); Wash. Rev. Code Ann. § 10.01.160(2).
110. *See* Wash. Rev. Code Ann. § 6.17.020(1). Pursuant to Wash. Rev. Code Ann. § 9.94A.760(4) for crimes committed on or after July 1, 2000, the judgment may be enforced against a convicted defendant who remains under the courts' jurisdiction. Defendants generally remain under the authority of the court, which has the power to limit a person's ability to travel outside a particular area, until they pay off their economic sanctions. Enforcement of judgments against defendants who commit offenses earlier than July 1, 2000 have ten years to enforce the judgment, at which point a superior court may add an additional ten-year period at its discretion.
111. Fla. Stat. Ann. § 938.30(5).
112. Fla. Stat. Ann. § 960.295.

113. Fla. Stat. Ann. § 960.292

114. Fla. Stat. Ann. §§ 960.291, 960.297.

115. Fla. Stat. Ann. §§ 939.04, 55.03.

116. Wash. Rev. Code Ann. § 19.52.020.

117. Fla. Stat. Ann. SA § 938.35.

118. Wash. Rev. Code Ann. § 10.82.010; Fla. Stat. Ann. §938.30(5), N.Y. Penal Law § 420.10(6).

119. N.Y. Penal Law § 420.10(3); Wash. Rev. Code Ann. § 10.82.030; Wash. Rev. Code Ann. §10.01.180; Fla. Stat. Ann. §938.30.

120. *See* Wash. Rev. Code Ann. §9.94A.634, Wash. Rev. Code Ann. § 9.94A.760(10); Wash. Rev. Code Ann. §9.94A.737; Wash. Rev. Code Ann. § 9.94A740.

121. Fla. Stat. Ann §948.01, Fla. Stat. Ann. §948.10, Fla. Stat. Ann. § 775.089.

122. *See* SEARCH, The National Consortium for Justice Information and Statistics, *Report of the National Task Force on the Commercial Sale of Criminal Justice Record Information* 11 (2005), available at http://www.search.org/files/pdf/RNTFCSCJRI.pdf.

123. *See* N.Y. Bar Ass'n, *Re-entry and Reintegration: The Road to Public Safety, Report and Recommendations of the Special Committee on Collateral Consequences of Criminal Proceedings* 202 (2006).

124. N.Y. Bar Ass'n, *Re-entry and Reintegration: The Road to Public Safety, Report and Recommendations of the Special Committee on Collateral Consequences of Criminal Proceedings* 177 (2006). *See also* Les Rosen, *Credit Reports and Job Hunting* (2000), http://www.esrcheck.com/articles/article7.php, cautioning employers against overuse of credit histories and noting a job applicant's rights with respect to her credit history, including the right to know when a credit history adversely influences a potential employer's decision.

125. Jennifer Bayot, *Use of Credit Reports Grows in Screening Job Applicants*, N.Y. Times, Mar. 28, 2004, at 1 (cited in N.Y. Bar Ass'n, *Re-entry and Reintegration: The Road to Public Safety, Report and Recommendations of the Special Committee on Collateral Consequences of Criminal Proceedings* 178 [2006]).

126. Sharon Dietrich, "Criminal Records in Employment," *in Every Door Closed* (A.E. Hirsch et al., eds., 2002); *see also* Marc Mauer & Meda Chesney-Lind, *Invisible Punishment* 22 (2002) (noting an expansion of prohibitions against hiring teachers, child care workers, and related professionals with criminal records).

127. N.Y. Bar Ass'n, *Re-entry and Reintegration: The Road to Public Safety, Report and Recommendations of the Special Committee on Collateral*

Consequences of Criminal Proceedings 204 (2006) (citing New York State Occupations License Survey, authored by the Legal Action Center (2001)).

128. Ibid.

129. Child support is such a common concern of incarcerated parents in West Virginia that the state's Bureau for Child Support Enforcement has written materials aimed at addressing the child support concerns of incarcerated parents. *See* West Virginia Dep't of Health and Human Resources, Bureau for Child Support Enforcement, *Administrative Modification of Child Support Orders: Working for West Virginia Inmates and Their Families*, Brochure, on file with the author, and West Virginia Dep't of Health and Human Resources, Bureau for Child Support Enforcement, *You Are a Parent: An Inmate's Guide to Child Support Modification & Other Services of the West Virginia Bureau for Child Support Enforcement*, Brochure, on file with the author.

130. Ann Cammett, New Jersey Inst. for Social Justice, *Making Work Pay: Promoting Employment and Better Child Support Outcomes for Low-Income and Incarcerated Parents* 8 (February 2005) (citations omitted). *See also* Jessica Pearson, *Building Debt While Doing Time: Child Support and Incarceration*, Am. Bar Ass'n, Judge's Journal, No. 1, vol. 43 (Winter 2004) (analyzing state approaches to address accumulation of child support arrears during incarceration).

131. U.S. Department of Health and Human Services, Office of Inspector General, *The Establishment of Child Support Orders for Low Income Non-custodial Parents*, 2000.

132. Mark H. Bergstrom & R. Barry Ruback, *Economic Sanctions in Criminal Justice: Purposes, Effects, and Implications*, 33 Crim. Justice & Behav. 242, 247 (2006).

133. Ibid., 246.

134. Ibid., 248.

135. Ibid.

136. Ibid.

137. Ibid.

"Prisons, Politics, and the Census" by Gary Hunter and Peter Wagner

1. Tracy Huling, "Building a Prison Economy in Rural America," in *Invisible Punishment: The Collateral Consequences of Mass Imprisonment*, Marc Mauer and Meda Chesney-Lind, eds. (New York: The New Press, 2002).

2. Bureau of Justice Statistics, Justice Expenditure and Employment in the United States, 2003, Table 3.

3. *Reynolds v. Sims*, 377 U.S. 533 (1964), at 562.

4. See for example, Arizona State Constitution, Article VII, Section 3; Nevada State Constitution Article II; and New York State Constitution, Article II, Section 4.

5. New York State Constitution, Article II, Section 4.

6. Rose Heyer and Peter Wagner, "Too Big to Ignore: How Counting People in Prisons Distorted Census 2000," Prison Policy Initiative, April 2004, available at http://www.prisonersofthecensus.org/toobig.

7. Ibid.

8. Ibid.

9. Ibid.

10. Peter Wagner, "Importing Constituents: Prisoners and Political Clout in New York," Prison Policy Initiative (April 2002).

11. Peter Wagner and Rose Heyer, "Importing Constituents: Prisoners and Political Clout in Texas," Prison Policy Initiative (November 2004).

12. Ibid.

13. Letter from Daniel Jenkins, Mark Flack Wells, and Norman Gervais to the director of the Census Bureau on July 9, 2004, in regards to the establishment of the 2010 Census Redistricting Data Program, available at http://www.prisonersofthecensus.org/news/2004/09/06/ruralcitizens/.

14. Peter Wagner, "Importing Constituents: Prisoners and Political Clout in New York (Further Research & Methodology)," Prison Policy Initiative (January 2005).

15. Ibid.

16. Ibid

17. Dale M. Volker, letter to the editor, *The Times Union* (Albany, NY), June 16, 2004.

18. Paul Finkelman, "The Founders and Slavery: Little Ventured, Little Gained," 13 Yale J.L. & Human. 413, 427, 442–43 (2001).

19. Peter Wagner, "Importing Constituents."

20. Ibid., figure 10.

21. Ibid., figures 10 and 13.

22. Jonathan Tilove, "Minority Prison Inmates Skew Local Populations as States Redistrict," Newhouse News Service (March 12, 2002).

23. Staff and AP reports, "Prisons a City Benefit," *Vacaville Reporter* (CA) (January 28, 2006, p. 1).

24. The most rigorous examination of how prisoner counts affect funding is Eric Lotke and Peter Wagner, "Prisoners of the Census: Electoral and Financial Consequences of Counting Prisoners Where They Go, Not Where They Come From," 24 Pace L Rev 587 (Spring 2004) available at http://www.library.law.pace.edu/PLR24-2/PLR218.pdf.

25. It is unearned because other costs associated with hosting a prison, such as burden on roads and sewerage, are typically accommodated in other parts of the budget.

26. Hearing before the Subcommittee on the Census of the Committee on Government Reform, 106th Congress 106–39 (1999) (statement of Kenneth Prewitt, Director, Bureau of the Census).

27. Kenneth Prewitt, foreword to "Accuracy Counts: Incarcerated People and the Census," Patricia Allard and Kirsten D. Levingston, Brennan Center for Justice (2004).

28. *New York Times* editorial (May 20, 2006).

"Behind Closed Doors" by Tara Herivel

1. For purposes of this analysis, the term "facilities" refers broadly to detention centers, boot camps, or training schools, unless otherwise specified.

2. This was not Edwards' first indictment for criminal financial malfeasance: he was also charged with corruption in 1985 for racketeering, but managed to fight off the charges. A bizarre slogan for Edwards' 1991 campaign against KKK member David Duke commanded: "Vote for the Crook! At Least He's Honest!"

3. Fox Butterfield, "Hard Time: A Special Report; Profits at a Juvenile Prison Come with a Chilling Cost," *New York Times*, July 15, 1998.

4. Fox Butterfield, "Privately Run Juvenile Prison in Louisiana Is Attacked for Abuse of 6 Inmates," *New York Times*, March 16, 2000.

5. Fox Butterfield, "Louisiana Seizes Management of Privately Run Youth Prison," *New York Times*, July 24, 1998.

6. Robert Travis Scott, "State Seeks to Buy Tallulah Facility," *Times-Picayune*, January 19, 2007.

7. Cecil Brown's conviction for extortion and related charges in his business dealings with Governor Edwards was upheld by the Court of Appeals Div. 5, Case No. 01-30771 (August 9, 2002). Fred Hofheinz pleaded guilty in 2000 for charges related to bribes he paid Edwards. He paid a $5,000 fine and was sentenced to one year of

probation. See the *New York Times*, "National News Briefs; Guilty Plea in Bribe Case For Houston Ex-Mayor." November 23, 2000.

8. Jane Austen, Ph.D, and Gary Coventry, Ph.D., U.S. Department of Justice, "Emerging Issues on Privatized Prisons," NCJ 181249, 2001.

9. Peter Ash, M.D., "Adolescents in Adult Court: Does the Punishment Fit the Criminal?" *Journal of American Academy of Psychiatry and the Law* 34:2:145-149 (2006) (quoting Howard N. Snyder, "Juvenile Arrest Rates 2002," Office of Juvenile Justice and Delinquency Prevention, NCJ 204608, 2004).

10. Howard N. Snyder and Melissa Sickmund, "Juvenile Offenders and Victims: 2006 Report," Washington, D.C., U.S. Office of Justice, Office of Juvenile Justice Programs, 2006.

11. While there are more juvenile facilities that are privately owned than the 40 percent that are publicly owned, the privately owned facilities tend to be smaller, and therefore account for less of the overall population. See the Office of Juvenile Justice and Delinquency Prevention, U.S. Department of Justice, "Juvenile Residential Facility Census, 2002" (2006).

12. National Mental Health Association, "Privatization and Managed Care in the Juvenile Justice System," 6 (citing Building Blocks for Youth 2002).

13. First Analysis Securities Corporation, "Offender Management: 2000 Outlook" (2000), 11.

14. Ibid., 4 (citing American Correctional Association 1999).

15. Carol Marbin Miller, "Florida Continues to Abuse Children," *Miami Herald* (2004).

16. Dan Fesperman, "Hickey Turns a Violent Page," *Baltimore Sun,* March 30, 2004.

17. See Paul von Zielbauer, "A Spotty Record of Health Care at Juvenile Sites in New York," *New York Times*, March 1, 2005.

18. Erin Sullivan, "Jail Sell," *AlterNet,* May 15, 2000.

19. First Analysis Securities Corporation, "Offender Management: 2000 Outlook" (2000), 4.

20. "Juvenile Residential Facility Census, 2002: Selected Findings," Juvenile Offenders and Victims, U.S. Department of Justice, National Report Bulletin, 2006, 3.

21. Ibid.

22. Justice and Delinquency Prevention Act of 2002, as amended, Pub. L. No. 93-415 (1974).

23. Aside from any federal standards, the privately run American Cor-

rections Association has also promulgated a series of standards for juvenile settings, but these "standards" are not mandatory and they are primarily concerned with lessening potential liability for corrections staff.

"Mapping the Prison Telephone Industry" by Steven J. Jackson

1. Names have been changed to protect identity.
2. A more detailed description of these firms and contracting patterns through this period can be found in Steven J. Jackson, "Ex-Communication: Competition and Collusion in the U.S. Prison Telephone Industry," *Critical Studies in Media Communication* 22, 4 (2005): 263–80.
3. In some states (e.g., New York, Florida, Michigan) inmate phone revenues are paid into the Department of Corrections, sometimes into inmate benefit or welfare funds. In others (e.g., California, Connecticut, Massachusetts) prison phone revenues go straight into general state funds and have no material connection to correctional activities. It should be noted that even where paid directly back into the prison system, phone revenues often go to offset the cost of services (e.g., AIDS medication) that the state is obligated to provide in any case.
4. Amanda Wunder, "Inmate Phone Use: Calling Collect from America's Prisons and Jails." *Corrections Compendium*, May 1995.
5. Instructive here is the Request for Proposals for Inmate Telephone Systems and Related Services issued by the Florida Department of Corrections in 2000. The document's evaluative criteria assigned three hundred points (out of one thousand total) on the basis of "commission rate"—a significantly higher weighting than either "corporate qualifications" or "project staff." Florida Corrections Commission, *2000 Annual Report* (accessed June 12, 2006 at http://www.fcc.state.fl.us/fcc/reports/final00/9concerns.htm).
6. Data from Florida House of Representatives, Justice Council Committee on Corrections (n.d.), "Maintaining Family Contact When a Family Member Goes to Prison: An Examination of State Policies on Mail, Visiting, and Telephone Access," retrieved March 24, 2005, from http://www.fcc.state.fl.us/fcc/reports/family/famv/html; and from the CURE Campaign Against Excessive Telephone Charges, retrieved March 24, 2005, from http://www.curenational.org/~etc/.

7. Though note also occasional instances of relief, as cited in the "Protests and Alternatives" section below.

8. In general, pricing across states follows a roughly bimodal distribution, with a large cluster of states (twenty-six) charging between $13 and $17 for a fifteen-minute interstate call and a somewhat smaller grouping (twelve) falling in the $3–7 range. In between lies a still smaller (seven) cohort filling out the midrange of $8–13. Current high-charging states (as measured by interstate long-distance charges) include Alaska, Alabama, Arkansas, Arizona, Colorado, Connecticut, Florida, Georgia, Illinois, Massachusetts, Maine, Michigan, Minnesota, Missouri, Mississippi, North Carolina, New Jersey, Nevada, Ohio, Oregon, Pennsylvania, Rhode Island, South Dakota, Tennessee, Washington, and Wyoming. Lower-charging states (though still well above standard consumer rates) include District of Columbia, Iowa, Indiana, Kentucky, Louisiana, Maryland, North Dakota, Nebraska, New Hampshire, West Virginia, Wisconsin, and, measured by interstate calling alone, New York (as noted in later sections, New York has moved to a flat-rate pricing scheme, which has reduced long-distance and especially interstate rates while inflating the cost of local calling). Falling in the midrange are Idaho, Missouri, New Mexico, South Carolina, South Dakota, Utah, and Vermont. Current rate data for California, Delaware, Hawaii, and Virginia are unavailable. Texas does not allow routine prisoner calling (collect or otherwise) and therefore falls outside the scope of this study. All data based on the CURE Campaign to Promote Equitable Telephone Charges, http://www.etc campaign.com/etc/current_status.php, accessed July 31, 2006.

9. The figure $11.57 references the debit intrastate long-distance rate in Kansas; regular collect calling runs even higher at $13.61.

10. Beyond issues of price, family members and prison advocates have expressed additional concerns around issues such as excessive "branding" (the message informing recipients that the call is originating from an inmate at a correctional facility), which cuts into the usable portion of already expensive and time-limited calls; poor service quality, including frequent disconnections, leading call recipients to incur multiple connection charges; billing irregularities (including assigning peak rates to off-peak hours); inappropriate disciplinary actions taken against inmate families who attempt to control costs through contracting with cheaper remote call forwarding services; and administrative actions against and the frequent and inappropriate placing of blocks on the lines of call recipients, particularly those

who have chosen not to retain the prison phone contractor as their general service provider. Moreover, even simple questions of access have in some cases not yet been resolved (e.g., in Texas, where prisoners continue to be limited to one fifteen-minute call every ninety days, and then as a condition of good behavior). This additional list of concerns is not exhaustively addressed here; interested readers are referred to advocacy sites such as the CURE Excessive Telephone Charges campaign, at http://www.curenational.org/~etc, and the New York Campaign for Telephone Justice, at http://www.tele phonejustice.org, for details.

11. See, for example, J. Petersilia, *When Prisoners Come Home: Parole and Prisoner Reentry* (New York: Oxford University Press, 2003); J. Travis and M. Waul, eds., *Prisoners Once Removed: The Impact of Incarceration and Reentry on Children, Families, and Communities* (Washington: Urban Institute Press, 2003).

12. See http://www.telephonejustice.org/, accessed June 15, 2006.

13. Federal Communications Commission, *Implementation of the Pay Telephone Reclassification and Compensation Provisions of the Telecommunications Act of 1996, Report and Order of September 20, 1996*, FCC Docket No. 96-128, para. 16.

14. Federal Communications Commission, *Second Report and Order on Reconsideration in the Matter of Billed Party Preference for Inter-LATA 0+ calls*, FCC Docket No. 92-77, adopted January 29, 1998, addendum.

15. To anticipate one common objection, it should be noted that security issues around prison calling are real and to be taken seriously. Interested readers are referred to the Department of Justice, Office of the Inspector General, *Criminal Calls: A Review of the Bureau of Prisons' Management of Inmate Telephone Privileges*, available at http://www.usdoj.gov/oig/special/9908. But these concerns have been exploited strategically and often disingenuously with regard to the more specific question of price, where a growing body of evidence suggests that lower-cost alternatives (e.g., the debit calling systems adopted by the Federal Bureau of Justice and several state-level correctional authorities) can be fully compatible with legitimate penal concerns around security. Most pointedly, under the terms of the prison phone contracts the commission portion of prison phone rates makes no material contribution to security (short of the highly improbable proposition that the high cost of calling itself is likely to dissuade inmates from placing, and outside conspirators from receiving, "criminal" calls).

16. See *Arsberry v. Illinois*, 244 F.3d 558 (7th Cir. App., 2001); *Bullard v. New York*, 307 A.D.2d 676 (New York SC, App. Div., 3rd Dep., 2003); *Wright v. Corrections Corporation of America*, C.A. No. 00-293 (GK) (D.D.C. Aug. 22, 2001).

17. A useful review and analysis of legal challenges to the prison phone industry can be found in Madeleine Severin, "Is There a Winning Argument Against Excessive Rates for Collect Calls from Prisoners?" *Cardozo Law Review* 25:1469 (2004).

18. Despite the commission reductions, the 2002 contracts remained controversial. The decision to award the contracts to MCI and Verizon on a noncompetitive (no-bid) process followed significant contributions by both companies to the election campaign of successful gubernatorial candidate Gray Davis.

19. At the time of writing, one year later, the bill awaits action in the New York Senate.

20. A very useful summary of recent state legislative action around the prison telephone issue may be found at http://www.curenational .org/~etc, retrieved July 31, 2006.

21. H.R. 4466 has been referred to the committee on Energy and Commerce, where it awaits action.

"For-Profit Transportation Companies" by Alex Friedmann

A more extensive version of this article was published in *Prison Legal News*, August 2006, which is available at http://www.prisonlegal news.org.

1. *Prison and Jail Inmates at Midyear 2005*," U.S. Dept. of Justice, Bureau of Justice Statistics, published May 2006 (http://www.ojp.us doj.gov/bjs/prisons.htm).

2. "Detainers" are requests filed by law enforcement or corrections agencies to have prisoners returned to their jurisdiction to face charges or complete jail or prison sentences; interstate compact transfers are used to move prisoners from one state to another.

3. U.S. Marshals Service Web site, http://www.usmarshals.gov/jpats/ index.html.

4. Hence TransCor's corporate slogan, "Because your officers have better things to do."

5. U.S. Constitution, Art. IV, Sec. 2, Clause 2.

6. 18 U.S.C. § 3182, 3194.

7. "Just Hop on the Van, Man," *Westword*, December 18, 1997.

8. TransCor's Web site (http://www.transcor.com); TransCor's responses to written questions dated May 31 and June 12, 2006.
9. CCA's Form 10-K (2005 Annual Report) filed with the SEC on March 7, 2006 (http://www.shareholder.com/cxw/EdgarDetail.cfm?CompanyID=cxw&CIK=1070985&FID=950144-06-1892&SID=06-00). Yet the company has been losing money for years; for example, TransCor's 2005 expenses were $21 million, for a net loss of $6.5 million. See CCA's First Quarter 2006 Supplemental Disclosure Information, Consolidated Statements of Operations (http://www.shareholder.com/cxw/downloads/Q12006_Supplemental.pdf).
10. "Interstate Inmates," *Mother Jones*, May/June 2000.
11. See http://www.prisonertransport.net.
12. Phone conversation with Con-Link owner Randy Cagle, June 2006.
13. See www.usextraditions.com.
14. See www.securitytransportservices.com.
15. See www.courtservices.org.
16. Based on phone conversations with Con-Link, Wackenhut, and U.S. Extraditions, and 2005 contracts between the state of Nevada, PTS, and TransCor (RFP/Contract #1383).
17. Ibid.; *Traveler* (TransCor internal newsletter), January/February 2006.
18. *Billings Gazette* (Montana), November 19, 2003.
19. *Orlando Sentinel*, December 7, 2005.
20. 2005 contracts between the state of Nevada, PTS, and TransCor (RFP/Contract #1383).
21. "Correctional Populations, 1980–2004," U.S. Dept. of Justice, Bureau of Justice Statistics (http://www.ojp.usdoj.gov/bjs/glance/tables/corr2tab.htm).
22. *Nashville Business Journal*, July 29, 1996 (quoting former TransCor CEO John Zierdt Jr.).
23. "Just Hop on the Van, Man"; "Interstate Inmates."
24. U.S. Rep. Bill McCollum, remarks on Jeanna's Law, December 7, 2000 (http://thomas.loc.gov/cgi-bin/query/R?r106:FLD001:H62033).
25. North Dakota legislative Criminal Justice Committee report, November 2000.
26. *Bismarck Tribune* (North Dakota), November 5, 1999.
27. "Road Hazard," Westword, February 14, 2002; ACLU press release, March 1, 1999.

28. Ibid.

29. ACLU press release, March 1, 1999.

30. Ibid.; "Just Hop on the Van, Man"; "Ticket to Ride," *Pitch Weekly* (Kansas City, MO), May 6, 2004; North Dakota legislative Criminal Justice Committee minutes, March 2, 2000.

31. "Just Hop on the Van, Man."

32. "Ticket to Ride."

33. *Billings Gazette*, September 4, 2004 (see quote by Jim Cashell, president of the Montana Sheriffs and Peace Officers Association).

34. "NHTSA Restates Rollover Warning for Users of 15-Passenger Vans," NHTSA, May 26, 2005 (http://www.yourlawyer.com/articles/read/9840).

35. Phone conversations with officials at Con-Link, U.S. Extraditions, and PTS, June 2006; invoices for Court Services, Inc., from Capps Van and Car Rental, 2006.

36. "The Prison Industrial Complex," *Atlantic Monthly*, December 1998; Associated Press newswires, July 9, 1999; Statement of Senator Dorgan, U.S. Senate, June 6, 2000 (http://thomas.loc.gov/cgi-bin/query/D?r106:5:./temp/~r106xSZNvL::).

37. Ibid.; "Just Hop on the Van, Man"; *Denver Post*, August 4, 1997.

38. United Press International, October 24, 1997; *Commercial Appeal* (Memphis, TN), October 24, 25, 1997.

39. *Prison Privatisation Report International* (PPRI), January 1998.

40. "The Prison Industrial Complex," *Bismarck Tribune* (North Dakota), October 31, 1999; *Oak Ridger* (Tennessee), December 9, 1997.

41. "The Prison Industrial Complex."

42. *Los Angeles Times*, January 24, 2000; *Daily News of Los Angeles*, January 24, 27, 2000.

43. *Las Vegas Review-Journal*, April 17, 2000; *San Diego Union-Tribune*, March 27, 2000.

44. Associated Press, November 3, 2000.

45. *Portsmouth Herald* (Massachusetts), May 25, 2000.

46. *Wine v. Dept. of Corrections*, USDC, WD WI, Case No. 00-C-704-C (2000 WL 34229819); Associated Press, November 21, 2000; *Milwaukee Journal Sentinel*, July 27, 2001.

47. "Private Transportation Firms Take Prisoners for a Ride," *Prison Legal News*, November 1997; *Commercial Appeal* (Memphis, TN), May 24, 1997.

48. *Commercial Appeal* (Memphis, TN), April 5, 10, 1997.

49. The reported jury award was $10.5 million, but according to court documents the award was reduced to $7 million. *Catalano v. Federal*

Extradition, USDC MD TN, Case No. 3:97-cv-00790; *Commercial Appeal* (Memphis, TN), March 1, 2001; *Tennessean*, May 25, 2001; James R. Omer and Assoc. Web site (http://www.tennlaw-omer .com/awards_verdicts.html); phone conversation with James R. Omer Sr., May 2006.

50. The reported jury award was $20 million, but according to court documents the award was $17.5 million. Cannon v. Federal Extradition Agency, USDC, MD TN, Case No.3:97-1183; James R. Omer and Assoc. Web site (http://www.tennlaw-omer.com/ awards_verdicts.html); phone conversation with James R. Omer Sr., May 2006.

51. Phone conversation with James R. Omer Sr., May 2006.

52. *Hirsch v. Zavaras*, USDC CO, Case No. 1:93-cv-01917 (see 920 F.Supp. 148 [D.Co. 1996]); Gwynn v. TransCor, USDC CO, Case No. 1:95-cv-02886; "Just Hop on the Van, Man."

53. *Nichols v. TransCor*, Circuit Court for Davidson Co., Tenn. (see appellate ruling, Case No. M2001-01889-COA-R9-CV, 2002 WL 1364059).

54. *Houston Chronicle*, October 26, 1999, October 6, 2001; see Edwards v. State, 97 S.W.3d 279 (Tex.App.-Houston, 2003).

55. *Houston Chronicle*, October 6, 2001; *Prison Legal News*, January 2004; see Edwards v. State, 97 S.W.3d 279 (Tex.App.-Houston, 2003).

56. *Tennessean*, May 3, 2002; CCA's Form 10-K filed with the SEC on March 22, 2002; Schoenfeld v. TransCor, USDC WD TX, Case No. 5:00-cv-00248.

57. *Jamison v. TransCor*, USDC CO, Case No. 1:99-cv-00390; ACLU press release, March 1, 1999; *Rocky Mountain News*, April 24, 2002.

58. Statement of Sen. Leahy, April 6, 2000; *Oregon Statesman Journal*, October 18, 1999; *Albuquerque Journal*, October 13, 14, 1999, November 6, 1999; *Albuquerque Tribune*, November 8, 1999; *Bismarck Tribune*, October 15 and November 5, 1999; Associated Press, January 9, February 8, and June 6, 2000.

59. Senate Bill 1898, 106th Congress.

60. Ibid.

61. Public Law 106-560; *Corrections Professional*, Oct. 19, 2001.

62. Press release from Sen. Dorgan's office dated December 20, 2002 (http://www.dorgan.senate.gov/newsroom/record.cfm?id=189498).

63. Ibid.

64. *Milwaukee Journal Sentinel*, July 27, 2001.

65. Associated Press, September 29, November 18, 2001; *Charleston Daily Mail* (West Virginia), September 28, 2001.

66. Associated Press, September 12, 2001; *Post-Standard* (Syracuse, NY), September 19, 2001.
67. "Road Hazard," *Westword*, February 14, 2002; ACLU press release, March 14, 2003 (http://www.aclu.org/prison/women/14711prs20030314.html).
68. Ibid.; *Darbyshire v. Extraditions International, Inc.* USDC CO, Case Number: 02-N-718; *Rocky Mountain News* (CO), April 12, 2002.
69. ACLU press release, March 14, 2003 (www.aclu.org/prison/women/14711prs20030314.html).
70. Ibid.
71. 28 C.F.R. § 97, et seq.
72. Ibid.
73. TransCor's responses to written questions dated May 31, 2006.
74. *Maggiolini v. TransCor*, Penn. State Court, Case No. 01-11-307.
75. 49 C.F.R. § 387.25, et seq.
76. See notes 47–51.
77. Press release from Sen. Dorgan's office dated December 20, 2002 (http://www.dorgan.senate.gov/newsroom/record.cfm?id=189498).
78. As stated by Randall Shelden, professor of criminal justice at the University of Las Vegas, "Private businesses adhere to the bottom line and will cut costs wherever they can. . . . It's pretty much inevitable that they will skimp on safety, hold down wages [and] cut back on training." "A Private Nightmare," *Las Vegas Mercury*, January 8, 2004.
79. *Denver Post*, August 5, 2004.
80. *Daily Mississippian*, Oct. 25, 26, 28 and December 1, 2004.
81. "A Private Nightmare."
82. *Jensen v. TransCor*, USDC NV, Case No. 2:03-cv-01359.
83. Associated Press, September 3, 2004; *Billings Gazette* (Montana), September 4, 2004; *Montana Standard*, September 9, 2004. Interestingly, despite being found guilty at trial, escape charges against two of the prisoners were dismissed in January 2005 because, according to the jury instructions that were used, due to a legal definition they weren't in "official detention" at the time of their escape because they were in the custody of private guards, not public law enforcement officers. *Helena Independent Record*, January 13, 19, 2005.
84. Private Corrections Institute, November 25, 2003, citing the *Register-Herald* (http://www.privateci.org/tennessee.htm).
85. *Orlando Sentinel*, December 6, 7, 2005; WSAV news, December 10, 2005; WFTV news, December 5, 2005 (http://www.wftv.com/

news/5469903/detail.html); Associated Press, December 11, 2005; *Gainesville Sun,* December 6, 2005.

86. *La Crosse Tribune* (Wisconsin), June 10, 2006.
87. Miami-Dade County Channel 10 News, November 10, 2005 (http://www.local10.com/news/5293758/detail.html).
88. *Houston Chronicle,* November 2, 2005. In an interview, Kidd stated that the guards had stopped for a lunch break and removed his restraints to make it easier for him to eat; he then escaped through the unsecured rear window in the van.
89. *Star Bulletin* (Honolulu), April 12, 14, 29, 2006.
90. Freedom of Information Act, 5 U.S.C. § 552.
91. Phone conversation with PTS founder Thor Catalogne, May 2006.
92. "Interstate Inmates," *Mother Jones* magazine, May/June 2000.
93. 28 C.F.R. 97.22.
94. ACLU press release, March 14, 2003 (www.aclu.org/prison/women/14711prs20030314.html). Also, Federal Extradition Agency lost its carrier license for about one month in 1996 when it failed to notify the Federal Highway Administration of its insurance coverage. *Commercial Appeal* (Memphis, TN), October 24, 1997.
95. Associated Press, November 3, 2000.
96. Governor Rowland was later convicted of accepting bribes involving juvenile prisons in Connecticut.
97. *Las Vegas Review-Journal,* April 17, 2000.
98. Associated Press, January. 19 2006; *Corrections Digest,* January 20, 2006.
99. See note 85 (re escape of Dominic Reddick); WKMG Local 6 News, February 6, 2006 (http://www.local6.com/money/6791732/detail.html) (security concerns over leaving loaded firearms in unsecured vans during prisoner transports to Florida jails). State Extraditions co-founder Dennis Warren refused to comment on the company's closure when contacted by phone.
100. See notes 47–51.
101. See notes 67–70.
102. See notes 52–57, 81–82.
103. "Private prisons or transport companies might be cheaper, but only in the short run. The money that public agencies spend on hiring employees, training them properly and being accountable to citizens is a good investment." Editorial, *Oregon Statesman Journal,* October 18, 1999.

Permissions

Jennifer Gonnerman's "Million-Dollar Blocks: The Neighborhood Costs of America's Prison Boom" and "The Riot Academy: Guards Stage Mock Prison Riots to Test the Latest High-Tech Gear" are reprinted with the permission of the *Village Voice*.

Samantha M. Shapiro's "Jails for Jesus" is reprinted with the permission of *Mother Jones*.

Wil S. Hylton's "Sick on the Inside: Correctional HMOs and the Coming Prison Plague" is reprinted with the permission of *Harper's Magazine*.

Paul von Zielbauer's "Private Heath Care in Jails Can Be a Death Sentence" is reprinted with the permission of the *New York Times*.

Portions of Steven J. Jackson's "Mapping the Prison Telephone Industry" appeared in Steven J. Jackson's "Ex-Communication: Competition and Collusion in the U.S. Prison Telephone Industry," *Critical Studies in Media Communication* 22, 4 (2005), 263–80. Reprinted here with the permission of *Critical Studies in Media Communication*.

Anne-Marie Cusac's "Shocked and Stunned: The Growing Use of Tasers" is reprinted with the permission of *The Progressive*.